STAGE 1 EXEMPTION

BUSINESS STUDIES

First edition 1990
Second edition May 1991

ISBN 0 86277 737 2 (previously 0 86277 717 8)

A CIP catalogue record for this book is available
from the British Library

Published by

BPP Publishing Limited
Aldine House, Aldine Place
London W12 8AW

We are grateful to the Chartered Institute of Management
Accountants, the Chartered Association of Certified Accountants, the
Institute of Chartered Accountants in England and Wales and the
Association of Accounting Technicians for permission to reproduce past
examination questions. The suggested solutions have been prepared by
BPP Publishing Limited.

CONTENTS

PREFACE

BPP's range of Study Texts provides a comprehensive course of study for the examinations set by the Chartered Institute of Management Accountants. However, knowledge of the topics covered by the syllabus is only one element of examination success. Equally important are an awareness of exam technique and practice in dealing with examination style questions. BPP's range of CIMA Practice and Revision Kits has been produced to meet these needs. The kits are an ideal supplement to BPP study texts but will also be useful to students using other texts.

The main section of this Business Studies kit contains a large bank of narrative questions and multiple choice questions covering each of the three sections of the Business Studies syllabus. All questions are provided with full suggested solutions.

To put the Business Studies paper in context, an introductory section of the kit sets out the syllabus and paper format. A study guide on pages 5 to 9 highlights the key points in each syllabus area as an aid to study and revision. This is followed by guidance on dealing with questions in multiple choice format and we have included the Specimen Paper with full suggested solutions to indicate the scope and nature of likely examination questions. Finally this section ends with a quiz to test your basic knowledge of the areas covered by the syllabus.

The main question bank in the kit represents the equivalent of sitting the examination several times over. If you are able to attempt all of the questions you should be very well prepared for anything you may meet in the examination itself.

BPP Publishing
May 1991

SYLLABUS

Aim

To test the candidate's ability:
(a) to use and interpret the simpler mathematical and statistical methods;
(b) to explain the basic principles of the law relating to business;
(c) to explain the basic principles of micro-economics.

Content	Ability required
1 *Statistics* (weighting 33⅓%)	
Role of statistics: uses and value to the practitioner	1
Sources, collection (including sampling methods) and tabulation: accuracy and approximation	2
Presentation, summary and interpretation of collected data; simple index numbers; charts, diagrams and graphs including histograms, Z-charts and Lorenz curves	3
Frequency distributions; measures of location and dispersion for grouped and ungrouped data	3
Compound interest, annuities, loans and mortgages	3
Elementary probability *	2

* *Elementary probability will be deleted from the syllabus with effect from the January 1992 examination*

2 *Business law* (weighting 33⅓%)	
Judicial precedent, statutes, delegated legislation; civil and criminal law	1
The nature of a contract; intention to create legal relations; agreement, certainty, consideration, form, capacity	2
Contractual terms, standard form contracts and exemption clauses	2
Mistake; misrepresentation; illegality and contracts contrary to public policy, including restraint of trade	2
Discharge of contract with special reference to frustration and breach	2
Remedies for breach	2
Liability in tort, with special reference to professional advice, dangerous goods, industrial accidents and dangerous premises	2
Principles of agency with special reference to the authority of persons to act on behalf of others, particularly companies and partnerships	2

3 *Economics* (weighting 33⅓%)	
For the July 1991 examination	
Demand, supply and price	1
The theory of value; consumer behaviour	1
Indifference curve analysis	1
The concept of elasticity	1
Economies of scale	1
Forms of market structures; perfect and imperfect competition, oligopoly, duopoly, monopoly	1

SYLLABUS

	Ability required
3 *Economics*	

With effect from the January 1992 examination
The foregoing detail in the economics section of the syllabus is
to be deleted and replaced by the following.

Basic concepts	2
Theory of value	2
Theory of production	3
Industrial organisation and location	1
Money and banking	2

The syllabus contains a ranking of the level of ability required in each topic, and a weighting for each syllabus area. The Institute has published the following explanatory notes on these points.

Abilities required in the examination

The rankings range from 1 to 4 and represent the following ability levels.

Ranking for
syllabus topics

Appreciation
To understand a knowledge area at an early stage of learning, or outside
the core of management accounting, at a level which enables the accountant
to communicate and work with other members of the management team.   1

Knowledge
To advise on such matters as laws, standards, facts and techniques
at a level of detail appropriate to a management accounting specialist.   2

Skill
To apply theoretical knowledge, concepts and techniques to the solution
of problems where it is clear what technique has to be used and the
information needed is clearly indicated.   3

Application
To apply knowledge and skills where candidates have to determine from
a number of techniques which is the most appropriate and select the
information required from a fairly wide range of data, some of which
might not be relevant; to exercise professional judgement and to
communicate and work with members of the management team and other
recipients of financial reports.   4

Study weightings

A percentage weighting is shown against each topic in the syllabus; this is intended as a guide to the amount of study time each topic requires.

All topics in a syllabus must be studied, as a question may examine more than one topic or carry a higher proportion of marks than the percentage study time suggested.

The weightings do not specify the number of marks which will be allocated to topics in the examination.

THE EXAMINATION PAPER

Paper format

The paper is divided into three sections, one for each section of the syllabus, each of which is allocated equal marks.

Up until and including the January 1990 sitting the paper was split approximately 55% objective testing and 45% longer computational and discursive questions. You will see later in this section that the specimen paper was in this format. However from July 1990 the split of the multiple choice questions against essay questions changed to 50:50. You should bear this point in mind when using the specimen paper for revision purposes.

Past papers

The Institute does not publish past question papers for the Stage 1 exemption examinations, but they have issued the specimen paper which we have reproduced later in this section. The CIMA has also made the following points which should help you in preparing for the examination.

(a)   'As the current syllabus has allowed examiners gradually to refine their approaches to their papers, it is natural to assume that some of the essay-type questions set will not necessarily be as easy as some of those in the pilot (specimen) papers. Those papers were intended to give an idea of the sort of approach taken, but that past Stage 1 papers may be a better guide.'

We have included many past Stage 1 questions in this kit to enable you to achieve the required standard.

(b)   'The exemption papers are set by the same examiners who set the Stage 1 papers and they are satisfied that the degree of difficulty is about the same.'

(c)   'There will normally be no choice of question for the essay answer. This certainly adds to the difficulty of the papers, because although the multiple choice questions allow candidates to show the wide reading they have done, and the extent to which they have understood the subject, the concentration of the compulsory essay answer on one or two areas penalises those who have not studied enough.'

(d)   'If the Business Studies examination only provides an hour for each of the non-accounting areas of Stage 1, it must require evidence of thorough knowledge.'

(e)   'It is necessary for all Business Studies candidates to complete (and obtain a minimum mark in) each section of that paper. This applies even if they have been given exemption from one or two of the related Stage 1 papers.'

(f)   'It is worth pointing out that the Institute is usually looking for a mark of about 50% on each paper for a pass, and that candidates who do poorly on the multiple choice and well on the essay (or vice versa) may be singled out for more detailed review.'

Using this kit

The more practice you can get in answering examination-style questions, the better prepared you will be for the examination itself. But if time is limited, remember that a serious attempt at one question is more valuable than cursory attempts at two. Avoid the temptation to 'audit' the answers: complete your attempt before checking with our solution. When you have had enough practice to be confident of your grasp of the material, try a few questions under exam conditions, timing yourself against the clock.

The mark allocations will give you an idea of how long each question should take, for example a question worth 20 marks should take approximately 30 to 35 minutes. Remember that the mark allocations for individual questions in your examination may not be the same.

To obtain the greatest benefit from the use of this study material you are recommended to do the following.

(a)   Test your knowledge in the basic test on page 33 to 43 and revise until you are really proficient. You must cover the whole syllabus in your work on this paper, and the test will help you to identify where your studies have been patchy.

(b)   Complete a thorough preparation of each subject before attempting the questions on that subject. Answering questions is a test of what you have learnt and also a means of practising so that you develop a skill in presenting your answers. To attempt them before you are ready is not a fair test of your proficiency and the result may discourage you.

(c)   Start with the longer computational and discursive questions on each subject. Write your answers in examination conditions without referring to books, manuals or notes. Then compare the suggested solutions with your own. Look to see how many points of similarity and difference there are between them. The suggested answers are only suggestions. They are correct and complete on essentials but there is more than one way of writing an answer.

If you find that your answer is basically incorrect or lacks essential points do not be discouraged. This result indicates that, while you still have time, this part of the syllabus requires further revision.

(d)   Lastly, you should attempt the relevant set of objective test questions. You will find some notes on dealing with this type of question later in this section of the kit.

The questions in this kit are designed to provide a wide coverage of the syllabus. By working through the questions, you should therefore be going over all the topics you ought to learn, and assessing your ability to answer examination-style questions well.

Notes on specific areas of the syllabus

The brief notes which follow highlight some of the key points which you should cover in your revision. We also recommend particular questions from the kit which you may wish to try.

STUDY GUIDE

1 Statistics

Sources, collection and tabulation of data

This area is concerned with collecting data, and then turning the data collected into something useable. If asked about sampling, think about the two aspects of representativeness (should we, for example, stratify the population?) and cost-effectiveness. If asked to present data, for example in a table, think about the reason for preparing the table so that you include all relevant information.

Questions to try: *Q3 Lever Limited; Q4 Complete tables*

Index numbers

In a numerical question, always show your workings, as it is very easy to pick up the wrong year's price or quantity from the question. In the multiple choice questions, you will not be able to show your workings so you must take extra care. In a written question asking you to compare alternative indices, think about the precise use to which the information will be put. No one index is best for all purposes.

Questions to try: *Q8 Sales indices; Q9 Retail prices index*

Charts, diagrams and graphs

Practice drawing each type of chart diagram and graph. In particular make sure that you can draw and interpret histograms, Z charts and Lorenz curves, which are mentioned specifically on the syllabus. Remember that presentation is vital. Use a ruler to draw straight lines!

Questions to try: *Q12 Zed Limited; Q13 Shareholdings*

Location and dispersion

You may well be asked to compute means, medians and standard deviations. If you cannot do these quickly, practice before the examination. If your calculator is too small to be easy to use, try to obtain the use of another one. Unless you are answering a multiple choice question, it is vital to set out your workings in a neat table. There is every chance that you will press a wrong button in the heat of the examination, so your answer will be wrong. If it is clear that you have used the right method, you will get most of the marks; if there are no workings you will get no marks.

Questions to try: *Q17 Transfer times; Q20 Executive*

Compound interest, annuities, loans and mortgages

Practice using the relevant formulae. Revise how to calculate the present value of an annuity by using present value discount factors. Questions often require a lot of arithmetical calculations and unless you are answering a multiple choice question you must always give full workings so that any slips will not lose you too many marks. Look carefully to see whether receipts or payments start immediately or after one year/quarter/month.

Questions to try: *Q23 Reserve fund; Q24 Instalments*

Elementary probability (for the July 1991 examination only)

It is sometimes hard to sort out what the possibilities are. Draw a tree diagram, a table, or anything else you find helpful, even if the question does not require it. You can then sort out the possible outcomes before you start to multiply or add probabilities. If the question requires a tree, do a rough sketch first then take a full page (and a ruler) to do your final version.

Questions to try: *Q28 Imperfect jackets; Q29 Software company*

2   *Business law*

The legal system
There are two important areas in this part of your syllabus: the sources of law and the distinction between civil and criminal law. You should make sure in particular that you are clear about today's legal sources of law - namely statute and case law - and about technical areas such as the laying down and use of judicial precedent and the interpretation of statutes. Delegated legislation and the role of EC law are also important areas.

The legal system includes other parts of the syllabus. For example if you can distinguish between civil and criminal issues you will be well equipped to deal with matters such as industrial accidents and the supply of dangerous goods.

Questions to try: *Q1 Precedent; Q4 Criminal law and civil law*

The law of contract
Contract law is the fundamental part of any study of business law and it is vital that you know, first of all, the basic rules determining whether or not a binding agreement has come into effect - namely offer and acceptance, intention to create legal relations and consideration. The nature and effect of a contract's terms, and the status of representations, are also important, as is the form which the contract takes. Examination questions often focus on the ways in which a contract may be deficient, as where there is mistake, misrepresentation, undue influence or illegality. Finally you must be clear in your mind about the ways in which a contract may be discharged, the remedies for breach and the circumstances in which a party's liability may be limited by exclusion clauses.

Questions to try: *Q5 Reid; Q12 Mort; Q20 Damages*

Tort
The law of tort greatly affects many different areas of business conduct, and must be thoroughly understood in relation to: negligence in giving professional advice, strict liability for supplying dangerous goods or operating dangerous premises, and employer's liability for industrial accidents. It is an area in which statute and case-law intertwine to a very large extent, and you must be careful also to distinguish between civil liability and criminal offences.

Questions to try: *Q21 Proffit; Q24 Dennis and Sam*

Agency
The law of agency is an important area to cover since it underlies much of the company law syllabus which you encounter in Stage 3. You should concentrate on the types of authority, actual and apparent, which an agent may have and on the authority of partners and of company directors and employees.

Questions to try: *Q28 Jack and Jill; Q29 Charles*

3   *Economics*

Basic concepts
Make sure that you are clear about:

- the nature of the economic problem
- the methods of allocating resources
- the development and advantages of the mixed economy.

Note carefully the definition of terms.

Questions to try: *Q3 The price mechanism; Q2 The study of wealth*

Economic structures
You should know something about each of the various types of organisation in the private and public sectors of the economy. Pay attention to the function of the entrepreneur and the nature of profit.

The reasons for the location of industries are important.

Questions to try: *Q8 Small firms; Q10 Entrepreneur's reward; Q13 Economic factors*

Supply and demand
It is very important that you understand the theory of value and the functioning of the price mechanism. Can you explain how price is determined in the various market structures from perfect competition through to monopoly?

Diagrams can be useful for clarity, as emphasised later in these notes.

Make sure that you understand the concept of elasticity of demand and supply, and note the practical significance of elasticities.

Study the relationship between costs and output carefully. Can you explain the reasons for growth and integration, and the economies of large scale production?

Questions to try: *Q14 Price takers and price makers; Q18 Short run and long run costs*

Money and banking
This subject area is introduced into the syllabus starting with the January 1992 examination.

On money, be clear about its nature and its functions, particularly with regard to the changing value or purchasing power of money.

On banking, cover the structure and functions of the central banks and of commercial banks. Note carefully the various sources of capital. You should ensure that you are familiar with the main UK financial institutions, especially the Stock Exchange, the Discount Market and the Capital Markets.

Questions to try: *Q24 Importance of money; Q30 Company finance*

Diagrams
Questions may be set which invite solutions with the aid of diagrams, for example, pricing and output decisions for a monopolist, oligopolist or a firm in monopolistic competition, price discrimination, or the elasticity of demand.

It may help, for example, to remember the following points about the theory of the firm:

(a)   A marginal cost curve (mainly upward sloping) cuts the average cost curve (basically U-shaped) at the lowest point on the AC curve.

(b)   In conditions of perfect competition, the demand curve for the industry as a whole is downward-sloping and the market price equilibrium is determined by supply and demand; but each individual firm must sell all its output at the ruling market price no matter how much it produces and sells, and so its demand curve is a horizontal line, and price = average revenue per unit sold = marginal revenue per extra unit sold; ie D = P = AR = MR. For equilibrium in the market, an individual firm's profits are maximised not only when MC=MR=AR, but when MC = AC, so that AC = AR and there are no superprofits.

(c)   A monopolist has a downward sloping demand curve, and enjoys supernormal profits because when MR=MC the MR of the firm must be below the price on the demand curve (AR) and AR is greater than AC.

(d)   To draw a downward-sloping demand curve and corresponding MR curve, it is often convenient to draw the demand curve as a straight line, because the MR curve could then be drawn accurately. The MR curve would start at the same place as the demand curve on the y axis of the graph, and would cut the x axis halfway along from the origin to where the demand curve cuts it.

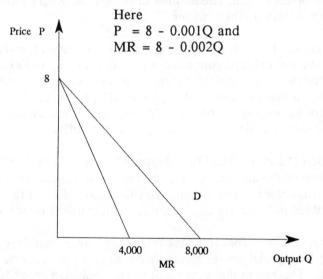

Here
P = 8 - 0.001Q and
MR = 8 - 0.002Q

Make sure that the axes of your diagrams are labelled, and that you explain the diagram properly in the text.

Current affairs
Keep up to date by reading the economic and financial sections of the good quality newspapers. Listen to or watch economics-related programmes on radio or television, of which there is a growing number. Try to relate current affairs to what you are learning.

A NOTE ON OBJECTIVE TEST (MULTIPLE CHOICE) QUESTIONS

Introduction

A multiple choice or objective test question consists of two elements.

(a) The *stem*. The stem sets out the problem or task to be solved. It may be in the form of a question, or it may be an unfinished statement which you have to complete.

(b) The *options*. These are the responses from which you must choose the one you believe to be correct. There is only one correct option; the other, incorrect, options are called *distractors*.

Example

An advertisement claims '80 per cent of dog owners buy Brand X'. Assuming the claim to be true, the probability that, of two dog owners chosen at random, exactly *one* buys Brand X is:

A 0.2   B 0.16   C 0.32   D 0.36

Discussion

The stem of the question ends at '... Brand X is'. This stem takes the form of an unfinished statement which must be completed by the student. Four options (A - D) are given and you must choose which you think is correct. In this case the correct answer is 0.32 (option C).

(a) The question above consists of a stem and *four* options. This means that there are three distractors and one correct option. The number of options may vary from one paper to another, but it will not vary within a single paper.

(b) Each option is identified by a letter A,B,C, etc. Once you have identified which you think is the correct option you must record your answer in whatever way the examiner instructs. In the specimen paper students are required to indicate their choice by circling the appropriate letter. For example, in the question above, you would place a circle 'O' around the letter C. But other methods of answering are possible, for example a tick by the appropriate letter. You should read the instructions on the question paper carefully.

(c) In some cases, option D has consisted of the words 'None of these' or 'None of the above'. If you believe that none of the options A - C is correct, you would then circle letter D. It would not be necessary in that case to submit your own calculation of what the true answer is. Indeed, the answer paper does not contain any space for calculations or workings.

One of the advantages claimed for multiple choice questions is that they remove the subjective element in marking. The special answer sheets are documents which can be read and electronically marked by computer. This means that your result on each question depends entirely on whether or not you have circled the correct option. No credit can be given for workings and, unlike with conventional questions, there is no point in submitting neat supporting calculations. Once you are satisfied that you know the correct option, draw a circle around the appropriate letter; if you later change your mind, *clearly* block out your original choice and encircle your new choice.

The use of multiple choice questions has some implications for the way you plan your study and your approach to the examination itself.

A NOTE ON OBJECTIVE TEST (MULTIPLE CHOICE) QUESTIONS

(a) Multiple choice questions are typically very short (perhaps worth one or two marks). A paper set entirely in this format would consist of some 60 to 70 questions, compared with the three to ten questions of a conventional paper. This permits the examiner to range much more widely over the syllabus. The practice of question spotting (ie revising only certain key areas of the syllabus, in the hope that the other areas will not be examined) is unwise even for a conventional examination; with a multiple choice approach, any gaps in knowledge are even more likely to be shown up.

(b) An advantage claimed for multiple choice testing is to some extent a corollary of (a) above. In conventional examinations, students are sometimes confronted with a lengthy question which they are unable to attempt (perhaps because of inadequate revision or because they can see no good way to get started or because the question is ambiguously worded). If this happens, they may fail the exam without having had enough scope to show how much they know. With multiple choice testing, failure to answer a question leads to the loss of only two marks at most. Well-prepared candidates will find they are able to show the extent of their knowledge.

(c) Multiple choice is an ideal format for testing factual knowledge and computational ability; it is much more difficult to test a student's skills in analysis and evaluation. For this reason, you will find that 50% of the marks on the paper will be allocated to conventional questions.

You must ensure that you are completely familiar with multiple choice questions, since 50% of the marks in your examination will relate to questions in this format. In this kit you will find a large bank of multiple choice questions on each section of the syllabus. If you would like some extra practice you may be interested in the **Password** series of books published by BPP Publishing Limited. Each book contains over 300 multiple choice questions, revision notes at the start of each chapter, and full solutions. The titles which are particularly relevant to this paper are **Foundation Business Mathematics, Business Law** and **Economics**. See the back of this kit for an order form.

Specimen paper: questions

Time allowed: 3 hours

Instructions to students

1. You will be allowed five minutes at the end of the examination to enter your examination number on the front of the answer book and at the top of every sheet used. Your name must not appear anywhere.

2. State XBS and the appropriate section identifying letter on the line marked subject. The full title of the paper is not required.

3. Attempt all questions.
    The paper is divided into three sections. Each section carries equal marks.
    Within each section the multiple choice questions represent 55% of available marks and the conventional questions 45%.*

4. Candidates are advised that allocation of marks between the two types of question does not indicate the Institute's assessment of the amount of time that is required to answer them. You are advised to devote no more than 75 minutes to the multiple-choice questions.

5. Use the special answer sheets provided for the multiple-choice questions. Begin each narrative answer on a separate page. Enter clearly the section letter on all answer sheets.

6. Answer the narrative questions using:

    - effective arrangement and presentation
    - clarity of explanation
    - logical argument
    - clear, concise and lucid English.

7. Ensure you have been handed a copy of 'Mathematical tables for students'.

---

* Tutorial note: remember that the allocation of marks in the examination has now changed to 50% for multiple choice and 50% for conventional questions. We have left the marks as shown in the specimen paper so that you can judge the relative weightings for this particular set of questions.

Section A: Statistics

Each of the questions numbered from 1 to 10 inclusive given below has only one correct answer. On the special answer sheet provided, you are required to place a circle O around the letter (either A, B, C or D) that gives the correct answer to each question.

If you wish to change your mind about an answer, block out your first attempt and then encircle another letter. If you do not indicate clearly your final choice, or if you encircle more than one letter, no marks will be awarded for the question concerned.

You are advised to spend no more than 25 minutes on these ten questions.

1. The number of rejects from eleven machines is as follows:

    7,   2,   2,   3,   1,   5,   6,   1,   6,   1,   10

    The median number of rejects is:

    A   1
    B   3
    C   4
    D   5

2. A small factory employs four groups of staff, totalling 60 people. The arithmetic mean earnings per week for all employees is £80. Earnings per week for three groups is given below.

Group	Number of employees	Mean earnings per week £
I	15	60
II	10	100
III	20	70

    The arithmetic mean earnings per week for group IV is

    A   not possible to find from the data provided
    B   £76.67
    C   £90.00
    D   £100.00

3. If we denote the probability of X by P(X) and $P(X) = 0.4$, $P(Y) = 0.3$, $P(X \text{ or } Y) = 0.7$ what is $P(X \cap Y)$, ie P(X and Y)?

    A   0
    B   0.12
    C   0.58
    D   0.70

13

4. An accountant is sampling invoices from a computer file. She randomly selects one week and investigates every invoice for that week. The sample of invoices selected for investigation is termed

    A   simple random
    B   stratified
    C   cluster
    D   quota

5. The price of a new product is to be £1.00 per unit, plus or minus 10%. The quantity sold is expected to be 1,000 units, plus or minus 20%. The maximum error in the estimated sales revenue will be

    A   20%
    B   28%
    C   30%
    D   32%

6.

	January 1980		January 1986	
	Price	Quantity sold	Price	Quantity sold
X	£1	15	£2	10
Y	£2	10	£3	15
Z	£3	5	£3	20

The all-items Laspeyre price index for January 1986, with January 1980 = 100, is (to two decimal places)

    A   133.33
    B   150.00
    C   166.67
    D   250.00

7. When each employee of a firm is given a 4% pay rise, the coefficient of variation of the distribution of the firm's wages will

    A   remain unaltered
    B   decrease by 4%
    C   decrease by 2%
    D   increase by 2%

8. | Age (years) | 0 – 15 | 15 – 25 | 25 – 30 |
    | Number of people | 15 | 30 | 45 |

A correct shape for the histogram of the above distribution would be:

A

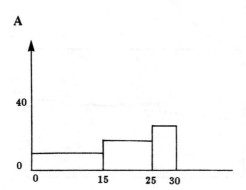

C

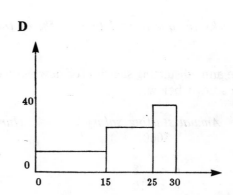

B

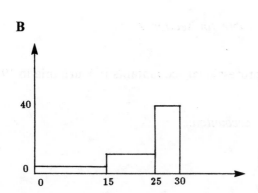

D

9. When each employee of a large firm is given a 9% increase in salary, the standard deviation of the new salary distribution

    A   is the same as before
    B   is 3% more than before
    C   is 4.4% more than before
    D   is 9% more than before

10.   £

15

The cumulative frequency curve for the above histogram could be represented as

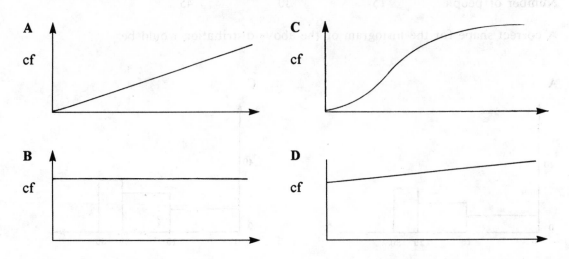

Total marks for questions 1 to 10: 55% of those available for section A

11. The annual starting salaries for newly-qualified professional accountants in Ruritania in 1985 are shown below.

Annual starting salary $000	Number of accountants
4 < 6	4
6 < 8	20
8 < 10	20
10 < 14	10
14 < 20	5
20 < 26	1

(Source: *First year after qualification, Ruritania*)

You are required:

(a) to calculate the arithmetic mean and standard deviation for this distribution, and explain their meanings in this case;

(b) to estimate an approximate value for the median and explain why it differs from the mean in (a).

45% of the marks available for section A

Section A: Statistics

Special answer sheet

1	A	B	C	D
2	A	B	C	D
3	A	B	C	D
4	A	B	C	D
5	A	B	C	D
6	A	B	C	D
7	A	B	C	D
8	A	B	C	D
9	A	B	C	D
10	A	B	C	D

Section B: Business law

Each of the questions numbered from 1 to 10 inclusive given below has only one correct answer. On the special answer sheet provided, you are required to place a circle 'O' around the letter (either A, B, C or D) that gives the correct answer to each question.

If you wish to change your mind about an answer, block out your first attempt, and then encircle another letter. If you do not indicate clearly your final choice, or if you encircle more than one letter, no marks will be awarded for the question concerned.

You are advised to spend no more than 25 minutes on these ten questions.

1. In relation to judicial precedent which of the following statements is incorrect?

   A The House of Lords is no longer bound by its previous decisions
   B The Court of Appeal is bound by decisions of the Judicial Committee of the Privy Council
   C The Court of Appeal will normally follow its own previous decisions
   D A High Court judge is not bound by decisions of other High Court judges

2. Which of the following acts emanating from the European Economic Community is immediately binding upon an English court?

   A Regulation
   B Directive
   C Decision of the European court
   D All of the above

3. An employee is injured by a machine which is not guarded in accordance with the Factories Act. He sues his employer for compensation on the grounds of strict liability.

   Which of the following defences could the employer successfully use?

   A That the machine had been delivered without a guard by the manufacturer
   B That a guard would render the machine inoperable
   C That, unknown to the employer, the guard had been removed
   D None of the above

4. With reference to the liability of one person for the torts of another person, which of the following statements is correct?

   A A company using the services of an independent contractor is never responsible for his actions

   B An employer who is found to be vicariously liable for the actions of his employee can be indemnified by that employee

   C An employer is never responsible if he has instructed an employee not to do the wrongful act

   D An employee has no liability in tort if his employer is vicariously liable

5. A offers to sell goods to B at a price of £100 per unit. B replies accepting A's offer but says he will only pay a price of £80 per unit.

    Which of the following statements is correct?

    A   A contract has been formed on A's terms

    B   No contract has been formed but, if A refuses B's counter offer, B may then insist on delivery at A's price

    C   No contract has been formed and, if A refuses B's counter price, B is not able to insist on delivery at A's price

    D   A contract has been formed on B's terms

6. On 1 April A agreed to lend £500 to B for a period of two months. A clause in the contract provided that if repayment was not made by 31 May B should immediately become liable to A to the extent of £2,000. This sum of £2,000 would be held by a court to be

    A   anticipatory damages
    B   a penalty
    C   liquidated damages
    D   unliquidated damages

7. In the case of most contracts silence does not constitute misrepresentation. Exceptionally, however, the law does impose a duty upon contracting parties to disclose all material facts.

    In which of the following types of contract is disclosure required?

    A   Carriage of goods
    B   Employment
    C   Sale of a business
    D   Insurance

8. Which of the following contracts will be valid if made orally?

    A   Sale of goods to the value of £10,000
    B   Sale of shares in a company
    C   A contract of guarantee
    D   A contract of hire purchase

9. The apparent authority of an agent would not be decided by reference to

    A   prior dealings between the parties
    B   the types of activity engaged in by the agent
    C   an undisclosed limitation on the agent's usual activity
    D   the custom of the trade or profession

10. In which of the following situations may the principal disclaim responsibility for the actions of his 'agent'?

   A   A partner in a firm of accountants orders stationery on credit. The supplier now requests payment from one of the other partners

   B   A salesman is instructed that discount should only be given on orders over 1,000 items. A customer who was promised discount by the salesman on his order for 500 items insists on paying the reduced price

   C   An insurance agent issues a policy to a client on behalf of his company and accepts payment of the full premium. The money is never sent to the company which claims that the client is not insured

   D   A gale causes severe damage to the roof of a house whilst the owner is away on holiday. A neighbour engages a builder to carry out repairs to avoid further damage. The owner later refuses to pay the builder for his work.

   Total marks for questions 1 to 10: 55% of those available for section B

11. Define a contract and explain the essential requirements for the formation of a valid contract. Why is an understanding of the principles of the law of contract of importance to businessmen?

   45% of the marks available for section B

Section B: Business Law

Special answer sheet

1	A	B	C	D
2	A	B	C	D
3	A	B	C	D
4	A	B	C	D
5	A	B	C	D
6	A	B	C	D
7	A	B	C	D
8	A	B	C	D
9	A	B	C	D
10	A	B	C	D

Section C: Economics

Each of the questions numbered from 1 to 10 inclusive given below has only one correct answer. On the special answer sheet provided, you are required to place a circle 'O' around the letter (either A, B, C or D) that gives the correct answer to each question.

If you wish to change your mind about an answer, block out your first attempt and then encircle another letter. If you do not indicate clearly your final choice or if you encircle more than one letter, no marks will be given for the question concerned.

You are advised to spend no more than 25 minutes on these ten questions.

1. Given a free market and a completely inelastic demand, a sudden increase in supply will most likely

    A   increase the total income of the producers
    B   increase the price of the commodity
    C   decrease the quantity demanded
    D   decrease the total income of the producers

2. If there is no change in supply, a leftward shift in the demand curve will

    A   increase price
    B   decrease price
    C   leave price unchanged
    D   alter price in proportion to the movement of the shift

3. A short-run average cost curve

    A   sometimes crosses the long-run curve
    B   always crosses the long-run curve
    C   always lies above all points on the long-run curve
    D   coincides with the long-run curve at one point

4. In the United Kingdom a statutory monopoly is defined as an industry in which

    A   one firm produces 25% of the industry's output
    B   one firm produces 33% of the industry's output
    C   there are fewer than three firms in the industry
    D   one firm dominates the industry

5. Trade Unions find it easier to gain wage increases when

    A   the employer is in a competitive industry
    B   labour supply is elastic
    C   the industry is capital-intensive
    D   the demand for labour is elastic

6. When the demand for a product in a freely competitive market has a price elasticity greater than unity, which of the following statements is true?

   A   A price fall results in a fall in the producers' total revenue
   B   A price fall does not alter the producers' total revenue
   C   A price rise results in a fall in the producers' total revenue
   D   A price rise results in a rise in the producers' total revenue

7. A free market economy implies the existence of all of the following conditions except which one?

   A   Equilibrium price is determined by the interaction of demand and supply
   B   The state intervenes to free the market from the distortions of imperfect competition
   C   Consumers and producers may enter and leave the market freely
   D   Prices will fluctuate as demand and supply change

8. Which of the following statements shows an inelastic demand for the product?

   A   At 10p 100 are bought; at 9p 125
   B   At 10p 100 are bought; at 11p 80
   C   At 10p 100 are bought; at 9p 110
   D   At 10p 100 are bought; at 11p 95

9. Rational economic behaviour involves all of the following actions except which one?

   A   Consumer will satisfy wants according to a scale of preferences
   B   Consumer will be consistent in choice of products
   C   Consumer will choose the cheaper of two identical products
   D   Consumer will maximise satisfaction where purchases give equi-marginal utility.

10. At which of the output points A, B, C or D in the diagram below will a firm in imperfect competition maximise profit?

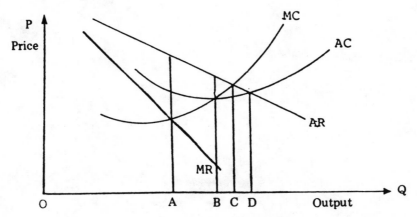

Total marks for questions 1 to 10: 55% of those available for section C

11. Explain how the price mechanism operates in an advanced industrial mixed economy.

    45% of the marks available for section C

Section C: Economics

Special answer sheet

1   A   B   C   D

2   A   B   C   D

3   A   B   C   D

4   A   B   C   D

5   A   B   C   D

6   A   B   C   D

7   A   B   C   D

8   A   B   C   D

9   A   B   C   D

10 A   B   C   D

REVIEW OF THE SPECIMEN PAPER

General remarks

The specimen paper is in three sections: Section A (Statistics), Section B (Business law) and Section C (Economics). Each section is identical in format, containing ten questions in multiple choice format and a single question in conventional format.

In each section, the multiple choice questions account for 55% of the total marks available. (*Note:* For your examination this proportion will be reduced to 50%.)

Despite the greater number of marks available for the multiple choice questions, candidates are advised in the rubric to the examination paper not to allocate more than 25 minutes per section to these questions (ie 75 minutes in total). This leaves 35 minutes available for each of the three conventional questions. It is worthwhile following this advice because the conventional questions require fairly lengthy answers to do them justice.

Section A

The Statistics section is almost entirely concerned with computations/diagrams in the multiple choice questions. But in question 11 students are required not only to perform calculations but also to explain their procedures and interpret their results.

Section B

Business law is a particularly difficult subject to examine by means of multiple choice questions because it abounds with exceptions and fine distinctions. Some of the questions set (eg Q1) avoid this problem by referring to matters of pure factual knowledge. In other questions (eg Q5) the facts given are taken from a specified decided case, so that again an unambiguously correct answer is available.

The conventional question in this section is a straightforward one on the essential elements of a valid contract. But the student is required to go beyond his book knowledge of contract law to think about why businessmen need to understand contract law at all.

Section C

The Economics section concentrates in its multiple choice questions on the theory of price and demand and the features of perfect and imperfect competition.

The conventional question seems at first sight to call for mere regurgitation of everything you know about the price mechanism. But as always it is important to read the question carefully. It is concerned specifically with 'advanced industrial mixed economies'. Only a proportion of the marks will be available for general remarks on the price mechanism; to score well, you must go on to deal with the specific features of these economies.

Specimen paper: suggested solutions

Section A: Statistics

1.   B   The median is the middle number when the scores are ranked:

$$1, 1, 1, 2, 2, 3, 5, 6, 6, 7, 10$$
$$\uparrow$$
Middle number = 3

2.   D   Let x be the arithmetic mean earnings per week for group IV

$$\frac{(60 \times 15) + (100 \times 10) + (70 \times 20) + 15x}{60} = 80$$

$$900 + 1,000 + 1,400 + 15x = 4,800$$

$$15x = 1,500$$

$$x = \underline{£100}$$

3.   A $P(X \text{ or } Y) = P(X) + P(Y) - P(X \text{ and } Y)$

so $P(X \text{ and } Y) = P(X) + P(Y) - P(X \text{ or } Y)$

$$= 0.4 + 0.3 - 0.7$$

$$= 0$$

4.   C   This is the definition of cluster sampling, when every item in the small area fitting the definition is examined.

5.   D   Maximum price = £1.10
Maximum quantity sold = 1,200
So maximum sales revenue = £1.10 x 1,200 = £1,320
This is 32% above the estimated sales revenue

6.   B

p_0	p_1	q_0	$p_0 q_0$	$p_1 q_0$
£	£			
1	2	15	15	30
2	3	10	20	30
3	3	5	15	15
			50	75

Laspeyre price index $= \dfrac{\Sigma p_1 q_0}{\Sigma p_0 q_0} \times 100\%$

$$= \frac{75}{50} \times 100\% = 150.00$$

7. A   Coefficient of variation = $\dfrac{\text{standard deviation}}{\text{mean}}$

If each wage is increased by 4%, both the mean and the standard deviation will increase by 4%, leaving the coefficient of variation unchanged.

8. B

Age (years)	Frequency	Adjustment to account for different widths of classes	Adjusted frequency
0 – 15	15	x $\frac{1}{3}$	5
15 – 25	30	x $\frac{1}{2}$	15
25 – 30	45		45

Graph B looks most like the histogram, with frequencies (heights of bars) of 5, 15 and 45.

9. D $\sigma = \sqrt{\dfrac{\Sigma\, f(x-\bar{x})^2}{\Sigma f}}$

If each x is increased by 9%, the mean $\bar{x}$ will also increase by 9%, and so the whole standard deviation will increase by 9%.

10. A   The cumulative frequency must start at the origin, and here increases evenly for increasing x values.

11.

Annual starting salary $000	Midpoint x	Number of accountants f	xf	fx²
4, < 6	5	4	20	100
6, < 8	7	20	140	980
8, < 10	9	20	180	1,620
10, < 14	12	10	120	1,440
14, < 20	17	5	85	1,445
20, < 26	23	1	23	529
		60	568	6,114

(a) Arithmetic mean $\bar{x}$ = $\dfrac{568}{60}$ = 9.467 thousand dollars

= $9,467

Standard deviation σ = $\sqrt{\dfrac{\Sigma f x^2}{\Sigma f} - (\bar{x})^2}$

= $\sqrt{\dfrac{6,114}{60} - (9.467)^2}$

= 3.505 thousand dollars

= $3,505

Any measure of average such as the arithmetic mean is a 'measure of central tendency' ie whereas a population may range in values, the mean is a value in the middle of this cluster of values and may be considered to be representative of the population as a whole. With the given example, although the annual starting salaries for newly-qualified professional accountants in Ruritania range through the given bands, they all cluster about some mid-point of $9,467 (or $9,500 to the nearest hundred dollars).

The standard deviation then gives us some idea of the spread of the salaries about this mean value. Most observations fall within one standard deviation below and above the arithmetic mean, and nearly all observations fall within three standard deviations of the mean.

(b) Median = $\left[\begin{array}{c} \text{value of lower limit of class} \\ \text{in which the median item falls} \end{array} \right] + \left[\dfrac{R}{f} \times c \right]$

where   R = the difference between the median ranking and the cumulative frequency up to the beginning of the median class
f = the frequency of the median class
c = the size of the median class

With 60 items in the population, the median item is 60/2th = 30th item. (It would also be possible to use the $30\frac{1}{2}$th which would give a slightly different answer). The 30th item is the 6th in the 8 to 10 thousand dollars class.

So the median = $8,000 + \left[\dfrac{30 - 24}{20} \times 2,000 \right]$

= $\underline{\$8,600}$

The median differs from the mean because the distribution is skewed, that is not perfectly symmetrical about its average value. In this case the distribution is positively skewed, ie is weighted towards the left hand side of the graph. It is a feature of positively skewed distribution that the mode is less than the median, which in turn is less than the arithmetic mean. In the given case we have a median of $8,600 which is indeed lower than the arithmetic mean calculated to be $9,467.

SPECIMEN PAPER: SUGGESTED SOLUTIONS

Section B: Business law

1. **B** Decisions of the Judicial Committee of the Privy Council may be cited as *persuasive* precedents, but are not binding on the Court of Appeal.

2. **A** Directives require member states to alter their law. Until the alteration is made, they are not binding. Decisions of the EC Commission are immediately binding, but these should not be confused with decisions of the European Court.

3. **D** In cases of strict liability, it need not be shown that the defendant employer acted negligently; the defences in A, B and C are therefore irrelevant.

4. **B** A is wrong because there are many circumstances in which a person is liable for the torts of an independent contractor (eg in cases of strict liability). C is also wrong: see, for example, *Limpus v London General Omnibus Co 1862*. D is wrong because the person who actually commits a tort (the *tortfeasor*) is *always* liable for his wrong.

5. **C** The facts are based on *Hyde v Wrench 1840*.

6. **B** See *Dunlop v New Garage & Motor Co 1915*.

7. **D** Insurance is a contract *uberrimae fidei*.

8. **A** Contracts of guarantee may be made orally but are not enforceable in a court of law unless there is written evidence of their terms. Contracts for the sale of shares and hire purchase agreements are void unless they are in writing.

9. **C** An undisclosed limitation affects the *actual* authority of an agent, but cannot affect his *apparent* authority.

10. **D** A is wrong because a partner is an agent of the firm and of the other partners. B is wrong because the salesman is acting within his apparent authority and his principal is therefore bound. The same applies to C. But in D the neighbour has neither actual nor apparent authority and his action is not binding. He is not an agent of necessity.

11. A contract is an agreement which legally binds the parties involved. Sometimes contracts are referred to as enforceable agreements, but this is rather misleading since one party cannot usually force the other to fulfil his part of the bargain. He will usually be restricted to the remedy of damages.

    The essential requirements for the formation of a valid contract are:
    (a) it is an agreement made by *offer and acceptance*;
    (b) the parties intend thereby to create *legal relations* between themselves; and
    (c) it is a bargain by which the obligations assumed by each party are supported by *consideration* given by the other. (But a gratuitous promise is binding if made by deed.)

Offer and acceptance

An offer is a definite promise to be bound on specific terms. It must be distinguished from the mere supply of information and from an invitation to treat. Acceptance may be by express words or by action; it may also be implied from conduct. But passive inaction is not acceptance. Acceptance must be unqualified agreement to the terms of the offer.

Legal relations

In domestic agreements (for example between husband and wife) it is presumed that there is no intention to create legal relations, although this can be rebutted. But when businessmen enter into commercial agreements it is presumed that there *is* an intention to enter into legal relations unless this is expressly disclaimed or the circumstances displace that presumption.

Consideration

Consideration is either an advantage to the promisor or a detriment incurred by the promisee. It must have some value, but the value may be nominal.

Assuming that these three essential requirements are present in an agreement a valid contract may exist. But the contract may still be vitiated in certain circumstances:

(a)   The contract must be sufficiently complete and precise in its terms. Any vagueness in the agreed terms may make it difficult to enforce.

(b)   Some contracts must be made in a particular form or supported by written evidence.

(c)   Agreements obtained through mistake, misrepresentation, duress or undue influence may not be valid contracts.

(d)   The courts will not enforce a contract which is deemed to be illegal or contrary to public policy.

(e)   Some persons (for example minors) have only restricted capacity to enter into contracts and are not bound by agreements made outside those limits.

The conduct of business is founded upon contract law. Most business transactions take the form of agreements involving the exchange of goods or services for money. The law relating to contracts provides a stable framework within which this economic activity can take place and enables businessmen to take decisions with a firm knowledge of the consequences.

Businessmen benefit from an understanding of contract law in two ways:

(a)   They need to know the implications of contracts undertaken by themselves and the consequences if they fail to honour their obligations.

(b)   They need to know what recourse is open to them in the event that the other party dishonours his contractual obligations.

Although professional legal advice is available, most business transactions are undertaken without any involvement by lawyers and it is important that businessmen should themselves realise the contractual implications.

SPECIMEN PAPER: SUGGESTED SOLUTIONS

Section C: Economics

1. **D** With completely inelastic demand, the additional quantities available will not be taken up by consumers.

2. **B**

3. **D** A long-run average cost curve can be drawn by joining up the minimum points on the short-run average cost curves of firms producing on different scales of output.

4. **A**

5. **C** In capital-intensive industries demand for labour is inelastic. Price rises, ie increased wage rates, do not reduce demand for labour from the consumer, ie employers.

6. **C** If price elasticity is greater than unity, a rise in price will lead to a more than proportionate fall in demand, so that producers' total revenue falls.

7. **B**

8. **D** A 10% price rise leads to only a 5% fall in demand. Contrast this with B (where the 10% price rise led to a 20% fall in demand) and with A and C (where a 10% price reduction leads to increases in demand of 25% and 10% respectively).

9. **B** This would be irrational behaviour: it implies that consumers will continue to buy a product even if a superior or cheaper alternative becomes available.

10. **A** Profits are maximised where marginal revenue equals marginal costs.

11. The price mechanism describes the interaction of demand and supply for goods in markets, whereby:

    (a) the price of a good determines the quantity that will be demanded;

    (b) the price of the good also determines the quantity that producers will be prepared to supply at that price.

    In a free market economy, the unrestricted interaction of demand and supply, given no change in demand or supply conditions, should result in an equilibrium price and output level for each good in each market. In a controlled economy, the government can try to determine the quantity that will be produced, regardless of price, and it can also try to determine the supply quantity, but it cannot control demand. The price mechanism therefore works imperfectly in a controlled economy, typically with supply shortages and sometimes black markets developing. In a mixed economy, some markets behave in a free market fashion and others are controlled, and so the allocation of scarce resources within the economy is partly attributable to the free workings of demand and supply, and partly to the allocation decision of government.

In an advanced industrial mixed economy, the government will supply a variety of goods free of charge, or below cost. Education, health, defence, police and fire services are typical examples.

Demand for goods in any market will be related to price, and the demand curve for a good is downward sloping. The reason why this is so is explained theoretically by utility theory and indifference theory. (Consumers will choose a mix of products with their income so that the amount of marginal utility obtained per penny spent on any marginal quantity of any product is the same.) If the price of a product goes up, its marginal utility per penny spent must fall, and so consumers will buy less of the product.

The supply of goods in a market is determined by the marginal costs of suppliers. Individual firms, seeking to maximise profits, will produce output up to the output level where MC = MR. Given diminishing returns to scale, the MC curve will rise. The supply curve of an industry is the sum of the supply curves of all the individual firms in it.

Advanced industrial societies are characterised by the imperfectly competitive market structures of monopoly, oligopoly and oligopolistic competition, whereby firms are able to achieve a downward sloping demand curve for their own output. (In perfectly competitive markets, the industry's demand curve is downward sloping, but the demand curve of each individual firm is perfectly elastic.) With a downward sloping demand curve, imperfectly competitive firms are likely to be able to achieve supernormal profits, and output levels will be lower and price higher than in perfectly competitive markets.

Prices are not stable in most markets, and the reason that a price might not remain the equilibrium price for long is that changes may occur in demand or supply conditions, causing shifts in the market demand or supply curve - for example changes in the price of substitute goods, changes in consumer income and changes in producers' costs.

The extent to which shifts in demand affect price and output depend on the scale of the shift, and the elasticity of supply. Similarly, the extent to which shifts in the supply curve affect price and output depend on the scale of the shift and the elasticity of demand.

In summary the price mechanism in an advanced industrial mixed economy can be described as the interaction of supply and demand, with free market forces operating to arrive at an equilibrium price in some markets, and government resource allocation decisions or price decisions affecting price and output levels in other markets. Prices in all markets are continually moving up or down as market conditions change.

Statistics

1 What is the difference between discrete variables and continuous variables? Give an example of each.

2 What is a random sample?

3 A factory owner estimates that a week's work will use 2,750kg of materials at £7 per kg. Either quantity or unit price could differ from his estimate by up to 13% of the estimate. What is the maximum error in total cost, as a percentage of the estimated total cost?

4 A business buys two components, the A and the B. In 19X1 each A cost £5, each B cost £8 and the numbers of each used were 2,000 of A and 3,000 of B. By 19X5 the prices were £6 and £10 and the numbers used 2,200 and 2,500.

   What is the Paasche price index for 19X5 based on 19X1?

5 The Retail Prices Index was 100.0 in January 19X7. Retail prices rose by 3.3% in the period from then until January 19X8, and by 11.8% between January 19X8 and July 19X9. What is the value of the Retail Prices Index for July 19X9?

6 In a histogram of salaries, the bar for the range £10,501 - £11,000 was 9cm high and there were 50 people in that class. If there were 30 people in the class £11,001 - £11,250, how high would the bar for that class be?

7 In a pie chart, what would be the angle of a sector representing 38% of the total?

8 What is the standard deviation of the following frequency distribution?

Value	Frequency
-6	20
2	30
4	50
5	20

9 The numbers of responses from nine different direct mail advertisements were as follows.

   70, 70, 20, 60, 70, 20, 30, 40, 70

   What was the median number of responses from an advertisement?

10 What amount will be in a bank account after five years if £2,000 is invested at 12% per annum compound with interest credited annually?

11 I can play a game by placing a £2 bet. I have an 0.35 probability of winning £3, and an 0.27 probability of having my name entered (free of charge) in a second game. In the second game, if my name is entered, I have an 0.47 probability of winning £1.30. What is the expected value of my entering the first game?

TEST YOUR KNOWLEDGE: QUESTIONS

Business law

12 Explain briefly 'common law' and 'equity'.

13 Distinguish *ratio decidendi* and *obiter dictum*.

14 In the law of contract, what is an offer and in what form is it made? Must an offer be communicated to a person who accepts it?

15 What is (i) executed and (ii) executory consideration?

16 What is the difference between a condition and a warranty?

17 Is it necessary that (i) a hire purchase agreement regulated by the Consumer Credit Act 1974 or (ii) a contract for the grant of a lease of land should be a written document?

18 In what circumstances (if any) may the condition of merchantable quality, implied by the Sale of Goods Act 1979, be excluded from the contract?

19 Distinguish between (i) common mistake and (ii) mutual mistake.

20 What are the remedies for misrepresentation in inducing a contract?

21 What is a restraint of trade?

22 How may the obligations arising from a contract be discharged?

23 What is the difference between (i) remoteness of damage and (ii) measure (or *quantum*) of damages?

24 What is specific performance?

25 What is strict liability in tort?

26 How are loss and wrong distinguished, and what is the importance of the distinction?

27 In what circumstances may 'economic loss' be grounds for an action for compensation for negligence?

28 What defences are possible to an action in tort?

29 How is agency created?

30 Is an agent entitled to be paid for his services or otherwise rewarded?

31 What is the difference between (i) actual and (ii) apparent (or ostensible) authority of an agent?

Economics

32 What are the four factors of production and the rewards associated with each factor?

33 List reasons why the government may intervene in a free market economy.

34 What is the formula for elasticity of demand? What is the significance of elasticity for total *revenue* when prices change?

35 What will be the effect of minimum price regulations on demand and supply? Give an example of minimum price legislation in practice.

36 (a) Define marginal cost.

    (b) Define marginal revenue.

37 What is the difference between the theory of diminishing returns and economies and diseconomies of scale? How are they consistent with each other?

38 Distinguish oligopoly and monopolistic competition.

39 What barriers to entry might protect a monopoly from competitors who would otherwise enter the market?

40 List the sources of capital available to a company.

41 What are the two basic types of inflation?

42 What are the functions of money?

43 What are the functions of the Bank of England?

Statistics

1   Discrete variables can only take on certain values (for example the number of students in a class cannot be 23.7).

Continuous variables may take on any value, and are measured rather than counted (for example the warmest temperature reached in a day can be 23.7 degrees).

2   A random sample is a sample selected in such a way that every item in the population has an equal chance of being included.

3   Estimated cost   =   2,750 x £7 = £19,250. Maximum cost = (2,750 x 1.13) x (£7 x 1.13)
                      =   3,107.5 x £7.91 = £24,580.33. Maximum error = £24,580.33 - £19,250
                      =   £5,330.33

Percentage error   = $\frac{5,330.33}{19,250}$ x 100% = 27.69%

4   Paasche price index number = $\frac{\Sigma p_1 q_1}{\Sigma p_0 q_1}$ x 100

	p_0	p_1	q_1	$p_0 q_1$	$p_1 q_1$
A	5	6	2,200	11,000	13,200
B	8	10	2,500	20,000	25,000
				31,000	38,200

Index for 19X5 based on 19X1   = $\frac{38,200}{31,000}$ x 100

                               =   123.23

5   The index in January 19X8 was 100.0 x (1 + 0.033) = 103.3.
     The index in July 19X9 is 103.3 x (1 + 0.118) = 115.5

6   The class is half the width of the preceding class (£250 as against £500), and the height must be correspondingly adjusted.

Height = 9 x $\frac{30}{50}$ x 2 = 10.8cm

7   Angle = 38/100 x 360° = 136.8°

8

x	f	fx	$x - \bar{x}$	$(x - \bar{x})^2$	$f(x - \bar{x})^2$
-6	20	-120	-8	64	1,280
2	30	60	0	0	0
4	50	200	2	4	200
5	20	100	3	9	180
	120	240			1,660

$\bar{x} = 240/120 = 2$

Standard deviation $= \sqrt{\dfrac{\Sigma f(x-\bar{x})^2}{\Sigma f}} = \sqrt{\dfrac{1,660}{120}}$

$= \sqrt{13.833} = 3.72$

TEST YOUR KNOWLEDGE: SOLUTIONS

9   The numbers must first be ranked in order

   20, 20, 30, 40, 60, 70, 70, 70, 70

The median is the fifth number, which is 60.

10   £2,500 x $(1.12)^5$ = £4,405.85

11   Expected value = -£2 + 0.35 x £3 + 0.27 x 0.47 x £1.30
                   = -£2 + £1.05 + £0.16
                   = -£0.79

Business Law

12   Common law was developed in mediaeval times by royal courts as a law common to the whole kingdom, through which the judges went on tour at regular intervals.

Equity was a system of relief from the rigidity and restricted scope of the common law developed by the Chancellor to whom the king referred petitions on legal matters.

13   *Ratio decidendi* are the reasons given (in terms of rules of law) in deciding a case. *Obiter dictum* are remarks, often on a hypothetical point, which appear in the judgement but are not the reasons for the court's decision. Only the *ratio decidendi* of a previous decision are relevant as a possible precedent in a later case.

14   An offer is a proposal to enter into a binding contract on the terms indicated in the offer. It may be in any form, written, spoken or by conduct. Display or advertisement of goods and indication of a selling price are generally not sufficient to constitute an offer.

The reward cases suggest that unless an offer has been communicated an act of 'acceptance' cannot be acceptance of the offer so far as to make a binding agreement.

15   (a)   Executed consideration is the act or forbearance which must be completed to render a contractual promise binding.
   (b)   Executory consideration is a promise made in return for a promise. Each party is bound although neither at that time has carried out (executed) his promise as consideration for the promise given to him. But the mutual promises suffice.

16   A condition is a fundamental term and if a party breaks it the other has the option of treating the contract as discharged by the breach. A warranty is a less important term, breach of which gives rise only to a claim for damages.

17   (i)   A regulated hire purchase agreement must be a document in writing complying with the Consumer Credit Act 1974.
   (ii)   A contract for the grant of a lease (a disposition of an interest in land) must be in writing following the Law of Property (Miscellaneous Provisions) Act 1989.

18   In a contract where the buyer is not a 'consumer' the implied condition may be excluded if it is 'reasonable' as provided by the Unfair Contract Terms Act 1977.

19 (i) Common mistake is where the parties are in complete agreement but are mistaken as to some fundamental thing, such as the existence of the subject matter.

    (ii) Mutual mistake is where each party believes that the other agrees with him but there is a misunderstanding and a latent disagreement over a point on which each puts a different interpretation.

20 The party misled may rescind, provided that he has not lost the right to do so. Except where the misrepresentation is innocent, there is usually a right to recover damages in addition to rescission. In negligent or innocent misrepresentation the court may award damages instead of ordering rescission.

21 Restraint of trade is a restriction by contract of the normal freedom of a person to carry on any gainful occupation including a profession, either as an employee or on his own account.

22 A contract may be discharged by performance, mutual agreement, at the option of one party (repudiation), by breach of condition by the other and by frustration (also called subsequent impossibility).

23 (i) Remoteness is the test (*Hadley v Baxendale*) of the kind of damage or loss caused by breach of contract for which compensation will be awarded in a court of law. Damages are not given for every consequence caused by the breach. There is a test of reasonable foreseeability.

    (ii) The measure of damages is the calculation of a monetary sum which is reckoned to be sufficient to put the innocent party in the same financial position as if the contract had been duly performed.

24 In some circumstances, particularly a contract for the sale of land, the court has power at its discretion to order the party at fault to perform the contract rather than pay damages for breaking it.

25 Where there is strict liability the tortfeasor does not have to be shown to have acted negligently or intentionally. He is liable purely by reason of having created a situation of inherent risk. Thus he cannot escape by showing that he used reasonable skill and care as he has breached an absolute duty. The most notable example is the keeping of potentially damaging substances on land, such as water (*Rylands v Fletcher*) or zoo animals.

26 A loss, or *damnum*, is a consequence of an action for which damages or compensation might be paid. That action may or may not be caused by a wrong or *injuria*. In most cases a loss suffered without the causative wrong is not actionable (*Electrochrome v Welsh Plastics*) while a wrong suffered without any proven loss will be. A wrong is the violation of a right vested in the injured party.

27 'Economic loss' is the amount of profits lost from, for example, losing working hours as a result of a tort. So a restaurant damaged by a flood from the office next door may sue for repairs but not for loss of profits while repairs are carried out.

28 A defence to an action in tort may be specific to the case or general, in which case it may be used in any action, including one involving strict liability:

    (i) consent, or *volenti non fit injuria*;
    (ii) accident;
    (iii) act of God, or unavoidable accident;
    (iv) statutory authority;
    (v) limitation, or the rule of *laches*, ie the action is bought too late;

(vi) capacity - in very limited circumstances want of capacity can be a defence; most notably diplomatic status may lead to immunity;

(vii) contributory negligence.

29　Agency is usually created by agreement, express or implied, between the principal and the agent. It may also be created by ratification, as agency of necessity or by estoppel.

30　There is no inherent right to payment or other reward for acting as an agent. It is often agreed that the agent shall receive a fee from the principal. If the agent obtains any 'profit' from the transaction or from the other party with whom he has dealings he should disclose to the principal what he has received. He is only entitled to retain it if the principal agrees.

31　(i)　Actual authority is what the principal agrees to give the agent. His agreement may be implied from employing an agent in a particular capacity.

　　(ii)　Apparent authority is that which the party dealing with the agent reasonably believes he has been given. This may be implied from what he does or the authority created by representation on the part of the principal which he is estopped from denying.

Economics

32　*Factor*　　　　　*Reward*
　Land　　　　　　Rent
　Labour　　　　　Wages
　Capital　　　　Interest
　Enterprise　　　Profits

33　The government may intervene in a free market economy for any of the following reasons:

- to moderate the trade cycle;

- to restrain the unfair use of economic power by monopolies or other bodies;

- to correct inequalities (eg to redistribute wealth between individuals and economic regions);

- to provide goods and services that private enterprise is reluctant or unable to provide;

- to remove any socially undesirable consequences of private production (eg pollution);

- to direct structural change;

- to manage price levels, employment levels, the balance of payments and economic growth in accordance with social objectives.

34　The responsiveness of demand to a change in price is termed the elasticity of demand. For a change in price: Elasticity of demand = $\dfrac{\text{\% change in quantity demanded}}{\text{\% change in price}}$

It is also possible to measure elasticity at a particular point on the demand curve. Point elasticity is defined as $\dfrac{dp}{dq} \cdot \dfrac{p}{q}$

For example with a demand curve $p = A - Bq^n$, where p is the price of the product and q is the quantity demanded then: $\dfrac{dp}{dq} = -nBq^{n-1}$

Therefore point elasticity of demand is measured by $- nBq^{n-1} \dfrac{p}{q}$.

(a) Elasticity greater than 1 (ie elastic demand):

   (i) Price goes up - demand falls so that total revenue falls;

   (ii) Price goes down - demand increases so that total revenue increases.

(b) Elasticity less than 1 (ie. inelastic demand):

   (i) Price goes up - demand falls, but total revenue goes up;

   (ii) Price goes down - demand rises, but total revenue falls.

(c) Elasticity is 1 (unity). If the price goes either up or down, there will be a counter-balancing change in quantity demanded so that total revenue remains the same.

(*Note:* Total *revenue* goes up, down or remains the same in the ways indicated here, but the effect on *profit* will depend also on changes in total costs.)

35 (a) If the minimum price set by regulation is below the equilibrium price, it will have no effect.

   (b) If the minimum price is above the equilibrium price, suppliers will want to produce more but consumers will want to buy less than they would do if the equilibrium price prevailed.

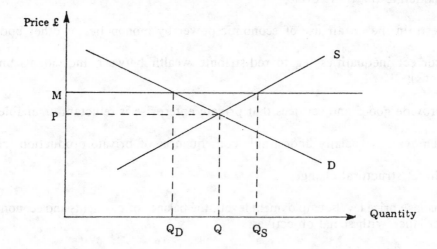

In the diagram, if the minimum price is M, suppliers will want to supply Q_S but consumers will demand Q_D.

An example of minimum price legislation is the minimum prices for agricultural produce set by the EEC. Since the EEC authorities will buy whatever suppliers produce, there will be production excess of demand equal to $Q_S - Q_D$ - ie. beef mountains, butter mountains, wine lakes etc.

36 (a) Marginal cost is the total cost of producing n units *less* the total cost of producing n-1 units.

    (b) Marginal revenue is the total revenue earned from the sales of n units *less* the total revenue earned from the sales of n-1 units.

37 (a) The 'law' of diminishing returns is that as a firm with an existing production capacity produces greater quantities of output, there will initially be increasing returns - ie. the marginal cost and average cost of producing extra units will fall - but there will eventually be diminishing returns and marginal costs of extra output and average unit costs will rise.

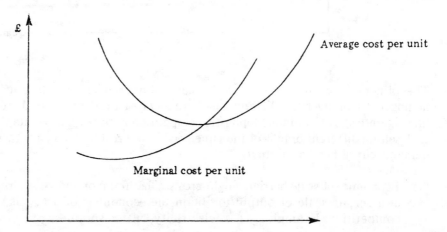

The *short run* average cost curve is therefore U-shaped and the marginal cost curve cuts the AC curve at its lowest point.

    (b) Economies of scale (and diseconomies of scale) refer to the reductions (and eventual increases) in average costs as a firm alters the scale of its operations. Since it takes time for a firm to grow bigger, the effect on costs of changes in scale can be described as a *long run* average cost curve.

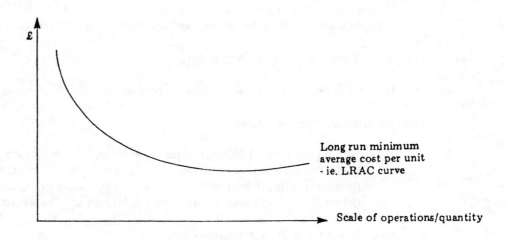

There is a short run average cost curve for every scale of operations. The LRAC curve is the 'envelope' of the series of short run AC curves, ie each short run AC curve will be tangential to the LRAC curve at the lowest average cost of producing that level of output in the long run.

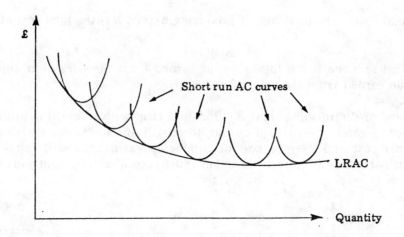

38 The oligopolistic firm is one of a small number of firms in a market, selling either a homogenous product or a differentiated product (ie a product where there are brand differences, like cigarettes). A firm in monopolistic competition is one of a large number of competing firms each selling different brands of the same goods. As a result, each firm faces a downward sloping demand curve for its product.

39 (a) Economies of scale barriers might create a 'natural monopoly'. A firm might need to operate at a certain scale of output to obtain the economies of scale that would make its costs competitive. Examples - gas, electricity, water supplies;

    (b) Patent laws;

    (c) Exclusive access to cheaper raw material sources (eg. exclusive supply contracts);

    (d) High costs of entry into the markets for a would-be competitor (eg. capital expenditure);

    (e) Government-awarded franchise or monopoly (eg. TV or radio companies);

    (f) Competitive action to give the monopolist's products a product differentiation advantage - eg. price wars or non-price competition such as advertising campaigns;

    (g) Taking over would-be competitors.

40 (a) Internal sources of capital - retained profits. Arguably also depreciation.

    (b) External sources of capital:

        (i)   New equity issues: Public companies can obtain new equity capital through the medium of the Stock Exchange (companies quoted on the SE) or the Unlisted Securities Market (companies quoted on the USM). A private company can raise new share capital privately or by 'going public' with a launch on the SE or USM.

        (ii) Issuing preference shares - rare.

        (iii) Issuing loan stock - fairly rare when interest rates are high. Some developments now in issuing 'floating rate notes' (ie. loan stock with a variable interest rate) on the eurobond market - very large companies only. Medium term notes (MTNs) are a medium term equivalent of commercial paper (CP).

      (iv)   Directors' loans (usually small owner-director companies).

      (v)   Bank loans (medium term as well as short term. Banks are now paying much more attention to the needs of larger corporate customers).

      (vi)   Short term finance: bank overdrafts, short term bank loans, money market loans, acceptance credits, commercial paper, multi-option facilities (MOFs), trade creditors, bills of exchange (payable), advances against debts (eg. from factoring organisations and from banks for some export debts), other creditors.

41   (a)   Demand-pull inflation. 'Too much money chasing too few goods'. Demand in the economy in money terms is rising faster than the increase in 'real' output by the economy.

      (b)   Cost-push inflation. Inflationary wage settlements or increases in import costs (perhaps due to a domestic currency that is falling in value against foreign currencies).

Expectations about future rates of inflation are thought to influence both wage demands and current demand.

42   Money acts as:

- a means of exchange;
- a unit of account;
- a standard of deferred payment;
- a store of value.

43   The functions of the Bank of England are:

- to be a banker to various limited categories of customer;
- to be the central note-issuing authority in the UK;
- to be manager of the national debt;
- to be manager of the exchange equalisation account;
- to be administrator of any exchange control regulations in force;
- to be an advisor to the government on monetary economic policy;
- to be the government's agent in carrying out monetary policy;
- to be the supervisor of the banking system;
- to be the informal supervisor of other financial institutions.

PRESENT VALUE OF £1

The table shows the value today of £1 to be received or paid after a given number of years

$$V_n.r = (1 + r)^{-n}$$

At rate r / After n years	1%	2%	3%	4%	5%	6%	7%	8%	9%	10%	11%	12%
1	·99	·98	·97	·96	·95	·94	·93	·93	·92	·91	·90	·89
2	·98	·96	·94	·92	·91	·89	·87	·86	·84	·83	·81	·80
3	·97	·94	·92	·89	·86	·84	·82	·79	·77	·75	·73	·71
4	·96	·92	·89	·85	·82	·79	·76	·74	·71	·68	·66	·64
5	·95	·91	·86	·82	·78	·75	·71	·68	·65	·62	·59	·57
6	·94	·89	·84	·79	·75	·70	·67	·63	·60	·56	·53	·51
7	·93	·87	·81	·76	·71	·67	·62	·58	·55	·51	·48	·45
8	·92	·85	·79	·73	·68	·63	·58	·54	·50	·47	·43	·40
9	·91	·84	·77	·70	·64	·59	·54	·50	·46	·42	·39	·36
10	·91	·82	·74	·68	·61	·56	·51	·46	·42	·39	·35	·32
11	·90	·80	·72	·65	·58	·53	·48	·43	·39	·35	·32	·29
12	·89	·79	·70	·62	·56	·50	·44	·40	·36	·32	·29	·26
13	·88	·77	·68	·60	·53	·47	·41	·37	·33	·29	·26	·23
14	·87	·76	·66	·58	·51	·44	·39	·34	·30	·26	·23	·20
15	·86	·74	·64	·56	·48	·42	·36	·32	·27	·24	·21	·18

At rate r / After n years	13%	14%	15%	16%	17%	18%	19%	20%	30%	40%	50%
1	·88	·88	·87	·86	·85	·85	·84	·83	·77	·71	·67
2	·78	·77	·76	·74	·73	·72	·71	·69	·59	·51	·44
3	·69	·67	·66	·64	·62	·61	·59	·58	·46	·36	·30
4	·61	·59	·57	·55	·53	·52	·50	·48	·35	·26	·20
5	·54	·52	·50	·48	·46	·44	·42	·40	·27	·19	·13
6	·48	·46	·43	·41	·39	·37	·35	·33	·21	·13	·09
7	·43	·40	·38	·35	·33	·31	·30	·28	·16	·09	·06
8	·38	·35	·33	·31	·28	·27	·25	·23	·12	·07	·04
9	·33	·31	·28	·26	·24	·23	·21	·19	·09	·05	·03
10	·29	·27	·25	·23	·21	·19	·18	·16	·07	·03	·02
11	·26	·24	·21	·20	·18	·16	·15	·13	·06	·02	·01
12	·23	·21	·19	·17	·15	·14	·12	·11	·04	·02	·008
13	·20	·18	·16	·15	·13	·12	·10	·09	·03	·013	·005
14	·18	·16	·14	·13	·11	·10	·09	·08	·03	·009	·003
15	·16	·14	·12	·11	·09	·08	·07	·06	·02	·006	·002

PRESENT VALUE TABLES

CUMULATIVE PRESENT VALUE OF £1

The table shows the Present Value of £1 per annum, Receivable or Payable at the end of each year for
N Years

Years	Net Rate of Interest Assumed											
	1%	2%	3%	4%	5%	6%	7%	8%	9%	10%	11%	12%
1	.99	.98	.97	.96	.95	.94	.94	.93	.92	.91	.90	.89
2	1.97	1.94	1.91	1.89	1.86	1.83	1.81	1.78	1.76	1.74	1.71	1.69
3	2.94	2.88	2.83	2.78	2.72	2.67	2.62	2.58	2.53	2.49	2.44	2.40
4	3.90	3.81	3.72	3.63	3.55	3.47	3.39	3.31	3.24	3.17	3.10	3.04
5	4.85	4.71	4.58	4.45	4.33	4.21	4.10	3.99	3.89	3.79	3.70	3.61
6	5.80	5.60	5.42	5.24	5.08	4.92	4.77	4.62	4.49	4.36	4.23	4.11
7	6.73	6.47	6.23	6.00	5.79	5.58	5.39	5.21	5.03	4.87	4.71	4.56
8	7.65	7.33	7.02	6.73	6.46	6.21	5.97	5.75	5.54	5.34	5.15	4.97
9	8.57	8.16	7.79	7.44	7.11	6.80	6.52	6.25	6.00	5.76	5.54	5.33
10	9.47	8.98	8.53	8.11	7.72	7.36	7.02	6.71	6.42	6.15	5.89	5.65
11	10.37	9.79	9.25	8.76	8.31	7.89	7.50	7.14	6.81	6.50	6.21	5.94
12	11.26	10.58	9.95	9.39	8.86	8.38	7.94	7.54	7.16	6.81	6.49	6.19
13	12.13	11.35	10.64	9.99	9.39	8.85	8.36	7.90	7.49	7.10	6.80	6.42
14	13.00	12.11	11.30	10.56	9.90	9.30	8.75	8.24	7.79	7.37	6.98	6.63
15	13.87	12.85	11.94	11.12	10.38	9.71	9.11	8.56	8.06	7.61	7.19	6.81

Years	Net Rate of Interest Assumed											
	13%	14%	15%	16%	17%	18%	19%	20%	30%	40%	50%	
1	.89	.88	.87	.86	.85	.85	.84	.83	.77	.71	.67	
2	1.67	1.65	1.63	1.61	1.59	1.57	1.55	1.53	1.36	1.22	1.11	
3	2.36	2.32	2.28	2.25	2.21	2.17	2.14	2.11	1.81	1.59	1.41	
4	2.97	2.91	2.86	2.80	2.74	2.69	2.64	2.59	2.17	1.85	1.61	
5	3.52	3.43	3.35	3.27	3.20	3.13	3.06	2.99	2.44	2.04	1.74	
6	4.00	3.89	3.78	3.69	3.59	3.50	3.41	3.33	2.64	2.17	1.82	
7	4.42	4.29	4.16	4.04	3.92	3.81	3.71	3.61	2.80	2.26	1.88	
8	4.80	4.64	4.49	4.34	4.21	4.08	3.95	3.84	2.93	2.33	1.92	
9	5.13	4.95	4.77	4.61	4.45	4.30	4.16	4.03	3.02	2.38	1.95	
10	5.43	5.22	5.02	4.83	4.66	4.49	4.34	4.19	3.09	2.41	1.97	
11	5.69	5.45	5.23	5.03	4.83	4.66	4.49	4.33	3.15	2.44	1.98	
12	5.92	5.66	5.42	5.20	4.99	4.79	4.61	4.44	3.19	2.46	1.99	
13	6.12	5.84	5.58	5.34	5.12	4.91	4.71	4.53	3.22	2.47	1.99	
14	6.30	6.00	5.72	5.47	5.23	5.01	4.80	4.61	3.25	2.48	1.99	
15	6.46	6.14	5.85	5.58	5.32	5.09	4.88	4.68	3.27	2.48	2.00	

STATISTICS

48

STATISTICS: INDEX TO QUESTIONS AND SUGGESTED SOLUTIONS

* Only those students taking the examination in July 1991 should attempt these questions. Elementary probability will be deleted from the syllabus with effect from the January 1992 examination.

STATISTICS
QUESTIONS

1 SAMPLING METHODS (20 marks)

(a) Sampling methods are frequently used for the collection of data. Explain the terms simple random sampling, stratified random sampling and sampling frame. (6 marks)

(b) Suggest a suitable sampling frame for each of the following in which statistical data will be collected:

(i) an investigation into the reactions of workers in a large factory to new proposals for shift working; (2 marks)

(ii) a survey of students at a college about the relevance and quality of the teaching for their professional examinations; (2 marks)

(iii) an enquiry into the use of home computers by school children in a large city. (3 marks)

(c) Explain briefly, with reasons, the type of sampling method you would recommend in each of the three situations given above. (7 marks)

2 SAMPLING TECHNIQUES (20 marks)

Statistical sampling techniques are widely used for the collection of data in industry and business. Explain four of the following, illustrating your answer with examples:

(a) sampling frame; (5 marks)
(b) simple random sampling; (5 marks)
(c) multi-stage sampling; (5 marks)
(d) stratification; (5 marks)
(e) quota sampling; (5 marks)
(f) sampling with probability proportional to size. (5 marks)

3 LEVER LIMITED (20 marks)

Lever Ltd, a large car manufacturer, has undertaken a large attitude survey of recent buyers of small cars in Great Britain. As a part of this study, 100 recent buyers of British cars and 100 recent buyers of German cars were asked to agree or to disagree with a number of statements. One of the summary tables from a computer print-out is shown below.

Statements	Buyers of British cars		Buyers of German cars	
	Agree	Disagree	Agree	Disagree
British cars are:				
easy to get serviced	65	35	46	54
economical	81	19	55	45
reliable	76	24	48	52
comfortable	69	31	61	39
German cars are:				
easy to get serviced	32	68	60	40
economical	61	39	83	17
reliable	74	26	85	15
comfortable	35	65	58	42

Draft an appraisal of the most significant features of these data, illustrating your analysis with simple, appropriate tables and/or diagrams.

4 COMPLETE TABLES (20 marks)

The following extract is part of a draft report for the second half of a UK company's financial year.

'Sales in the second half of the year were £14m, up 40% on the first half, equally split between the home and the export market. Of the export sales, £4m was due to North America, with the rest being evenly spread between Africa, Asia, and the EEC. Compared to the first half-year, export sales of each product division to each of the four overseas markets doubled in the second half-year.

The three main product divisions of the company, A, B and C, experienced very different trading conditions throughout this second half-year period. Overall, A's sales were the most important, being twice those of B which, in turn, were twice those of C. At home, 60% of sales were due to A, double those of B, the pattern of the first half being repeated.

The most important export market was again North America, to which sales of A were worth £2m, with B and C sharing equally the remaining sales to that area. Exports of A to the EEC and Asia were the same, each representing 10% of all export sales. There is, as yet, no market for C in Asia or the EEC, though your board have recently begun to look for suitable opportunities there.'

Required

(a) Prepare two complete tables of actual sales data (one for each half-year), suitable for a management report. (16 marks)

(b) State the percentage growth in sales over the year
(i) at home, and
(ii) in the fastest growing product division. (4 marks)

5 ABSOLUTE AND RELATIVE ERROR (20 marks)

(a) Define and give an example of each of the following:

(i) absolute error;
(ii) relative error. (8 marks)

(b) A builder has quoted £25,000 to his customer for the erection of a small building to house storage tanks of a potentially dangerous chemical. The materials are expected to cost £13,000 to the nearest £1,000 and the construction time is estimated at 500 hours to the nearest 20. The wage rate is £5 per hour but this might rise by 10% as a result of an impending wage award.

Required

Calculate:
(i) the estimated gross profit;
(ii) the minimum gross profit;
(iii) the maximum gross profit. (12 marks)

6   PRODUCTION PLANS (20 marks)

A company is preparing future production plans for a new product. Research findings suggest that next year the company could make and sell 10,000 units (± 20%) at a price of £50 (± 10%), depending on size of order, weather, quality of supply, discounts etc.

The variable costs of production for next year, given these data, are also uncertain but have been estimated as follows.

Type	Costs £	Margin of error
Materials	150,000	± 2%
Wages	100,000	± 5%
Marketing	50,000	± 10%
Miscellaneous	50,000	± 10%

You are required to find the range of possible error in next year's revenue, costs of production, contribution and contribution per unit, in each case stating your answer both in absolute (actual) and in relative (%) terms.

[Relative error (%) = 100 x maximum error/estimated total.]

7   RURITANIAN SHAVERS (20 marks)

In Ruritania a company produces and sells four types of electric shaver. The prices and quantities sold for 1983 and 1985 are shown below.

| | 1983 | | 1985 | |
Type	Price £	Quantity 000	Price £	Quantity 000
Mini	10	20	12	15
Standard	20	40	25	25
De-luxe	30	30	30	50
Super XL	50	10	55	10

The Index of Retail Prices (1974: 100) for 1983, 1984 and 1985 in Ruritania is as follows.
1983: 315;   1984: 336;   1985: 350.

Required

(a)   Calculate four all-items aggregate index numbers (1983 = 100), Laspeyre and Paasche price and quantity, to measure overall changes between 1983 and 1985.   (12 marks)

(b)   Comment briefly on your results.   (4 marks)

(c)   Calculate an expenditure index for electric shavers for 1985 with 1983 = 100.
          (2 marks)

(d)   Find how much expenditure on this company's electric shavers has changed in real terms between 1983 and 1985.   (2 marks)

8   SALES INDICES (20 marks)

A rapidly growing company produces computer software of four types. Data on prices and sales volumes for last year and the current year are given below.

| Type | 19X8 | | 19X9 | |
	List prices	Sales volume	List prices	Sales volume
	£	thousands	£	thousands
A	300	1.5	300	2.0
B	100	2.0	100	2.5
C	50	3.5	40	4.0
D	30	5.0	20	5.0

Required

(a) Calculate two aggregate index numbers for 19X9 (19X8 = 100), one for sales volume and one for sales revenue.   (10 marks)

(b) Explain which you would recommend as an indicator of sales.   (5 marks)

(c) Explain briefly why it would be inappropriate to calculate a price index number in (a).   (5 marks)

9   RETAIL PRICES INDEX (20 marks)

(a) Explain the principles and methods involved in the compilation and construction of the UK General Index of Retail Prices under the following headings.

    (i)   Base year.
    (ii)   Weights.
    (iii) Items included.
    (iv)   Data collection.
    (v)   Calculation.   (16 marks)

(b) Give two specific business applications of the index.   (4 marks)

10 GROSS DOMESTIC PRODUCT (20 marks)

The following table shows data for gross domestic product (GDP), gross earnings and retail prices for the UK, 1980-1989.

	Gross domestic product (market price, £billion)	Average gross earnings (1985 = 100)	Retail prices (1985 = 100)
1980	231	65	71
1981	255	73	79
1982	278	80	86
1983	303	87	90
1984	323	92	94
1985	354	100	100
1986	379	108	103
1987	414	116	108
1988	430	126	113
1989	*436	*136	*122

*provisional

[Source: *British business*, 1 September 1989 and *Economic trends* (various)]

Required

(a) Convert the GDP series to index numbers with 1985 = 100. (4 marks)

(b) Calculate deflated index numbers for GDP and average gross earnings, with 1985 = 100. (6 marks)

(b) Plot the *two* deflated indicators against time on the same graph and comment critically upon the meaning of these data. (10 marks)

11 FREEZERS (20 marks)

A manufacturer of domestic freezers has produced the following sales figures for the last six months.

	Last quarter 19X7		First quarter 19X8	
	Units sold (hundreds)	Sales value (£'000)	Units sold (hundreds)	Sales value (£'000)
Small	8	80	11	110
Medium	5	70	7	105
Large	2	40	3	60

The manufacturer has requested you to provide one summary figure which will show how overall sales have increased over the period.

Required

(a) Calculate four alternative index numbers that could be provided.   (14 marks)

(b) For the benefit of management select one of these four alternatives for its suitability, and explain briefly why you have chosen it in preference to the others.   (6 marks)

12 ZED LIMITED (20 marks)

Monthly sales of Zed Ltd for the years 19X1 and 19X2 were as follows.

Sales (000's units)

	19X1	19X2
January	30	30
February	40	45
March	50	65
April	55	65
May	50	55
June	45	45
July	50	50
August	55	60
September	65	75
October	65	80
November	50	60
December	40	50

You are required to draw a Z chart showing the sales for 19X2, and interpret each line.

13 SHAREHOLDINGS (20 marks)

Size of shareholding in British Telecom. May 1986

	Shareholders		Interests in ordinary shares of £0.25 each	
Class interval	Number of holdings	Percentage of total	Number of shares held (millions)	Percentage of total
1 - 399	457,144	28.9	90	8.0
400 - 799	760,582	48.1	347	30.8
800 - 1,599	337,773	21.3	274	24.3
1,600 - 9,999	23,173	1.5	55	4.9
10,000 - 99,999	1,855	0.1	59	5.2
100,000 - 999,999	957	0.1	302	26.8
Totals	1,581,484	100	1,127	100

(Source: *British Telecom annual report*, July 1986)

Note: American, Japanese and HM Government holdings are excluded.)

Required

(a) Draw a Lorenz curve for these data. (8 marks)
(b) Calculate the arithmetic mean and median size of shareholding. (8 marks)
(c) Explain your results. (4 marks)

14 TAKEOVER (20 marks)

Your company is considering the takeover of a company in the instrument engineering sector. You have been asked to prepare some background information on this sector, based on the following data.

Summary statistics for instrument engineering

Year	Index of production (19X0 = 100)	Sales of principal products*	Export *	Imports *	UK market *	Employment
			*£million current prices			thousands
19X0	100	1,597	868	768	1,496	122
19X1	94	1,558	905	871	1,524	114
19X2	98	1,772	993	970	1,749	100
19X3	108	1,962	986	1,176	2,152	103
19X4	122	2,178	1,100	1,382	2,460	103
19X5	132	2,377	1,175	1,495	2,697	104
19X6	130	2,522	1,210	1,611	2,923	104
19X7	138	2,654	1,346	1,695	3,003	102

Required

(a) Explain clearly the term 'current prices'. (2 marks)

(b) Draw a suitable graph of the four variables measured at current prices so as to highlight the important points. (8 marks)

(c) Comment on the following, using further calculations to support your reasoning where necessary:
   (i) productivity in the industry; (5 marks)
   (ii) trading position of the industry. (5 marks)

15 ECONOMIC TRENDS (20 marks)

(a) Real consumers' expenditure in 1984 - component categories
   (Seasonally adjusted, £000 million, 1980 prices)

Durable goods	Food	Alcohol and tobacco	Clothing and footwear	Energy products	Other goods	Rent and rates	Other services
16	22	14	11	11	16	17	37

(Source: *Economic trends*, August 1985)

Required

(i) Draw an appropriate diagram to illustrate the relative shares of real consumers' expenditure in 1984. (8 marks)

(ii) State one item/category of expenditure which falls under the heading *Other goods*, and one item which falls under the heading *Other services*. (2 marks)

(b) Comparative profit before tax (1980 = 100) of six Scotch whisky companies

Company	1980	1981	1982	1983	1984
Bells	100	116	160	183	208
Distillers	100	93	98	110	104
Highland	100	87	100	122	144
Invergordon	100	87	91	85	not available
Macallan	100	106	120	161	174
MacDonald	100	107	146	170	171

(Source: *Datastream*, September 1985)

Required

Draw an appropriate graph to compare the profit performance of the six companies. (10 marks)

16 STUDENTS (20 marks)

CIMA students and membership in relation to the profession:

Year	CIMA students	All accountancy bodies' students	CIMA members	All accountancy bodies' members
1973	29,062	104,464	13,398	116,700
1974	32,298	124,393	14,171	122,357
1975	34,681	144,271	14,969	128,162
1976	34,873	148,328	15,837	133,646
1977	36,150	149,299	16,571	139,960
1978	36,082	155,759	17,843	148,834
1979	36,706	156,968	18,337	155,292
1980	38,249	160,243	19,285	162,465
1981	39,252	162,297	20,328	167,979
1982	39,557	159,953	21,227	176,551
1983	41,100	158,168	22,300	182,132

(Source: Management accounting. August 1984)

Required

(a) Find the mean annual increase in each of the four series, summarising your results in one simple table. (4 marks)

(b) Draw two appropriate graphs/diagrams to highlight the pattern of (i) CIMA students and (ii) CIMA members in relation to all accountancy bodies from 1973 to 1983. (12 marks)

(c) State briefly two specific conclusions which may be drawn from the graphs and/or data. (4 marks)

17 TRANSFER TIMES (25 marks)

A sample of the transfer times of data from an intelligent terminal, in microseconds, are as follows.

Time (microseconds)	Frequency
10 and less than 20	6
20 and less than 30	12
30 and less than 35	9
35 and less than 40	12
40 and less than 45	9
45 and less than 55	9
55 and less than 65	3

Required

(a) Express each frequency as a percentage of the total frequency and tabulate these data against each class.

(b) Using the percentages found in (a) draw a histogram of the data.

(c) Find the mean and standard deviation of the data.

(d) Draw an ogive of the data.

(e) Using your ogive (or otherwise) find the median and semi-interquartile range of the data.

(f) Which measures of location and dispersion are most appropriate to these data and why?

18 MOTOR VEHICLE COMPONENTS (21 marks)

Your company manufactures components for use in the production of motor vehicles. The number of components, produced each day over a forty day period is tabulated below.

553	526	521	528	538
523	538	546	524	544
532	554	517	549	512
528	523	510	555	545
524	512	525	543	532
533	519	521	536	534
541	535	531	551	535
519	530	549	518	531

Required

(a) Group the data into five classes.   (3 marks)

(b) Draw the histogram of the frequency distribution that you have obtained in (a). (4 marks)

(c) Establish the value of the mode of the frequency distribution from the histogram and calculate the mode.   (5 marks)

(d) Establish the value of the mean of the distribution.   (4 marks)

(e) Establish the value of the standard deviation of the distribution.   (5 marks)

19 MANUFACTURING DEPARTMENT (20 marks)

The production of each manufacturing department of your company is monitored weekly to establish productivity bonuses paid to the members of that department.

250 items have to be produced each week before a bonus will be paid. The production in one department over a forty week period is shown below.

382	367	364	365	371	370	372	364	355	347
354	359	359	360	357	362	364	365	371	365
361	380	382	394	396	398	402	406	437	456
469	466	459	454	460	457	452	451	445	446

Required

(a) Form a frequency distribution of five groups for the number of items produced per week.   (5 marks)

(b) Construct the ogive or cumulative frequency diagram for the frequency distribution established in (a).   (5 marks)

(c) Establish the value of the median from the ogive.   (2 marks)

(d) Establish the value of the semi-interquartile range.   (4 marks)

(e) Interpret the results that you obtain in (c) and (d).   (2 marks)

(f) Contrast the use of the median and the mean as measures of location.   (2 marks)

20 EXECUTIVE (20 marks)

The table below shows the results of a random sample of 100 daily expense claims made by a firm's executives.

Amount of claim	Number of claims
Under £5	9
£5.00 to under £7.50	22
£7.50 to under £10.00	25
£10.00 to under £12.50	17
£12.50 to under £15.00	11
£15.00 to under £17.50	8
£17.50 to under £20.00	5
£20 and over	3
	100

Required

(a) Draw the histogram and frequency curve and estimate the mode. (10 marks)

(b) Calculate the mean and the standard deviation of the claims. (8 marks)

(c) Calculate the coefficient of variation. (2 marks)

21 HORTICULTURAL SHOP (20 marks)

A client company of your firm is a horticultural shop selling a wide variety of products to its customers. The analysis of weekly sales of plants throughout the year is summarised in the following frequency distribution.

Weekly sales of plants £	No of weeks
1255 but less than 1280	9
1280 but less than 1305	9
1305 but less than 1330	10
1330 but less than 1355	8
1355 but less than 1380	6

Required

(a) Construct a fully labelled histogram of the frequency distribution. (6 marks)

(b) Establish (to the nearest £) the value of the mode from the histogram using a graphical method. (2 marks)

(c) Calculate the mean weekly sales of plants over the 52 weeks to the nearest £. (4 marks)

(d) Compare and contrast the mode and mean of this frequency distribution. (2 marks)

(e) Calculate the standard deviation of the frequency distribution. (6 marks)

22 COMPUTER DOWNTIME (20 marks)

The time when a computer is out of action due to breakdown or failure is called 'downtime'. The following data show the total downtimes (minutes) of computer A for the last 70 working days.

Downtimes	Number of days
Never	10
Less than 10	24
Less than 20	44
Less than 30	54
Less than 40	62
Less than 60	68
Less than 120	70

Required

(a) Find the arithmetic mean, standard deviation, and coefficient of variation of downtimes for computer A over the last 70 working days and interpret these results.   (14 marks)

(b) Computer B having had a mean downtime of 41 minutes with a standard deviation of 18 minutes over the same period, compare A and B.   (4 marks)

(c) Computer A being down for less than X minutes on one half of the days, estimate X.   (2 marks)

23 RESERVE FUND (20 marks)

(a) In two years from now some machinery in your company will need replacing. It is estimated that £500,000 will then be required. To provide for this, £X is to be allocated *now*, invested at 12% nominal per year, with interest compounded *quarterly*. What should £X be?   (6 marks)

(b) Assume that the money required in (a) is not immediately available, but that the company can put £30,000 into a reserve fund every quarter, starting now (ie 9 quarterly amounts can be set aside in two years). Annual interest of 12% nominal is payable, compounded quarterly.

   (i) How much short of the target figure of £500,000 will the reserve fund be in exactly two years from now?   (8 marks)

   (ii) What quarterly amount should be put into the reserve fund, starting now, to ensure that £500,000 is available in exactly two years' time?

   (6 marks)

   Note: You may use the formula $S = A(R^n - 1)/(R - 1)$

24 INSTALMENTS (20 marks)

A £50,000 mortgage is arranged now for 15 years at a rate of interest of 10%. Interest is compounded on the balance outstanding at the end of each year. The loan is to be repaid by 15 annual instalments, the first being due after the end of one complete year.

Required

(a) Find the gross annual instalments:
   (i) using tables; (4 marks)
   (ii) using any other method but without using tables. (6 marks)

(b) Find the amount outstanding after two complete years, using either solution to (a) above. (6 marks)

(c) If the rate of interest changes to 13% after two complete years, find the revised annual instalments. (4 marks)

Note: The sum, S, of a geometric progression of n terms, with first term A and common ratio R is given by: $S = A(R^n - 1)/(R - 1)$.

25 MORTGAGE (20 marks)

A mortgage of £40,000 is to be repaid by 80 equal quarterly instalments (in arrears) of £X. Interest of 4% is charged each quarter on the remaining part of the debt.

(a) Show mathematically that after six months the amount owed is:
£$(40,000R^2 - RX - X)$, where R = 1.04 (4 marks)

(b) Find £X, stating why your answer is reasonable. (12 marks)

(c) Without carrying out any calculations, briefly explain why the repayments on a mortgage of £80,000 would or would not be £2X. (4 marks)

Note: The sum, S, of a geometric progression of n terms, with first term A and common ratio R is $S = A(R^n - 1)/(R - 1)$.

26 ANNUITY (20 marks)

(a) How much is it worth paying for an annuity of £3,000 a year for ten years, payable twice a year in arrear, assuming a nominal interest rate of 9% per annum and ignoring taxation. (5 marks)

(b) A mortgage of £50,000 has to be repaid by equal quarterly instalments in arrear over 25 years at a nominal annual interest rate of 10%. What is the amount of each quarterly instalment? (5 marks)

(c) A savings scheme specifies payments of £300 at the start of each month for five years, with interest guaranteed to be compounded at a minimum rate of 1% a month. What sum will be guaranteed at the end of the five-year term? If inflation is 5% a year what will be the 'real' value of this sum? (7 marks)

(d) For each of (a), (b) and (c) above give a different reason, apart from taxation, why your answer may in practice be only approximate. (3 marks)

Questions 27 to 30 are relevant only to those students taking the examination in July 1991

27 ACE (15 marks)

What are the chances of the following events.

(a) Drawing two aces from a pack of 52 playing cards in two successive draws (with and without replacement).

(b) Drawing the ace of hearts and the ace of spades in that order (assuming replacement).

(c) Selecting from a list of respondents to a questionnaire used in a sample survey from which it was estimated that 50% owned their own homes, 60% owned a car and 90% had a television set, a respondent who owned.

    (i)   his home and a car;
    (ii) all three of the above assets; and
    (iii) none of the above assets.

28 IMPERFECT JACKETS (20 marks)

From an analysis of past records a manufacturer has discovered that 20% of his jackets have imperfections in them. Two inspectors are to be employed to check the jackets before they leave the factory. Each inspector will have to check all the jackets and grade them as 'OK' or 'reject' and will make his decision independently. The probability that an inspector will mis-classify a jacket is 0.1. The company has decided to grade as 'fail' any jacket which *either* inspector rejects and to grade as 'pass' the remainder.

Required

(a) Draw a tree diagram to represent this situation. (10 marks)

(b) Find the percentage of jackets which will be correctly classified by this inspection system. (5 marks)

(c) Find the probability that a jacket is actually imperfect, *given* the fact that it has been passed by the inspection system. (5 marks)

29 SOFTWARE COMPANY (20 marks)

A software company has just won a contract worth £80,000 if it delivers a successful product on time, but only £40,000 if this is late. It faces the problem now of whether to produce the work in-house or to sub-contract it. To sub-contract the work would cost £50,000, but the local sub-contractor is so fast and reliable as to make it certain that successful software is produced on time.

If the work is produced in-house the cost would be only £20,000 but, based on past experience, would have only a 90% chance of being successful. In the event of the software *not* being successful, there would be insufficient time to re-write the whole package internally, but there would still be the options of either a 'late rejection' of the contract (at a further cost of £10,000) or of 'late sub-contracting' the work on the same terms as before. With this late start the local sub-contractor is estimated to have only a 50/50 chance of producing the work on time or of producing it late. In this case the sub-contractor still has to be paid £50,000, regardless of whether he meets the deadline or not.

Required

(a) Draw a decision tree for the software company, using squares for decision points and circles for outcome (chance) points, including all relevant data on the diagram.

(8 marks)

(b) Calculate expected values as appropriate and recommend a course of action to the software company with reasons.

(12 marks)

30 COMPUTER GAMES (20 marks)

A company could sell a new package of computer games. It has two possible courses of action to test market on a limited scale or to give up the project completely. A test market would cost £160,000 and current evidence suggests that consumer reaction is equally likely to be 'positive' or 'negative'. If the reaction to the test marketing were to be 'positive' the company could either market the computer games nationally or still give up the project completely. Research suggests that a national launch might result in the following sales.

Sales	Contribution £ million	Probability
High	1.20	0.25
Average	0.30	0.50
Low	-0.24	0.25

If the test marketing were to yield 'negative' results the company would give up the project. Giving up the project at any point would result in a contribution of £60,000 from the sale of copyright etc to another manufacturer. All contributions have been discounted to present values.

Required

(a) Draw a decision tree to represent this situation, including all relevant probabilities and financial values.

(8 marks)

(b) Recommend a course of action for the company on the basis of expected values.

(8 marks)

(c) Explain any limitations of this method of analysis.

(4 marks)

STATISTICS
SUGGESTED SOLUTIONS

1 SAMPLING METHODS

(a) *Simple random sampling* means that the sample is selected in such a way that every item in the population has an equal chance of being included in the sample.

Stratified random sampling means that the population is first divided into strata (ie component groups) and then simple random sampling is applied to each stratum. The advantage is that at least some representative items will be selected from each section.

A *sampling frame* is simply a list of all the items in a population.

(b) (i) The sampling frame should be a list of all workers who will be affected by the new proposals. The personnel or wages departments should be able to provide such a list.

(ii) The college registration department should be able to provide a list of all students attending courses to prepare them for their professional examinations.

(iii) The education department of the local authority should be able to provide a school roll, ie a list of all schoolchildren in the city. If not, the health department may be able to help.

(c) In the large factory, the recommended type of sampling method will depend on whether the workers affected by the new proposals were all homogeneous in one department, or whether they logically fitted into separate levels of seniority, different departments, etc. In the former case, simple random sampling would be appropriate. In the latter case, stratified random sampling would be appropriate.

In the college it is likely that the different years of each course would be given separate tuition which was more or less relevant to the professional examinations. Stratified random sampling should therefore be performed from the strata of each year of each course.

In the large city, each of simple random sampling and stratified random sampling would be prohibitively expensive to carry out. A system such as multi-stage sampling would be more appropriate, in which a random sample is taken from a random selection of schools from throughout the city.

2 SAMPLING TECHNIQUES

Tutorial note: an answer is given here to each part of the question, although you are only required to explain four of the six terms given.

(a) A sampling frame is a list of all the items in a population. For example, the sampling frame if collecting a sample of voting intentions in the United Kingdom would be an aggregation of the Electoral Registers of all the Constituencies. A further example would be the membership list of the CIMA, if the required knowledge was the average pay of a qualified CIMA member.

(b) Simple random sampling means that the sample is selected in such a way that every item in the population has an equal chance of being included.

A random sample can be selected from the sampling frame by two main methods:

(i)   the lottery method, eg picking numbers out of a hat;

(ii)   the use of random number tables. This method is to be preferred as it provides a high guarantee against bias.

In many practical situations it is more convenient to use a computer to generate the random numbers to select the items, especially where a large sample is required.

For example, if a random sample of six people from one hundred people is required, first the people must be numbered from 00 to 99. A sequence of random numbers is then generated, for example

93716   16894   98953   and so on

and the random numbers are examined in pairs. The first six people identified therefore are numbers:

93, 71, 61, 68, 94, 98.

(c)   This method is normally used to cut down the number of investigators and the costs of travelling etc. An example will serve to illustrate the principles.

A national survey of cheese consumption is to be carried out. The country is divided into a number of areas and a small sample of these is selected at random. Each of the areas selected is subdivided into smaller units and again, a small number of these is selected at random. This process is repeated as many times as necessary and finally, a random sample of the relevant people living in each of the smallest units is made. A fair approximation to a random sample can be obtained.

Thus, we might choose a random sample of eight areas, and from each of these areas, select a random sample of five towns. From each town, a random sample of 200 people might be selected so that the total sample size is $8 \times 5 \times 200 = 8,000$ people.

(d)   In many situations this is the best method of choosing a sample when the population is capable of being divided into strata. With a *random* sample there is a small probability that all the items selected will come from one stratum. If seeking a random sample of BPP students, it is possible that the sample selected are all Business Studies students. Stratified sampling removes this possibility, as first the population is stratified (ie divided up into its component sections) and then random samples are taken from each stratum. At least some representative items will therefore be selected from each section.

(e)   Investigators are told to interview all the people they meet up to a certain quota. A large degree of bias can be introduced. For example, an interviewer may fill his quota by only meeting housewives out shopping. In practice, this problem is partially overcome by sub-dividing the quota into different types of people, eg on the basis of age and sex.

Quota sampling is thus like stratified sampling but without the samples being random within each quota.

(f)   Sampling with probability proportional to size is another form of stratified sampling, in which the strata are weighted according to the number of items contained in each.

For instance, if seeking a random sample of BPP students, the sample frame is first split into the numbers of students studying each subject. A number of students is then selected from each stratum, where the total number of students from each course is selected in proportion to the number studying that subject.

3   LEVER LIMITED

Let us first of all look at the overall opinions of the 200 people surveyed regarding both British and German cars. For British cars, the percentage who agreed with each of the four statements made was as follows.

British cars are:	% agree
Easy to get serviced	55.5
Economical	68
Reliable	62
Comfortable	65

It can be seen from these figures that the overall percentage who were happy about the economy, reliability and comfort of British cars was more or less the same, but rather fewer people agreed that servicing was easy.

Turning to German cars, the overall opinion expressed was as follows.

German cars are:	% agree
Easy to get serviced	46
Economical	72
Reliable	79.5
Comfortable	46.5

The picture here is somewhat different in that about the same proportion (46%) agreed that the cars were easy to get serviced and that they were comfortable whereas a markedly higher proportion (about 75%) were happy with economy and reliability.

Comparing British and German cars overall, the picture can be represented by the following bar chart.

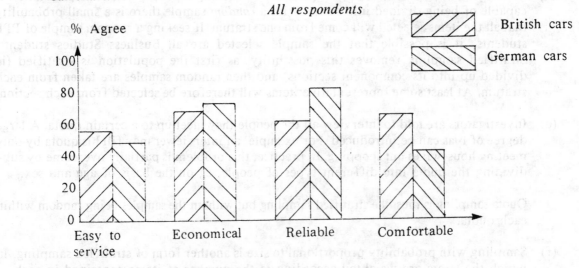

70

It can be seen that there is not much difference between the two in terms of both ease of servicing and economy, but German cars seem to score more highly for reliability whereas British cars seem to be more acceptable as regards comfort.

Looking more closely at the data, it is possible to contrast the opinions of those respondents who bought British cars with those who bought German. For the purchasers of British cars, their attitudes as regards British and German cars are represented in the following bar chart:

Buyers of British cars

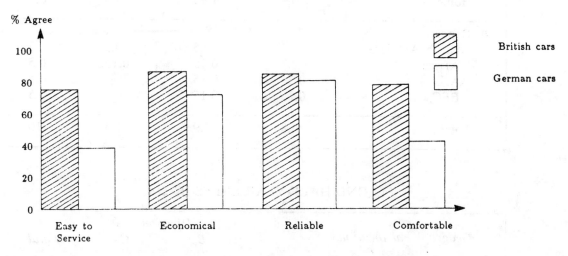

As would be expected, the attitudes of this group are biased towards British cars, and the only factor where British and German cars are at all close is reliability. When one looks at the same comparison but for purchasers of German cars, the same sort of picture emerges. As can be seen from the following bar chart, buyers of German cars favour German cars for all features except comfort where, as with reliability in the previous case, there is very little to choose between British and German cars.

Buyers of German cars

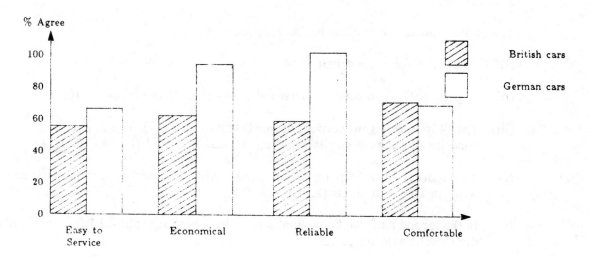

71

4 COMPLETE TABLES

(a) Two tables are shown below as required (one for each half year).

FIRST HALF YEAR SALES IN £M

| Geographical location | Division | | | |
	A	B	C	Total
Home	3.9	1.95	0.65	6.5
Export				
North America	1	0.5	0.5	2
Africa	0.2	0.15	0.15	0.5
Asia	0.35	0.15	–	0.5
EEC	0.35	0.15	–	0.5
Total	5.8	2.9	1.3	10

SECOND HALF YEAR SALES IN £M

| Geographical location | Division | | | |
	A	B	C	Total
Home	4.2	2.1	0.7	7
Export				
North America	2	1	1	4
Africa	0.4	0.3	0.3	1
Asia	0.7	0.3	–	1
EEC	0.7	0.3	–	1
Total	8	4	2	14

Tutorial note

The above figures are worked out as follows.

(i) Total sales for second half = 14.

(ii) This is 40% up on total for first half, which must therefore be 10.

(iii) The 14 is equally split between Home (7) and Export (7). The Export is split North America 4, balance equally between Africa, Asia and the EEC (1,1,1).

(iv) All export figures are twice in the second half what they were in the first half, so write in first half totals (2, 0.5, 0.5, 0.5).

(v) In the second half, we know total sales = 14. These are split 4:2:1 for A:B:C, so the divisional totals are 8,4,2.

(vi) Of the 7 total home sales, 60% (4.2) are A. This is double B (2.1). C must be the balance (0.7).

(vii) This pattern is the same in the first half. Total home sales are 6.5 (10 - total export sales of 3.5). These are split 60% (3.9) to A, which is double B (1.95) and balance (0.65) to C.

(viii) Second half North America A = 2. Balance of North America sales (2) is split equally between B and C (1,1). Sales of A to the EEC and Asia are both 10% × 7 (0.7). Sales of C to Asia and the EEC are zero.

(ix) All other figures in the second half table are balancing figures.

(x) The export figures in the first half table are half the export figures in the second half table.

(b) (i) Home sales in first half = £6.5m.
Home sales in second half = £7m.

$$\text{Percentage growth} = \frac{7 - 6.5}{6.5} \times 100\% = 7.7\%$$

(ii) Growth in sales for each division are:

$$A \quad \frac{8 - 5.8}{5.8} \times 100\% = 37.9\%$$

$$B \quad \frac{4 - 2.9}{2.9} \times 100\% = 37.9\%$$

$$C \quad \frac{2 - 1.3}{1.3} \times 100\% = 53.8\%$$

Division C is therefore growing the fastest, enjoying a 53.8% growth in sales from the first half of the year to the second half.

5 ABSOLUTE AND RELATIVE ERROR

(a) (i) Absolute error is the difference between the estimated or approximated value and the actual value.

For example if the estimated population of a town is 250,000 and the actual population is 249,800, the absolute error is 200 people.

(ii) Relative error is the absolute error shown as a percentage of the estimated value.

In the above example the relative error is:

$$\frac{200}{250,000} \times \frac{100}{1} = \underline{0.08\%}$$

(b) Building – costs and profits

Costs	Estimate £	Minimum £	Maximum £
Materials	13,000	12,500	13,500
Labour	2,500	2,450	2,805
	15,500	14,950	16,305
Sale price quoted	25,000	25,000	25,000

(i) Estimated gross profit   9,500

(ii) Minimum gross profit   8,695

(iii) Maximum gross profit   10,050

6 PRODUCTION PLANS

Tutorial note: the method which you should use is as follows.

Step 1: determine the estimate and the minimum and maximum possible true values for each variable.

Step 2: use these values to calculate the other maxima and minima. It is important to note that the final answers required at each stage are the *maximum* absolute and relative errors.

	Estimate	Minimum	Maximum
Number of units sold	10,000	8,000	12,000
	£	£	£
Price per unit	50	45	55
Materials	150,000	147,000	153,000
Wages	100,000	95,000	105,000
Marketing	50,000	45,000	55,000
Miscellaneous	50,000	45,000	55,000
	350,000	332,000	368,000

(a) Estimate of revenue = 10,000 × 50 = £500,000

Actual revenue could range from
minimum of 8,000 × 45 = £360,000 ie – 28%
to maximum of 12,000 × 55 = £660,000 ie + 32%
∴ Maximum error is £160,000 or 32%

(b) Estimate of costs of production = £350,000

Actual costs of production could range from
minimum of £332,000   ie – 5%
to maximum of £368,000 ie + 5.1%
∴ Maximum error is £18,000 or 5.1%.

(c)   Estimate of contribution = revenue - costs = £150,000

Actual contribution could range from
  minimum of £360,000 - £368,000 = loss of £8,000 ie -105%
  to maximum of £660,000 - £332,000 = £328,000 ie + 119%
∴ Maximum error is £178,000 or 119%.

(d)   Estimate of contribution per unit = £150,000/10,000 = £15

∴ Actual contribution per unit could range from
  minimum of £45 - (£368,000/8,000) = loss of £1 per unit
  to maximum of £55 - (£332,000/12,000) = £27 per unit (to nearest £)

These are relative errors of -107% and + 80% respectively.
∴ Maximum error is £16 or 107%.

7   RURITANIAN SHAVERS

Tutorial note: you must memorise the formulae for Laspeyre and Paasche price and quantity index numbers. But memorising them is only one step in the right direction. Use this question to ensure that you know how to *apply* the formulae.

(a)   Laspeyre price index $= \dfrac{\Sigma p_1 q_0}{\Sigma p_0 q_0} \times 100$

Paasche price index $= \dfrac{\Sigma p_1 q_1}{\Sigma p_0 q_1} \times 100$

We are computing an index number for 1985 based on 1983, and take the current prices/quantities as 1985 and the base prices/quantities as 1983.

p_0 £	q_0 '000s	p_1 £	q_1 '000s	$p_1 q_0$	$p_0 q_0$	$p_1 q_1$	$p_0 q_1$
10	20	12	15	240	200	180	150
20	40	25	25	1,000	800	625	500
30	30	30	50	900	900	1,500	1,500
50	10	55	10	550	500	550	500
				2,690	2,400	2,855	2,650

So, a Laspeyre price index for 1985 based on 1983 will be

$\dfrac{2,690}{2,400} \times 100 = 112.08$

A Paasche price index for 1985 based on 1983 will be

$\dfrac{2,855}{2,650} \times 100 = 107.74$

In a similar way, a Laspeyre quantity index is defined as

$\dfrac{\Sigma q_1 p_0}{\Sigma q_0 p_0} \times 100 = \dfrac{2,650}{2,400} \times 100 = 110.42$

And a Paasche quantity index defined as:

$$\frac{\Sigma q_1 p_1}{\Sigma q_0 p_1} \times 100 = \frac{2,855}{2,690} \times 100 = 106.13$$

(b)   Laspeyre indices use base period weightings, while Paasche indices use current period weightings. With the given numbers we see that each Laspeyre index is larger than the corresponding Paasche index, which is the usual situation. In practice, Laspeyre indices are more common, since they do not require the recomputation of the denominators of the indices each year.

(c)   Total spent in 1985 = $\Sigma p_1 q_1$ = £2,855 thousand
Total spent in 1983 = $\Sigma p_0 q_0$ = £2,400 thousand

Expenditure index for 1985 based on 1983 is therefore

$$\frac{2,855}{2,400} \times 100 = 118.96$$

(d)   Changes in real terms are changes after the effects of general price changes have been removed.

RPI for 1983 = 315
RPI for 1985 = 350

The adjusted expenditure index for 1985 based on 1983 is now

$$118.96 \times \frac{315}{350} = 107.06$$

This means that expenditure on this company's electric shavers has increased in real terms between 1983 and 1985 by just over 7%.

8   SALES INDICES

(a)   The Laspeyre sales volume (or quantity) index for 19X9 with 19X8 = 100 is as follows.

$$\frac{\Sigma P_0 Q_n}{\Sigma P_0 Q_0} \times 100$$

$$= \frac{(300 \times 2) + (100 \times 2.5) + (50 \times 4) + (30 \times 5)}{(300 \times 1.5) + (100 \times 2) + (50 \times 3.5) + (30 \times 5)} \times 100$$

$$= \frac{600 + 250 + 200 + 150}{450 + 250 + 175 + 150} \times 100$$

$$= \frac{1,200}{975} \times 100$$

$$= 123.1$$

The ratio of the two revenues ($\times$ 100) will be used as a sales revenue index.

$$100 \times \frac{\Sigma P_n Q_n}{\Sigma P_o Q_o} = \frac{(300 \times 2) + (100 \times 2.5) + (40 \times 4) + (20 \times 5)}{975} \times 100$$

$$= \frac{1,110}{975} \times 100$$

$$= 113.8$$

Tutorial note: the Paasche sales volume index (124.7) could be given instead of the Laspeyre index.

(b) A sales volume index is a better indicator of sales than a sales revenue index, as the latter is affected not only by changes in quantities sold but also by changes in prices. In this case, some prices have fallen and none have risen, which is why the 19X9 sales revenue index (113.8) is lower than the 19X9 sales volume index (123.1). Although the sales volume index uses prices, it does so only as weights, and uses the same set of prices in both the numerator and the denominator.

(c) Because of the falls in prices for software of types C and D, a price index for 19X9 would (using 19X8 as the base year) be slightly below 100. One might conclude that the company was doing badly, whereas as the indices computed in part (a) show, both sales volume and sales revenue are growing. Indeed, it may even be that price reductions are part of a marketing strategy.

9 RETAIL PRICES INDEX

(a) (i) *Base year*

The original base date for the RPI was July 1914. However the index has been rebased to 100 several times since then. Currently the base date for the RPI is January 1987, which month was given an index of 100. The index for later months is then given in terms of the January 1987 level. For example the index for January 1989 is 110.0, indicating that prices in January 1989 were in general 10% higher than in January 1987.

(ii) *Weights*

The weights used in calculating the RPI are designed to reflect the relative importance of the different sorts of expenditure of households. Information for this purpose is collected by the Family Expenditure Survey, which is a massive annual exercise involving many thousands of UK households, who are asked to keep a detailed record of their expenditure over a period of time.

(iii) *Items included*

The items included in the calculation of the index are designed to give a representative selection of goods and services bought in the UK. Items are combined in sections, which in turn are combined in groups.

(iv) *Data collection*

The collection of data on prices is carried out for each of the items monthly. Officials visit a set sample of shops, geographically spread across the UK, to record the prices actually being charged. Up to 1,000 separate prices could be collected for each item, and the total number of prices collected is likely to be around 150,000.

(v) *Calculation*

The first step to calculate the RPI for a month is to calculate each of the price relatives (being the ratio of the current price for one item to the price at the base date). These price relatives are then weighted using the weights explained in (ii) to give each of the section indices. The calculation for a section index is as follows.

$$\text{Section index} = \frac{\Sigma \text{ price relative} \times \text{weighting}}{\Sigma \text{ weighting}} \times 100$$

The section indices are in turn combined together using section weights to give the group indices. The group indices are combined together to give the final RPI figure for the month.

(b) *Business applications of the index*

(i) Wages contracts could be agreed to tie in with increases in the RPI. For example, a three year contract could be agreed with the workforce to increase their salaries each year by at least the percentage rise in the RPI + 1%.

(ii) Current value accounting methods could use the RPI to restate asset values in the balance sheet. Rather than retain fixed assets, say, in the balance sheet at historical cost less accumulated depreciation, the net book value could be indexed up by the RPI movement from the date of acquisition of the asset to the balance sheet date, to present a fairer picture of the true value of the asset.

10 GROSS DOMESTIC PRODUCT

Tutorial note: there are two steps to be taken in converting the GDP to index numbers with 1985 = 100.

Step 1: divide each value by the value for the base year (ie by 354).

Step 2: multiply the result by 100.

The two series are then deflated as follows.

Step 3: multiply the value for each year by the retail price index for 1985 (ie by 100).

Step 4: divide the result by the retail price index for the year in question.

For example in (a) the index number for 1980 is $\frac{231}{354} \times 100 = 65$.

In (b) the index number for GDP is $\frac{65}{71} \times 100 = 92$.

Suggested solution

(a)	GDP (1985 = 100)	(b)	At constant 1985 prices	
			GDP (1985 = 100)	Average gross earnings (1985 = 100)
80	65		92	92
81	72		91	92
82	79		92	93
83	86		96	97
84	91		97	98
85	100		100	100
86	107		104	105
87	117		108	107
88	121		107	112
89	123		101	111

(c) Up to and including 1987 the GDP and average gross earnings increased at very similar rates in real terms. However the GDP fell in 1988 whilst earnings continued to rise. The provisional 1989 figures show the gap increasing even though earnings also began to fall. However it is not advisable to place too much reliance on the final provisional figures.

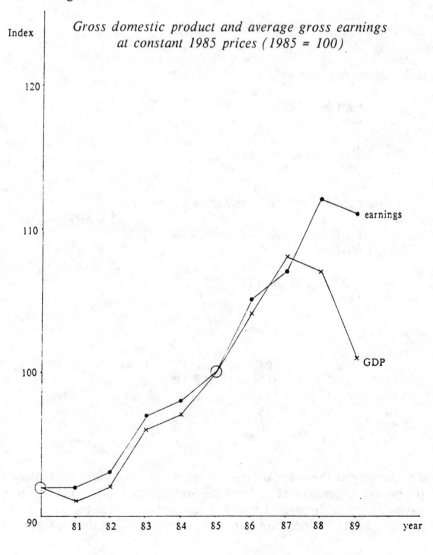

*Gross domestic product and average gross earnings
at constant 1985 prices (1985 = 100)*

Sources: 'British Business', 1 Sept 1989 and 'Economic Trends' (various)

11   FREEZERS

(a)   Possible index numbers that could be provided are as follows.

    (i)   *Aggregate sales units index*

$$\frac{\text{Units sold } 1/X8}{\text{Units sold } 4/X7} \times 100$$

$$= \frac{11 + 7 + 3}{8 + 5 + 2} \times 100$$

$$= \frac{21}{15} \times 100 = 140$$

    (ii)   *Aggregate sales value index*

$$\frac{\text{Sales value } 1/X8}{\text{Sales value } 4/X7} \times 100$$

$$= \frac{110 + 105 + 60}{80 + 70 + 40} \times 100$$

$$= \frac{275}{190} \times 100 = 144.7$$

    (iii)   *Laspeyre (base weighted) quantity index*

$$\frac{\Sigma q_1 p_0}{\Sigma q_0 p_0} \times 100$$

$$= \frac{268}{190} \times 100 = 141.1$$

    (iv)   *Paasche (current weighted) quantity index*

$$\frac{\Sigma q_1 p_1}{\Sigma q_0 p_1} \times 100$$

$$= \frac{275}{195} \times 100 = 141.0$$

Workings

p_0 (£0)	q_0 (00s)	p_1 (£0)	q_1 (00s)	$p_0 q_0$	$p_0 q_1$	$p_1 q_0$	$p_1 q_1$
10	8	10	11	80	110	80	110
14	5	15	7	70	98	75	105
20	2	20	3	40	60	40	60
				190	268	195	275

(b)   The purpose of the index we are seeking is to show how overall sales have increased over the period. Index (i) suffers from the problem that it does not differentiate between the various sorts of freezers. Large freezers sell for twice the price of small freezers, and this sort of difference should be recognised in the index number we are looking for.

Index (ii) shows how the total value of sales has risen from the base period to the current period. This statistic is certainly of interest, but suffers from the disadvantage of not looking at the individual sales performances of each sort of freezer.

Indexes (iii) and (iv) do take account of these individual sales performances. They take the individual volume increases (eg small freezers up from 8 to 11) and weight these increases according to the prices charged. (Alternatively weights of sales values could be taken, but this approach is less satisfactory.) The Laspeyre index uses the prices charged in the base period as the weights, and has the advantage that the denominator will not have to be recalculated each quarter as a new index is required. The Paasche index uses the prices charged in the current period as the weights. Although the denominator will have to be recalculated each time a new index is required, the weights used are the most recent information, and so on balance the Paasche quantity index (number (iv) above) is recommended.

12   ZED LIMITED

Tutorial note: make sure that your graph is neatly presented, with an appropriate title and so on. Remember to show all your workings.

Z-Chart: Sales for 19X2

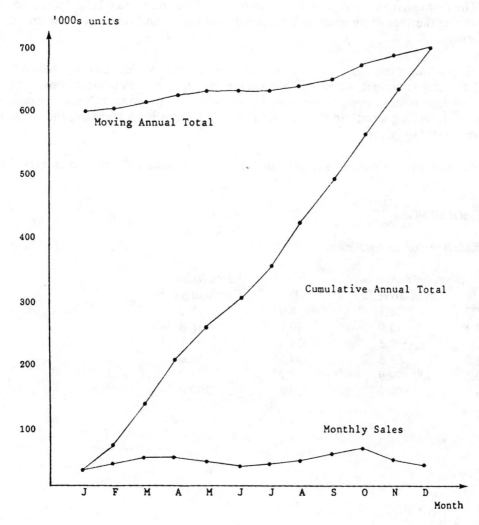

Workings

	19X1	19X2	CAT	MAT	
J	30	30	30	595 - 30 + 30	= 595
F	40	45	75	595 - 40 + 45	= 600
M	50	65	140	600 - 50 + 65	= 615
A	55	65	205	615 - 55 + 65	= 625
M	50	55	260	625 - 50 + 55	= 630
J	45	45	305	630 - 45 + 45	= 630
J	50	50	355	630 - 50 + 50	= 630
A	55	60	415	630 - 55 + 60	= 635
S	65	75	490	635 - 65 + 75	= 645
O	65	80	570	645 - 65 + 80	= 660
N	50	60	630	660 - 50 + 60	= 670
D	40	50	680	670 - 40 + 50	= 680
	595	680			

The Z Chart conveys three pieces of information at a glance.

(1)   The monthly sales curve shows the monthly and seasonal fluctuations in sales; in this example there appears to be a seasonal pattern with peaks in spring and autumn. The autumn peak is higher than the spring peak, but this may be simply due to the rising trend.

(2)   The cumulative annual total curve shows whether the annual total builds up steadily during the year or by leaps and bounds due to surges and relapses in the monthly sales levels.

(3)   The moving annual total curve shows the general tend in sales levels viewed on an annual basis; this is more informative than simple month by month comparisons. At the same time it provides a comparison between the sales in a given month and the sales for the corresponding month in the previous year - if there is an increase, the curve rises at the relevant point.

The actual data can be plotted against budget values if such information is available.

13   SHAREHOLDINGS

(a)   *Tabulation for Lorenz curve*

Shareholders		No of shares held	
%	Cumulative %	%	Cumulative %
28.9	28.9	8.0	8.0
48.1	77.0	30.8	38.8
21.3	98.3	24.3	63.1
1.5	99.8	4.9	68.0
0.1	99.9	5.2	73.2
0.1	100.0	26.8	100.0

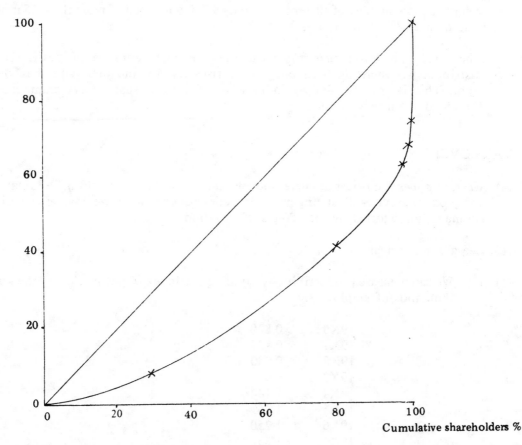

Cumulative
shares held
%

Lorenz curve showing the distribution of BT shareholders

Cumulative shareholders %

(b) Arithmetic mean $\bar{x} = \dfrac{\Sigma xf}{\Sigma f}$

where x = number of shares held

f = number of persons holding that many shares

Σxf = the total number of shares held = 1,127 million
Σf = the total number of shareholders = 1,581,484

So $\bar{x} = \dfrac{1{,}127 \text{ million}}{1{,}581{,}484}$ = 713 shares

Median = $\dfrac{1{,}581{,}484}{2}$th item = 790,742th item.

This lies within the 400-799 interval. Using the formula,

Median = $400 + (\dfrac{790{,}742 - 457{,}144}{760{,}582}) \times 400$

= 400 + (0.4386 × 400)

= 575 shares.

83

(c)   The Lorenz curve shows that BT shares are not evenly held amongst the shareholders. The curve lies significantly away from the diagonal line of uniform concentration. We can explain this by the large number of small shareholders in the company who bought their shares when the company was privatised, and by the small number of institutions who comprise a low number of shareholders (only 957 from a total of more than 1.5 million) but who own 26.8% of the shares.

The median is lower than the mean. This is representative of positively skewed distributions, where the frequency curve rises rapidly and then 'stretches' out to the right. This is true for BT again because of the unusually large number of small shareholders on privatisation.

14   TAKEOVER

(a)   *Current prices* are prices at current levels, that is, what one would have to pay now for the goods or services. Restating past transactions at current prices enables comparisons to be made, undistorted by the effects of inflation.

(b)   See graph overleaf.

(c)   (i)   We can measure productivity by dividing the index of production by the number of thousands of employees:

19X0	0.820
19X1	0.825
19X2	0.980
19X3	1.049
19X4	1.184
19X5	1.269
19X6	1.250
19X7	1.353

Productivity has improved every year except 19X6. One should not, however, assume that these annual improvements will go on indefinitely. Eventually, a limit of productivity will be reached.

(ii)   The trading position of the industry can be measured by the difference between exports and imports.

Exports - imports
(£ m current prices)

19X0	101
19X1	34
19X2	23
19X3	-190
19X4	-282
19X5	-320
19X6	-401
19X7	-349

From being a substantial net exporter in 19X0, the industry has become a substantial net importer in 19X7. The fact that the deterioration has (apart from 19X7) been consistent over the years suggests that there are serious long-term problems. More years' figures will be needed before one can say whether the improvement in 19X7 marks the solution of these problems.

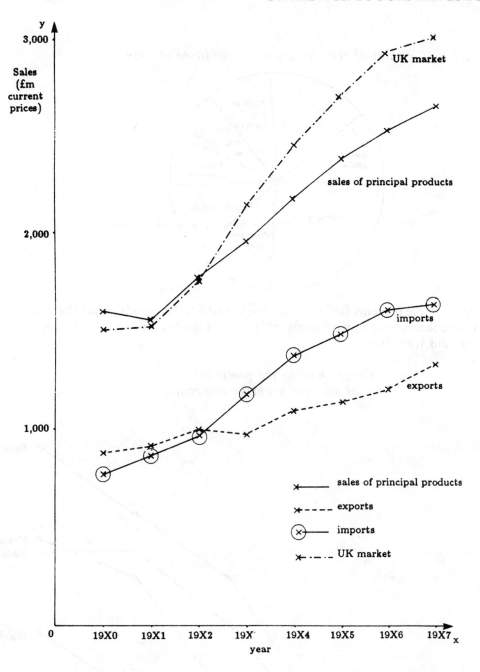

15 ECONOMIC TRENDS

(a)   (i)The 1984 expenditure is:

	£000 million	Degrees in sector
Durable goods	16	40.0
Food	22	55.0
Alcohol and tobacco	14	35.0
Clothing and footwear	11	27.5
Energy products	11	27.5
Other goods	16	40.0
Rent and rates	17	42.5
Other services	37	92.5
	144	360.0

Pie chart of real consumers' expenditure in 1984

(ii)   An example of items falling under the heading 'other goods' would be accountancy textbooks. An example of items falling under the heading 'other services' would be bus and train fares.

(b)

*Graph showing the profit before tax
of six scotch whisky companies*

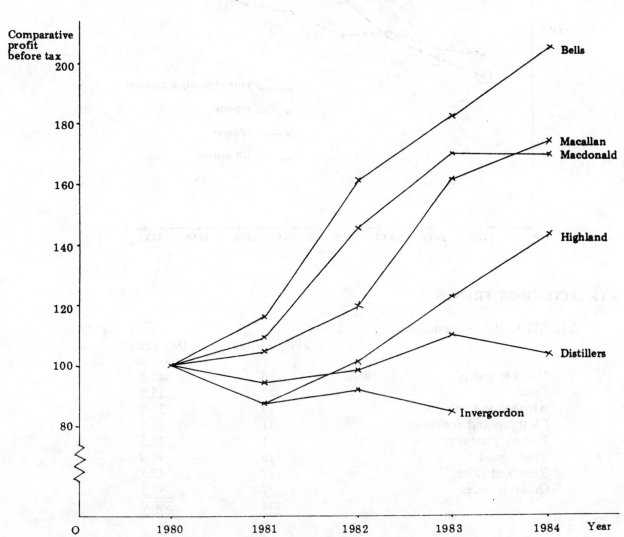

16 STUDENTS

(a) Over 10 years,

CIMA	students have risen by	41,100	−	29,062	=	12,038
All	students have risen by	158,168	−	104,464	=	53,704
CIMA	members have risen by	22,300	−	13,398	=	8,902
All	members have risen by	182,132	−	116,700	=	65,432

So the mean annual increase for each of the four series is:

CIMA   students $\dfrac{12,038}{10}$ = 1,204

All   students $\dfrac{53,704}{10}$ = 5,370

CIMA   members $\dfrac{8,902}{10}$ = 890

All   members $\dfrac{65,432}{10}$ = 6,543

(b) Graphs can be drawn for the numbers in both absolute terms and in terms of the proportions that the CIMA figures constitute of the figures for the whole profession.

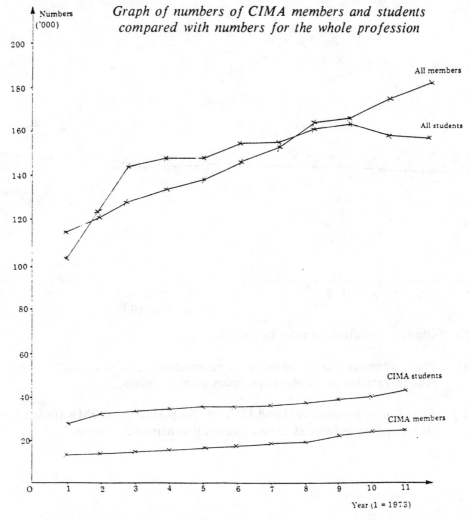

Graph of numbers of CIMA members and students compared with numbers for the whole profession

Year	CIMA students as a percentage of all students	CIMA members as a percentage of all members
1973	27.8	11.5
1974	26.0	11.6
1975	24.0	11.7
1976	23.5	11.8
1977	24.2	11.8
1978	23.2	12.0
1979	23.4	11.8
1980	23.9	11.9
1981	24.2	12.1
1982	24.7	12.0
1983	26.0	12.2

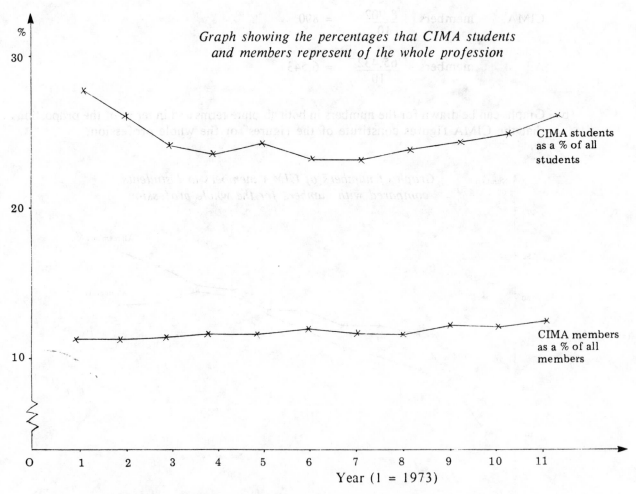

Graph showing the percentages that CIMA students and members represent of the whole profession

Year (1 = 1973)

(c) The following conclusions may be drawn.

(i) The growth rate for all members of accountancy bodies is much smoother than the growth rate for all students of accountancy bodies.

(ii) After falling between 1973 and 1976, the proportion that CIMA students represent of all accountancy body students has been consistently rising.

17 TRANSFER TIMES

Tutorial note: when answering part (b), remember that in a histogram the *area* of each bar is proportional to the class frequency. If a class has a different width from whatever you choose as the standard width, the height of the bar must be adjusted. In order to draw the ogive (cumulative frequency diagram) in (d), you must tabulate the cumulative frequencies up to the upper limit of each class (how many *in total* less than 20, less than 30, less than 35 and so on). The cumulative frequencies are then plotted against the upper limits of the classes.

(a) Total observations = 60

Time (microseconds)	%
10 and less than 20	10
20 and less than 30	20
30 and less than 35	15
35 and less than 40	20
40 and less than 45	15
45 and less than 55	15
55 and less than 65	5

(b) *Workings for histogram*

We will use 10 microseconds as the standard width of a bar.

Time (microseconds)	%	Adjustment	Adjusted %
10 and less than 20	10	x 10/10	10
20 and less than 30	20	x 10/10	20
30 and less than 35	15	x 10/5	30
35 and less than 40	20	x 10/5	40
40 and less than 45	15	x 10/5	30
45 and less than 55	15	x 10/10	15
55 and less than 65	5	x 10/10	5

Histogram of transfer times

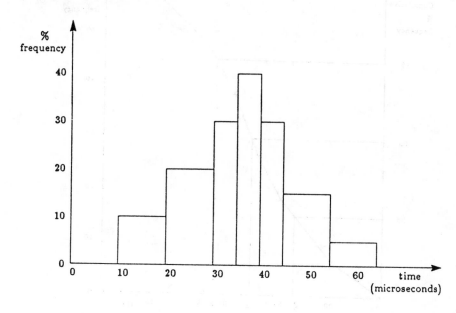

(c)

Class	Midpoint x	Frequency f	fx	$(x - \bar{x})$	$f(x - \bar{x})^2$
10 – 20	15.0	6	90.0	-20.76	2,583.3750
20 – 30	25.0	12	300.0	-10.75	1,386.7500
30 – 35	32.5	9	292.5	-3.25	95.0625
35 – 40	37.5	12	450.0	1.75	36.7500
40 – 45	42.5	9	382.5	6.75	410.0625
45 – 55	50.0	9	450.0	14.25	1,827.5625
55 – 65	60.0	3	180.0	24.25	1,764.1875
		60	2,145.0		8,103.75

$$\bar{x} = \frac{\Sigma\, xf}{\Sigma f} = \frac{2,145}{60} = 35.75 \text{ microseconds}$$

$$\sigma^2 = \frac{\Sigma\,(x - \bar{x})^2 f}{\Sigma f} = \frac{8,103.75}{60} = 135.0625$$

$$\sigma = \sqrt{135.0625} = 11.622 \text{ microseconds}$$

(d) Table of data for ogive

Time	Frequency	Cumulative frequency	% frequency	Cumulative % frequency
10 – 20	6	6	10	10
20 – 30	12	18	20	30
30 – 35	9	27	15	45
35 – 40	12	39	20	65
40 – 45	9	48	15	80
45 – 55	9	57	15	95
55 – 65	3	60	5	100

Ogive of transfer times

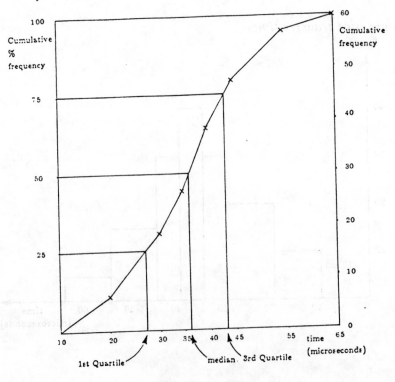

90

(e) Median   = 36.25 microseconds
      First quartile   = 27.5 microseconds
      Third quartile = 43.33 microseconds

Semi-interquartile range $= \dfrac{43.33 - 27.5}{2} = 7.915$ microseconds

(f) As the data are not markedly skewed, the mean and the standard deviation, which take account of all values, are preferable.

18 MOTOR VEHICLE COMPONENTS

(a) The data range from 510 to 555 and so the five classes into which it is split have a class interval of 10 units.

Number per day	Tally	Frequency
510 and less than 520	⧼⧽ //	7
520 and less than 530	⧼⧽ ⧼⧽	10
530 and less than 540	⧼⧽ ⧼⧽ //	12
540 and less than 550	⧼⧽ //	7
550 and less than 560	////	4
		40

(b)

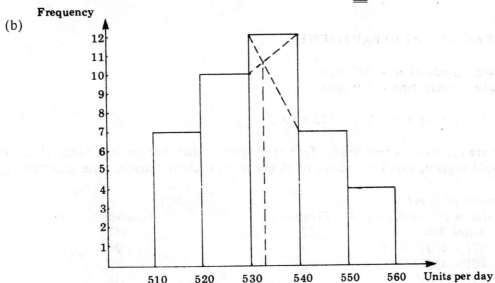

(c) The mode is estimated using the formula:

$$\text{Mode} = L + \left(\frac{fb - fa}{2fb - fa - fc} \times c \right)$$

where   L = lower limit of modal class   = 530
                 fa = frequency of class below modal class   = 10
                 fb = frequency of modal class   = 12
                 fc = frequency of class above modal class   = 7
                 c = class interval   = 10

So mode $= 530 + (\dfrac{12 - 10}{2 \times 12 - 10 - 7} \times 10) = 532.86$

say 533 units

(d)

Number per day	Mid point	Frequency			
	x	f	fx	$x - \bar{x}$	$f(x - \bar{x})^2$
510 and less than 520	515	7	3,605	-17.75	2,205.4375
520 and less than 530	525	10	5,250	-7.75	600.6250
530 and less than 540	535	12	6,420	2.25	60.7500
540 and less than 550	545	7	3,815	12.25	1,050.4375
550 and less than 560	555	4	2,220	22.25	1,980.2500
		40	21,310		5,897.5000

Arithmetic mean, $\bar{x}$ $= \dfrac{\Sigma fx}{\Sigma f} = \dfrac{21,310}{40} =$ 532.75 units

(e) Standard deviation, $\sigma = \sqrt{\dfrac{\Sigma f(x-\bar{x})^2}{\Sigma f}} = \sqrt{\dfrac{5,897.5}{40}}$

$=$ 12.14 units

19 MANUFACTURING DEPARTMENT

(a) Lowest production = 347 items
Highest production = 469 items

So the range is 469 - 347 = 122 items.

We are establishing five groups for our frequency distribution, so a range of 122 items would suggest, say, five groups of thirty items each as suitable class intervals.

Number of items produced per week	Frequency	Cumulative frequency
below 370	17	17
371 - 400	9	26
401 - 430	2	28
431 - 460	10	38
461 or more	2	40

(b) *Ogive of weekly production*

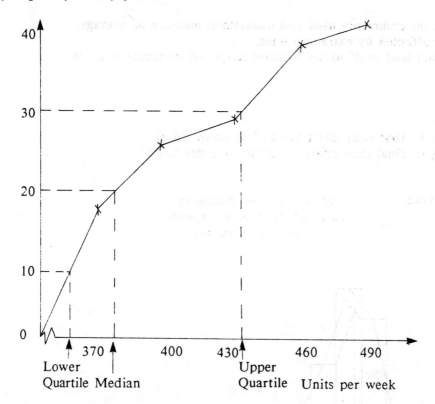

(c) Reading off from the ogive,

   median ≃ 382 units per week.

(d) Semi-interquartile range = $\dfrac{\text{upper quartile - lower quartile}}{2}$

   Reading off from the ogive, upper quartile = 441 units
   lower quartile = 359 units

   Therefore semi-interquartile range = $\dfrac{441 - 359}{2}$ = 41 units

(e) The median gives us the middle number in a distribution when the readings are ranked in order. The value of the median read off our ogive will therefore be an estimate of the middle number, if the forty readings given were to be ranked.

   The interquartile range is the range within which the middle 50% of readings fall, when they are ranked in order. The semi-interquartile range is defined as half of this range, and is a measure of the dispersion of the readings.

(f) The median has the following advantages and disadvantages.

   (i)   It is fairly easy to obtain, although it may be time-consuming to rank raw data.
   (ii) It is not affected by extreme values.
   (iii) It does not lend itself to use in more advanced statistical analysis.

The mean has the following advantages and disadvantages.

(i)   It is the commonly used and understood measure of average.
(ii) It is affected by extreme values.
(iii) It does lend itself to use in more advanced statistical analysis.

20 EXECUTIVE

Assumptions (i) first class taken as £2.50 to under £5.00
(ii) final class taken as £20.00 to under £22.50

(a)

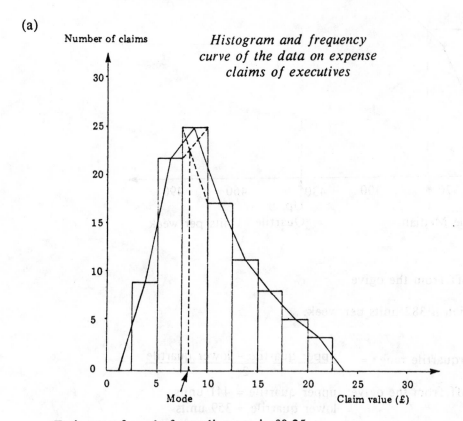

Histogram and frequency curve of the data on expense claims of executives

Estimate of mode from diagram is £8.25.

(b)

Midpoint of class x	Number of claims f	fx	$x - \bar{x}$	$f(x - \bar{x})^2$
3.75	9	33.75	-6.45	374.4225
6.25	22	137.50	-3.95	343.2550
8.75	25	218.75	-1.45	52.5625
11.25	17	191.25	1.05	18.7425
13.75	11	151.25	3.55	138.6275
16.25	8	130.00	6.05	292.8200
18.75	5	93.75	8.55	365.5125
21.25	3	63.75	11.05	366.3075
	100	1,020.00		1,952.2500

Arithmetic mean, $\bar{x}$ = $\dfrac{\Sigma fx}{\Sigma f}$ = $\dfrac{1,020}{100}$ = £10.20

Standard deviation, σ = $\sqrt{\dfrac{\Sigma f(x-\bar{x})^2}{\Sigma f}}$ = $\sqrt{\dfrac{1,952.25}{100}}$ = £4.42

(c) Coefficient of variation = $\dfrac{\text{standard deviation}}{\text{mean}}$ = $\dfrac{£4.42}{£10.20}$ = 0.43

21 HORTICULTURAL SHOP

(a) (b) *Histogram of plant sales*

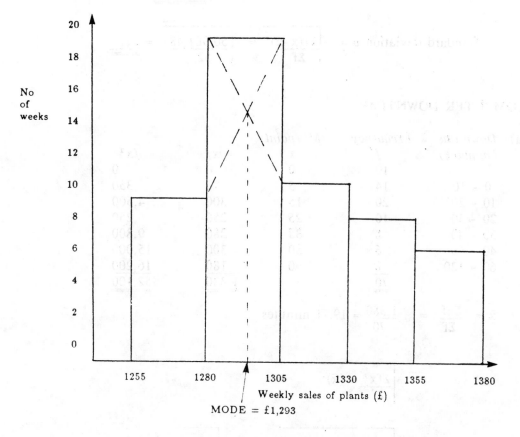

MODE = £1,293

(c)

Class £	Midpoint x £	Frequency of weeks	fx £
1255–1280	1267.5	9	11,407.5
1280–1305	1292.5	19	24,557.5
1305–1330	1317.5	10	13,175.0
1330–1355	1342.5	8	10,740.0
1355–1380	1367.5	6	8,205.0
		52	68,085.0

Mean $\bar{x}$ = $\dfrac{\Sigma fx}{\Sigma f}$ = $\dfrac{£68,085}{52}$ = £1,309.3

= £1,309 (to the nearest pound)

(d)   Mean = £1,309
       Mode = £1,293

The mode being lower than the mean reflects the fact that the distribution is positively skewed, ie weighted to the left hand side. The mean is a measure of central tendency which takes into account all the values of the parameter, while the mode is purely a measure of the most common value of the parameter.

(e)

x £	$(x - \bar{x})$ £	$(x - \bar{x})^2$	$f(x-\bar{x})^2$
1267.5	(41.8)	1,747.24	15,725.16
1292.5	(16.8)	282.24	5,362.56
1317.5	8.2	67.24	672.40
1342.5	33.2	1,102.24	8,817.92
1367.5	58.2	3,387.24	20,323.44
			50,901.48

$$\text{Standard deviation } \sigma = \sqrt{\frac{\Sigma f(x-\bar{x})^2}{\Sigma f}} = \sqrt{\frac{50,901.48}{52}} = \underline{£31.3}$$

22   COMPUTER DOWNTIME

(a)

Downtime (minutes)	Frequency f	Midpoint x	xf	fx^2
0	10	0	0	0
0 – 10	14	5	70	350
10 – 20	20	15	300	4,500
20 – 30	10	25	250	6,250
30 – 40	8	35	280	9,800
40 – 60	6	50	300	15,000
60 – 120	2	90	180	16,200
	70		1,380	52,100

$$\bar{x} = \frac{\Sigma xf}{\Sigma f} = \frac{1,380}{70} = 19.71 \text{ minutes}$$

$$\sigma = \sqrt{\frac{\Sigma fx^2}{\Sigma f} - (\bar{x})^2}$$

$$= \sqrt{\frac{52,100}{70} - (19.71)^2} = \sqrt{355.80} = 18.86 \text{ minutes}$$

$$\text{Coefficient of variation} = \frac{\sigma}{\bar{x}} = \frac{18.86}{19.71} = 0.96$$

The arithmetic mean of 19.71 minutes gives an average downtime around which the observed downtimes are expected to be clustered. The standard deviation gives a measure of how dispersed the observed data are about the arithmetic mean in absolute terms, and the coefficient of variation gives this measure in relative terms to the mean. The given data have a standard deviation nearly of the same magnitude as the mean, so we can deduce that the dispersion is fairly wide about the mean. About 68% of observations would normally be expected to lie within ± 1 standard deviation from the mean, which here is the interval 0.85 minutes up to 38.57 minutes. However, the fact that the lower limit of this interval lies so close to 0 minutes indicates that such conclusions, based on a normal distribution, are unlikely to apply in this case.

(b)

	Mean	Standard deviation	Coefficient of variation
Computer A	19.71	18.86	0.96
Computer B	41.00	18.00	0.44

Computer B has a larger expected downtime per day, but much the same standard deviation about this expected value. In relative terms therefore, the dispersion for B is less than the dispersion for A.

(c) With 70 days observations, the median item will be the $\frac{70}{2}$ = 35th item. This lies $\frac{11}{20}$th of the way up the 10 to 20 class.

Median = $10 + \frac{11}{20}(20 - 10) = 15.5$ minutes.

We estimate that computer A will be down for less than 15.5 minutes on one half of the days.

23 RESERVE FUND

Tutorial note: there is a lot of arithmetic involved in this question, as in all compound interest questions. You will lose marks if you do not show all your workings. Don't be tempted to simply write down the final answer from your calculator, without showing the interim stages in the calculations.

(a) Let £X be the amount of money allocated now.

$X(1 + 0.03)^8 = 500,000$

$X \times 1.2668 = 500,000$

$X = \frac{500,000}{1.2668} = £394,705$

(b) (i) $S = \frac{A(R^n - 1)}{R - 1}$ where: S = final sum accumulated
A = amount invested each time
R = interest rate of growth
n = number of investments made

In two years (ie eight quarters time), the reserve fund will have grown to

$S = \frac{30,000(1.03^9 - 1)}{1.03 - 1}$

$= \frac{30,000(1.30477 - 1)}{0.03}$

$= £304,773.$

The fund will be £500,000 - £304,773 = £195,227 short of the target figure.

(b) (ii) $\quad 500,000 \quad = \dfrac{A(1.03^9 - 1)}{1.03 - 1}$

$\qquad\qquad 500,000 \quad = \dfrac{A(1.30477 - 1)}{0.03}$

$\qquad\qquad A \quad = \dfrac{0.03 \times 500,000}{0.30477} = \text{£}49,217$

A quarterly amount of £49,217 should be put into the reserve fund, starting now, to ensure that £500,000 is available in exactly two years' time.

24 INSTALMENTS

(a) (i) The cumulative present value factor for r = 10% for 15 years is, from tables, 7.61. Thus, if x denotes the annual payment:

$$7.61x = \text{£}50,000.00$$
$$x = \text{£}6,570.30$$

(ii) At the end of year 1, the value of payments = x
At the end of year 2, the value of payments = $x(1 + r) + x$
At the end of year 3, the value of payments = $x(1 + r)^2 + x(1 + r) + x$

At the end of year 15, the value of payments = $x(1 + r)^{14} + ... + x$

This is a geometric progression with $A = x$
$$R = (1 + r)$$
$$n = 15$$

and so the total $\quad = \dfrac{x[(1 + r)^{15} - 1]}{(1 + r) - 1}$

If the initial loan was P, this will have increased in value in 15 years to

$$P(1 + r)^{15}$$

For the loan to be paid off, these two amounts must be equal.

$$\dfrac{x[(1 + r)^{15} - 1]}{r} = P(1 + r)^{15}$$

$$x = \dfrac{rP(1+r)^{15}}{[(1+r)^{15} - 1]}$$

Substituting r = 0.1, P = £50,000 we get

$$x = \dfrac{0.1 \times 50,000(1.1)^{15}}{(1.1)^{15} - 1}$$

$$= \dfrac{5,000 \times 4.177248}{3.177248}$$

$$x = \text{£}6,573.69$$

(b) Using x = £6,570.30

After one year Add 10% interest: £55,000
repay £6,570.30
balance = £48,429.70

After two years Add 10% interest: £53,272.67
repay £6,570.30
balance = £46,702.37

(c) The cumulative present value factor for r = 13% for 13 years is 6.12. Thus:

6.12 × new repayment = £46,702.37
New repayment = £7,631.11

25 MORTGAGE

(a) Let P = £40,000.

Time 0: amount owed = P

After 1 quarter 4% is added to amount owing, giving $P(1 + 0.04) = PR$

X is paid, leaving amount owed = PR - X

After two quarters 4% is added to amount owing, and X is paid.

$$\text{Amount now owed} = (PR - X)R - X$$
$$= PR^2 - XR - X$$
$$\text{or} \quad £(40,000\, R^2 - XR - X)$$

(b) After three quarters, amount owed

$$= (PR^2 - XR - X)R - X$$
$$= PR^3 - XR^2 - XR - X$$

And so on, until after 80 quarters, the amount owed

$$= PR^{80} - XR^{79} - XR^{78} - ... - X$$
$$= PR^{80} - X(R^{79} + R^{78} + ... + R + 1)$$
$$= PR^{80} - X\left(\frac{R^{80} - 1}{R - 1}\right) \text{ from the geometric progression formula given.}$$

Now as the mortgage is to be paid off in this period, this amount owed must be zero, and so

$$PR^{80} = X\left(\frac{R^{80} - 1}{R - 1}\right)$$

$$PR^{80}\left(\frac{R - 1}{R^{80} - 1}\right) = X$$

$$0.0418141\, P = X \quad (*)$$

Since P = £40,000, the quarterly repayment is £40,000 × 0.0418141 = £1,672.56.

This is a reasonable figure, because an interest-free mortgage would involve payments of £500 (£500 × 80 = £40,000).

(c) Using (*), if P is doubled from £40,000 to £80,000, the factor 0.0418141 would be unaltered, and so the quarterly repayment would double to £2X.

26 ANNUITY

The problem can be expressed as having to find the value of X in the table below.

(a)

Time	Flow	Discount factor at 9%	Present value
	£		£
0.5	1,500		
1	1,500		
1.5	1,500		
2	1,500		
10	1,500		£X

$$X = \frac{1,500}{1.09^{0.5}} + \frac{1,500}{1.09^{1}} + \text{-----------} + \frac{1,500}{1.09^{10}}$$

This is a geometric progression with the following terms.

$$a = \frac{1,500}{1.09^{0.5}}$$

$$r = \frac{1}{1.09^{0.5}}$$

$$n = 20$$

$$\text{So } X = \frac{1,500}{1.09^{0.5}} \left(\frac{(\frac{1}{1.09^{0.5}})^{20} - 1}{\frac{1}{1.09^{0.5}} - 1} \right)$$

$$= \frac{1,500 \ (\frac{1}{1.09^{10}} - 1)}{1 - 1.09^{0.5}}$$

$$= \frac{1,500 \times (-0.5776)}{1 - 1.0440}$$

$$= \frac{-866.4}{-0.044} = \underline{£19,691}$$

Tutorial note

An alternative approach would be to make the following approximation.

$\simeq$ $\dfrac{\text{Discount factor at time 0.5 given an interest rate of 9\%}}{\text{Discount factor at time 1 given an interest rate of } 4\frac{1}{2}\%}$

The geometric progression to sum is then

$$X \quad = \quad \frac{1,500}{1.045} + \frac{1,500}{1.045^2} + \text{---------------} + \frac{1,500}{1.045^{20}}$$

Using the formula as above,

$$X \quad = \quad \frac{1,500}{1.045} \left(\frac{(\frac{1}{1.045})^{20} - 1}{\frac{1}{1.045} - 1} \right)$$

$$= \quad \frac{1,500 \,(0.4146 - 1)}{1 - 1.045}$$

$$= \quad \frac{-878.04}{-0.045} \quad = \quad £19,512$$

We can see that the second method gives a very similar answer and is slightly easier to calculate. However it is not as accurate as the first method.

(b)   Let the quarterly instalments paid be £X.

After 25 years, first instalment has grown to $X(1.025)^{99}$
After 25 years, second instalment has grown to $X(1.025)^{98}$
After 25 years, third instalment has grown to $X(1.025)^{97}$
and so on.

The total amount to pay off after 25 years $= 50,000\,(1.025)^{100}$

The amounts paid must equal the amount to be paid off. So

$$X(1.025)^{99} + X(1.025)^{98} + \text{-------------} + X = 50,000\,(1.025)^{100}$$

$$\therefore \quad X[(1.025)^{99} + (1.025)^{98} + \text{-------------} + 1] = 50,000\,(1.025)^{100}$$

The left hand side is the sum of a geometric progression. The expression in square brackets comes to

$$1 \left(\frac{(1.025)^{100} - 1}{1.025 - 1} \right)$$

So $\quad X \left(\dfrac{(1.025)^{100} - 1}{1.025 - 1} \right) = 50,000\,(1.025)^{100}$

$$X \ \frac{(11.8137 - 1)}{0.025} \ = \ 50,000 \times 11.8137$$

$$X \ \frac{(10.8137)}{0.025} \ = \ 590,686$$

$$X \ = \ \frac{0.025 \times 590,686}{10.8137}$$

$$= \ \underline{£1,365.60}$$

(c) After five years, first payment has become $300 \, (1.01)^{60}$
After five years, second payment has become $300 \, (1.01)^{59}$
and so on.

The guaranteed sum at the end of the five years is
$300 \, (1.01)^{60} + 300 \, (1.01)^{59} \ + \ \text{------------------} \ + \ 300 \, (1.01)^{1}$

This is a geometric progression.

$$\text{Sum} \ = \ 300 \, (1.01) \left(\frac{(1.01)^{60} - 1}{1.01 - 1} \right)$$

$$= \ 300 \, (1.01) \left(\frac{(1.8167 - 1)}{1.01 - 1} \right)$$

$$= \ 303 \, \frac{(0.8167)}{0.01}$$

$$= \ \underline{£24,746}$$

The 'real' value of this sum after five years is

$$\frac{24,746}{(1.05)^{5}} \ = \ \frac{24,746}{1.2763} \ = \ £19,389$$

(d) The above answers will only be approximate for these reasons.

(i) Annuities generally cease to be paid immediately on the death of the beneficiary, and this has not been taken into account. There may also be administrative fees or charges which have not been considered.

(ii) We have assumed a constant interest rate of 10%. In practice, mortgage rates usually fluctuate in line with general market rates throughout the term of the mortgage.

(iii) The interest actually awarded may be greater than the minimum 1% per month stated. The prediction of a 5% inflation rate over the five years is also likely to prove inaccurate.

27   ACE

Tutorial note: you must try to develop a systematic approach to probability calculations. Reason each problem through in stages and write down the steps as you go. This approach will help both you and the examiner.

(a)   *Assuming replacement*

Pr(ace) = 4/52 = 1/13
Pr(ace on second draw) = 1/13

∴ Pr(ace followed by ace with replacement) = 1/169

Without replacement

Pr(ace) = 1/13
Pr(ace on second draw) = 3/51 = 1/17
Pr(ace followed by ace without replacement) = 1/221

(b)   Pr(drawing ace of hearts) = 1/52
Pr(drawing ace of spades) = 1/52 (if replacement is assumed)

∴ Pr(ace of hearts followed by ace of spades)

= (1/52)(1/52) = 1/2704

(c)   Pr(own home)   = 0.5
Pr(own car)   = 0.6   NB Not mutually exclusive events
Pr(own TV)   = 0.9

   (i)   Pr(home and car)   = Pr(home) x Pr(car) = 0.3

   (ii)   Pr(all three owned)   = Pr(home) x Pr(car) x Pr(TV) = 0.27

   (iii)   Pr (none owned)   = Pr(not home) x Pr(not car) x Pr (not TV)
                = 0.5 x 0.4 x 0.1
                = 0.02

28   IMPERFECT JACKETS

(a)   See next page for diagram.

(b)   Correct classifications have occurred at the branches marked with an asterisk (*). The total probability is

$$0.648 + 0.018 + 0.018 + 0.162 = 0.846$$

A correct classification is therefore made on 84.6% of occasions.

Tree diagram

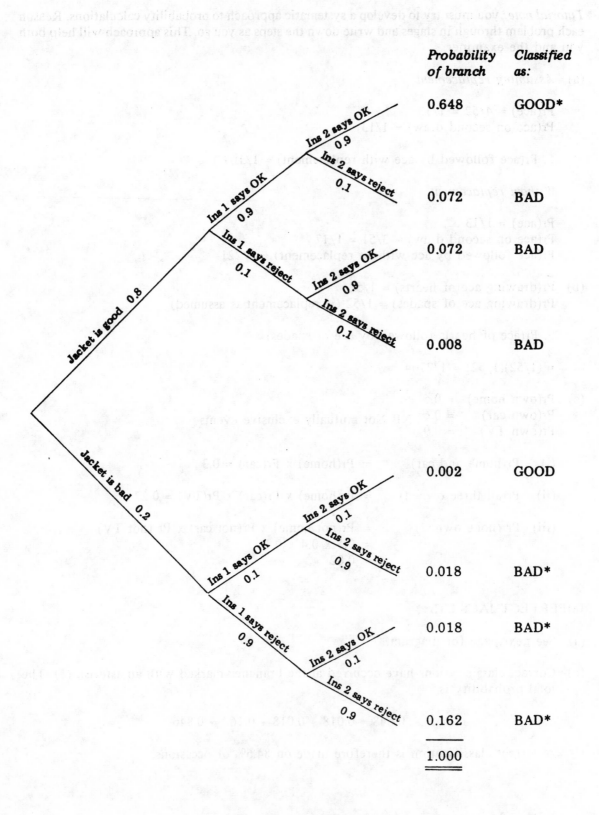

	Probability of branch	Classified as:
	0.648	GOOD*
	0.072	BAD
	0.072	BAD
	0.008	BAD
	0.002	GOOD
	0.018	BAD*
	0.018	BAD*
	0.162	BAD*
	1.000	

(c)   The tree shows that there are only two branches by which a jacket can be passed by the system: when the jacket is good, with an overall probability of 0.648, and when the jacket is bad with an overall probability of 0.002.

The probability that, given we are down one of these branches, that we are down the second of them, is

$$\frac{0.002}{0.648 + 0.002} = 0.00308$$

29   SOFTWARE COMPANY

Tutorial note: the Stage 1 examiner provided a useful step by step approach in his report which we reproduce here for your guidance.

' (i)   Begin the tree with a decision point on the left hand side of the page.
 (ii)   Distinguish carefully between chance outcome nodes and decision nodes, and write in probabilities and payoffs on the appropriate branches.
 (iii) Working backwards from right to left, calculate the expected values and 'roll back' until the decision points are encountered.
 (iv)   Explain the choice of the largest expected values at the end.'

(a)   *All values in £'000*

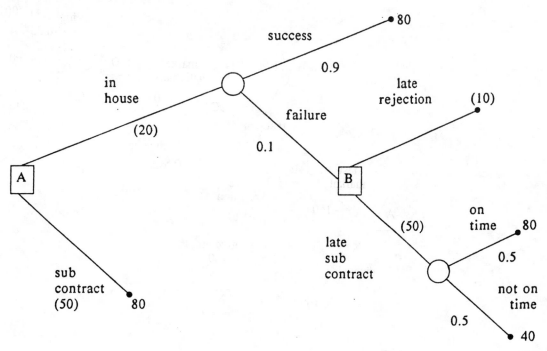

(b)   *At decision point B*

EV of late rejection = -10
EV of late sub contract = (80 x 0.5) + (40 x 0.5) - 50 = 10
The optimum strategy at B is therefore to subcontract with EV = 10.

At decision point A

EV of sub contract = 80 – 50 = 30
EV of in-house = (80 x 0.9) + (10* x 0.1) – 20 = 53
The optimum strategy at A is therefore to produce in-house with EV = 53.

* This is the optimum EV at decision point B.

Conclusions

The decisions which will maximise expected profits are to attempt initially to produce in-house and if this fails to sub contract. The expected profit is £53,000.

Assuming that the probabilities have been correctly estimated, the company has a 90% chance of making a profit of £60,000, a 5% chance of making £10,000 and a 5% chance of making a £30,000 loss. If the company is not willing to risk making a loss, the initial option of subcontracting should be taken since this offers a guaranteed profit of £30,000.

30 COMPUTER GAMES

(a)

Decision tree

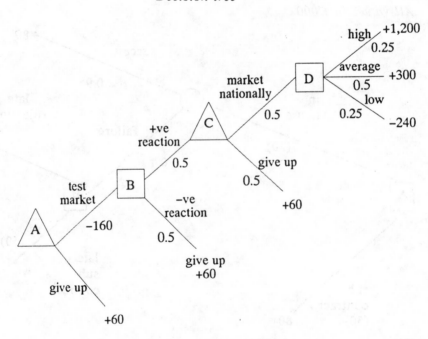

(b) EMV_D = $(0.25 \times 1200) + (0.5 \times 300) + (0.25 \times -240)$

= 390.

At C, the decision is therefore to market nationally, with an expected monetary value of £390,000.

EMV_B = $(0.5 \times 390) + (0.5 \times 60)$

= 225.

At A, the decision is therefore whether to test market, expected to yield

225 - 160 = 65

or to give up, expected to yield 60. The choice is to test market.

Conclusion: the company should test market, If the reaction is positive, market nationally. If the reaction is negative, give up.

(c) (i)   It is unlikely that sales will split into just three possible levels of high, average or low. It is more likely that they would form a practically continuous distribution rather than a discrete distribution as here.

(ii) We have assumed that we know the probabilities and discounted contributions for certain, though in practice, there will be significant uncertainties in each of these parameters.

(iii) This form of analysis considers a 'snapshot' of the possibilities at a given moment – it is likely that various possibilities are emerging and leaving through time, so a new decision tree should really be drawn at the time that each decision is being taken, rather than fixing future decisions now.

STATISTICS
OBJECTIVE TEST

Basic mathematics

1   There are two quantities, X and Y. X = -1 and Y = -2.

     Therefore:
     A $2X^2 > Y^2 < 0$ B $2X^2 < Y^2 < 0$ C $2X^2 < Y^2 > 0$

     D $2X^2 > Y^2 > 0$ E $2X^2 = Y^2$

2   The following formula is used in the calculation of loan repayments:

     $R = 2PC/B(N + 1)$

     Rearranging the terms, it follows that

     A $N = (2PC - R)/B$ B $N = (2PC - 1)/BR$ C $N = 2PC - 1$

     D $N = 2PC/B(R + 1)$ E $N = (2PC/BR) - 1$

Collection of data

3   Accountants are trying to estimate the extent of computer usage amongst small businesses in the UK. Which of the following sampling frames would be expected to provide the least biased results?

     A   Telephone directories of businesses.
     B   Those attending a computer exhibition for small businesses.
     C   Small businesses which have ever contacted computer equipment suppliers for advice.
     D   The Electoral Register.
     E   A list of members of all Rotary Clubs.

4   Read the following statements about the use of stratified random sampling, cluster sampling and simple random sampling in the checking of invoices for errors.

     I   Stratified random sampling is likely to provide, in general, more representative samples than cluster sampling.

     II   Simple random sampling is likely to provide, in general, the most representative samples.

     III Cluster sampling is more prone to bias than simple random sampling.

     Which is true?

     A I only   B II only   C I and III only   D II and III only   E I, II and III

5   An accountant is sampling from a computer file. The first sample number is selected randomly and is item 41: the rest of the sample is selected automatically and comprises items 91, 141, 191, 241, 291, 341, ... This type of sample is termed

     A simple random   B stratified   C multi-stage   D quota   E systematic

110

Accuracy and approximation

6   A street trader plans to buy 500 umbrellas and 1,000 pairs of sunglasses, each at a unit price of £2. All quantities are subject to an error of ±10%: all prices to ±5%.

The maximum error on the street trader's total outlay will be

A ±4.5%   B ±5.0%   C ±14.5%   D ±15.0%

E none of these

7   The revenue from the sale of Q units at a unit price of £P is £PQ. If the estimated revenue from next week's sales is quoted as +/-20%, and the price is quoted as +/-10%, the number of units sold, Q, is liable to an error of (to the nearest whole percentage)

A +2 to -2   B +9 to -11   C +10 to -10   D +33 to -27   E none of these

Index numbers

8   In the UK Index of Retail Prices for December 1989 (January 1987 = 100) the approximate index for beer was 138 and that for cheese was 110. Consider the following statements about December 1989:

I   The price of beer was lower than the price of cheese.
II   The price of beer was higher than the price of cheese.
III   The change in the price of beer was 20% greater than the change in the price of cheese since January 1987.

Which is true?
A   I only   B   II only   C   III only   D   II and III only

E   none of the above is necessarily true

9   Expenditure at actual (current) prices is given in £ below.

1981	*1982*	*1983*	*1984*	*1985*
3,000	3,500	3,600	4,050	4,200

The retail price index for the years 1981 to 1985 is respectively 100, 120, 125, 150, 150.

The expenditure series is to be deflated by the retail price index so that a 'real' expenditure series can be produced. 'Real' expenditure for 1984 would then be

A   £2,025   B   £2,700   C   £3,240   D   £4,050   E   £6,075

10 An index of industrial production in Xavia is calculated from four groups, with January 1984 = 100.

Groups	Weight	Index for May 1985
Agriculture	6	110
Chemicals	3	120
Oil etc	10	105
Engineering	1	109
All items	20	?

The all–items aggregate index of industrial production for May 1985 in Xavia is (to the nearest whole number):

A   22   B   105   C   109   D   111   E   120

11 For a certain product, data are available on last quarter's sales, by value, and on the current quarter's prices and sales volume. Which one of the following index number types can be calculated using the last quarter as base?

A   Laspeyres price index   B   Laspeyres quantity (volume) index
C   Paasche price index   D   Paasche quantity (volume) index
E   Sales value index

Charts, diagrams and graphs

12 The graph below is an ogive of invoice values

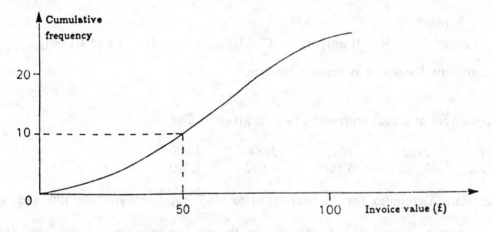

Read the following statements.

(i)   There are ten invoices for sums of £50.
(ii) There are more than ten invoices for sums of £50 or more.
(iii) There are ten invoices for sums of less than £50.

Which is true?

A   (i) only   B   (ii) only   C   (iii) only   D   (i) and (iii) only

E   (ii) and (iii) only

13   Where do the following lines intersect?

$$2Y = 92 + X$$
$$Y = 88 - 3X$$

A (-1,91)   B (12,40)   C (52,12)   D (12,104)   E (12,52)

14

Value of invoices (£)		Frequency
At least	Less than	
0	10	4
10	15	8
15	20	12
20	25	10
25	40	6
		40

The histogram which accurately represents these data is:

Blank for graphs – page 104 – business studies kit – 1990

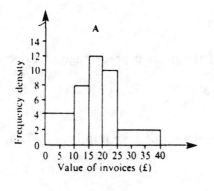

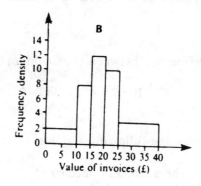

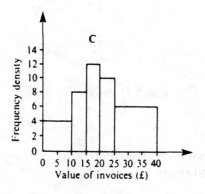

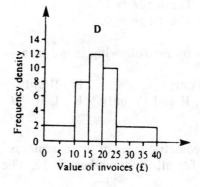

Location and dispersion

15 A wholesaler spends an equal amount on each of five different types of stock. The unit prices of the stock are £4, £8, £10, £16 and £20 respectively.

The mean price per unit (to two decimal places) is

A   £8.51   B   £10.00   C   £11.60   D   £17.02

E   impossible to calculate without further information

16 In the last three consecutive months the amounts of sand used by a company were 22, 18 and 29 tonnes, respectively. The arithmetic mean amount used for the nine-month period immediately before this was 19 tonnes. The arithmetic mean amount of sand used (in tonnes) for the whole of the last twelve months is

A 20   B 21   C 22   D 23   E impossible to calculate

17 The percentage of rejects in a quality control check is as follows

    1   1   5   7   2   8   3   5   5   3

The difference between the arithmetic mean and the median percentage of rejects is

A 0   B 1   C 2   D 3   E 4

18 Consider the following statements about the population of five numbers 2, 2, 5, 0, 11.

    I   The arithmetic mean is 5
    II   The median is 5
    III   The mode is 2
    IV   The range is 9.

Which of the following is *not* true?

A   I only   B   II only   C   I and II only
D   I, II and IV only   E   I, II, III and IV

19 The geometric mean of three numbers is 6. A fourth number is included so that the geometric mean for all four numbers is 12. The fourth number is

A   4   B $\sqrt{96}$ C   16   D   30   E   96

20 The variance of the population of numbers:

1, 2, 5, 8, 9 is (to two decimal places)

A   2.80   B   3.16   C   3.54   D   10.00   E   12.50

21 The following statistics (in £) have been calculated for five wages groups, A, B, C, D and E.

Group	Arithmetic mean	Standard deviation
A	150	30
B	48	8
C	100	10
D	80	20
E	72	9

An accountant has to compare the relative variation of the five groups. The group with the largest coefficient of variation is

A A   B B   C C   D D   E E

Compound interest, annuities, loans and mortgages

22 A unit trust used the following statement in its advertising:

'£1,000 invested on 1 January 1975 in the Recovery Fund was worth £20,157 on 1 January 1990.'

The annual percentage growth rate (to 2 decimal places) is equivalent to

A 21.76   B 22.17   C 27.71   D 34.38

E none of the preceding options

23 An investment quadruples in value in eight years. The annual percentage compound interest growth rate is closest to

A 15   B 19   C 22   D 37   E 50

24 An asset is purchased for £50,000 and will have a residual value of £2,000 at the end of its useful life of ten years. Using the reducing balance (constant percentage) method of depreciation, the asset's book value after five years will be closest to

A £10,000   B £14,000   C £19,000   D £22,000   E £26,000

25 An investor places £8,000 into an investment for ten years. The compound rate of interest earned is 8% for the first four years and 12% for the last six years. At the end of the ten years the investment (to the nearest £) is worth

A £16,320   B £21,483   C £21,517   D £26,854   E £27,252

26 Jill invests £700 on 1 January each year, starting in 19X0. Compound interest of 10% is credited on 31 December each year. To the nearest £, the value of her investment on 31 December 19X9 will be

A £10,456   B £11,156   C £12,272   D £12,972   E £12,992

27 One thousand pounds is invested on the same day each year for three years. The nominal annual rate of interest is 8% and interest is compounded every quarter. The value of the investment after three complete years is (to the nearest £)

A £3,480   B £3,506   C £3,522   D £3,805   E £4,522

28 A bank has granted a £12,000 loan at 14% interest per annum. The borrower is to repay the loan in eight equal annual instalments, starting one year from now. To the nearest £, how much must she repay each year?

Tutorial note: use cumulative present value tables to calculate your answer.

A £1,710   B £2,586   C £3,180   D £4,279   E £6,960

Elementary probability

Tutorial note: only those students taking the exam in July 1991 should attempt these questions. Elementary probability will be deleted from the syllabus with effect from the January 1992 examination.

29 A manufacturer has ten production lines. On past evidence there is an independent probability of 1% of a breakdown on any line each day. The probability that there will be no breakdown on a given day equals

A $10(0.01)(0.99)^9$ B $(0.99)^{10}$ C $1 - (0.01)^{10}$
D $(0.01)^{10}$ E none of these

30 A salesman makes four calls in a day. At each call there is a probability of 1/5 of making a sale. Assuming these probabilities to be independent, the probability the salesman will make at most one sale in the day is

A 1/625   B 16/625   C 256/625   D 4/5   E 512/625

31 X and Y are two mutually exclusive events. $\overline{X}$ signifies 'not X' and $\overline{Y}$ signifies 'not Y'.

$P(X) = 0.6$ $P(\overline{X} \text{ and } \overline{Y}) = 0.1$
$P(X \text{ or } Y)$ equals

A 0.18   B 0.50   C 0.72   D 0.90

E none of the preceding options

32 An audit requires a team of four qualified people. If there are ten such qualified people in the audit department, the number of different teams which could be found to carry out the audit is

A 24   B 210   C 1,600   D 5,040   E none of these

1   C $2X^2 = 2$, $Y^2 = 4$, $2 < 4$, $4 > 0$.

2   E   R   =   2PC/B(N+1)
        N+1   =   2PC/BR
        N   =   (2PC/BR) - 1

3   A   A is biased, because not all small businesses necessarily have a telephone, but the proportion of small businesses without is surely very small, so the degree of bias will be very small.

        A lower proportion of small businesses will have attended an exhibition or will have contacted suppliers for advice. The Electoral Register is a list of individual people, not of businesses. A lower proportion of small businesses will belong to local Rotary Clubs.

4   C   Stratification generally leads to more representative samples than either simple random or cluster sampling, so (I) is true and (II) is false.

        Cluster sampling is more prone to bias than other random sampling methods, so (III) is true.

5   E   This is how systematic samples are chosen, by selecting every nth item after a random start.

6   E   Highest amount he could pay is

        $(550 \times £2.10) + (1,100 \times £2.10)$
        $= £3,465$.
        This represents a 15.5% error on the expected outlay of $1,500 \times £2 = £3,000$.

7   D   Revenue, R   =   PQ
        $\therefore$ Estimate of Q   = $\dfrac{R}{P}$

        Maximum value of Q   = $\dfrac{1.20R}{0.90P}$ = $1.33 \dfrac{R}{P}$

        Minimum value of Q   = $\dfrac{0.80R}{1.10P}$ = $0.73 \dfrac{R}{P}$

        Therefore the range of error is +33% to -27%.

8   E   Index numbers give proportionate changes in prices, rather than any information about the absolute level of those prices, so I and II are not necessarily true.

        Beer has risen from 100 to 138; cheese has risen from 100 to 110. Beer has risen an extra 28 points on top of the 110 points cheese has reached. This is a 25% increase, not 20%.

9   B   £4,050 x $\frac{100}{150}$ = £2,700

10   C   Aggregate index = $\frac{6 \times 110 + 3 \times 120 + 10 \times 105 + 1 \times 109}{20}$

= 109 (to the nearest whole number)

11   E   Our only information from last quarter is the value of sales therefore it is only possible to calculate a value index. The current quarter's information makes it possible to calculate such an index.

12   E   (i)   is false, because the ogive tells us that there are ten invoices cumulatively for sums of £50 or less.
     (ii)   is true, because the graph exceeds 20 on the cumulative frequency axis.
     (iii)   is true, from the meaning of the ogive.

13   E   2Y = 92 + X
     ∴ 6Y = 276 + 3X
     Y = 88 - 3X

Adding gives
     7Y = 364
     ∴   Y = 52
     X = 2Y - 92 = 12

14   D   In a histogram the frequencies of the data are represented by the *areas* of the bars. If we choose a standard class interval of £5, we then need to divide the first class frequency by two, and the final class frequency by three. The graph for these adjusted frequencies is option D.

15   A

Unit price		*Weight*		
£				£
4	20/4	=	5.00	20
8	20/8	=	2.50	20
10	20/10	=	2.00	20
16	20/16	=	1.25	20
20	20/20	=	1.00	20
			11.75	100

Mean = £100/11.75 = £8.51

16   A   The mean of the first nine months is 19 tonnes, so the total for this period must be 9 x 19 = 171 tonnes. The total for the 12 months is therefore (171 + 22 + 18 + 29) tonnes = 240 tonnes, giving an average of 240 ÷ 12 = 20 tonnes.

17 A Arithmetic mean $= (1 + 1 + 5 + 7 + 2 + 8 + 3 + 5 + 5 + 3)/10 = 40/10 = 4$

Percentages in order: 1 1 2 3 3 5 5 5 7 8

Median $= (3 + 5)/2 = 4$

Difference $= 4 - 4 = 0$

18 D The arithmetic mean is $\dfrac{\Sigma x}{n} = \dfrac{2 + 2 + 5 + 0 + 11}{5} = 4$

The median is the middle number when the population has been ranked:

$$0, 2, 2, 5, 11$$

median $= 2$
The mode is 2
The range is $11 - 0 = 9$

19 E Let the three numbers be x, y, z and the fourth be a.

$\sqrt[3]{xyz} \quad = \quad 6$

$xyz \quad = \quad 6^3 \quad = 216$

$\sqrt[4]{xyza} \quad = \quad 12$

$xyza \quad = \quad 12^4 \quad = 20{,}736$

$a = \dfrac{xyza}{xyz} \quad = \quad \dfrac{20{,}736}{216} = 96$

20 D Variance $\sigma^2 = \dfrac{\Sigma(x - \bar{x})^2}{n}$

$\bar{x} = \dfrac{\Sigma x}{n} = \dfrac{1 + 2 + 5 + 8 + 9}{5} = \dfrac{25}{5} = 5$

$\sigma^2 = \dfrac{(-4)^2 + (-3)^2 + (0)^2 + (3)^2 + (4)^2}{5} = \dfrac{50}{5} = 10.00$

21 D Coefficient of variation $= \dfrac{\text{standard deviation}}{\text{mean}}$

Group	Mean	S.D.	Coeff. of variation
A	150	30	0.2
B	48	8	0.167
C	100	10	0.1
D	80	20	0.25
E	72	9	0.125

22 B The number of years' growth = 15.
Let r be the annual percentage growth rate.

$$1{,}000(1+r)^{15} = 20{,}157$$

$$(1+r)^{15} = \frac{20{,}157}{1{,}000} = 20.157$$

$$1+r = \sqrt[15]{20.157} = 1.2217$$

$$r = 0.2217 = 22.17\%$$

23 B Eight year ratio = 4
One year ratio = $4^{\frac{1}{8}}$ = 1.189
Annual rate = 18.9%

24 A Ten year ratio = 2,000/50,000 = 0.04
One year ratio = $0.04^{1/10}$ = 0.7248

∴ Value after five years = £50,000 × 0.7248^5 = £10,000

25 B The investment will be worth £8,000 $(1 + 0.08)^4$ $(1 + 0.12)^6$ = £21,483

26 C The £700 invested at the beginning has earned 10% interest for ten years, the £700 invested in 19X1 has earned 10% interest for nine years and so on. The last £700 invested in year 10 (19X9) will have earned interest for one year. Therefore we need to find the sum of the geometric progression:

$$£700 (1.1 + 1.1^2 + 1.1^3 + \ldots\ldots + 1.1^{10})$$

The first term, a, is equal to (£700 x 1.1). The common ratio, r = 1.1

Using the formula $S_n = \dfrac{a(r^n - 1)}{(r - 1)}$

$$S_n = (£700 \times 1.1) \times \frac{(1.1^{10} - 1)}{(1.1 - 1)}$$

$$= £12{,}272$$

27 C The quarterly rate of interest is 2%.

The first £1,000 will have been invested for a total of 12 quarters, the second £1,000 for eight quarters and the third £1,000 for four quarters.

Value of investment after
three complete years = £1,000 $(1.02^{12} + 1.02^8 + 1.02^4)$
= £3,522

28 B   The amount to be repaid each year = $\dfrac{£12,000}{\text{PV factor of £1 per annum at 14\% for 8 years}}$

$$= \frac{£12,000}{4.64}$$

$$= £2,586$$

29 B   p (breakdown in a line) = 1% = 0.01

∴   p (no breakdown in a line) = 0.99

∴   p (no breakdown in 10 lines) = $(0.99)^{10}$

30 E   p (at most one sale)

=   p (no sale or one sale)

=   p (no sale) + p (one sale)

$$= \left(\frac{4}{5}\right)^4 + 4\left(\frac{4}{5}\right)^3\left(\frac{1}{5}\right)$$

$$= \frac{256}{625} + \frac{256}{625}$$

$$= \frac{512}{625}$$

31 D $P(X \text{ or } Y) = 1 - P(\overline{X} \text{ and } \overline{Y}) = 1 - 0.1 = 0.9$

32 B $_{10}C_4 = \dfrac{10!}{6!4!} = \dfrac{10 \times 9 \times 8 \times 7}{4 \times 3 \times 2 \times 1} = 210$

BUSINESS LAW

BUSINESS LAW: INDEX TO QUESTIONS AND SUGGESTED SOLUTIONS

BUSINESS LAW
QUESTIONS

1   **PRECEDENT (20 marks)**

Explain the operation and significance of the doctrine of precedent in English law.

2   **INTERPRETATION OF STATUTES (20 marks)**

(a) The following are rules used by the courts to interpret statutes:

   (i)   the mischief rule;
   (ii)   the literal rule;
   (iii) the golden rule.

By means of examples where appropriate, explain the meaning of each of these rules.

(b) Describe the canons or presumptions which may assist the courts in the task of statutory interpretation.

3   **DELEGATED POWER (20 marks)**

Many of the statutory rules governing business operations were not laid down by Parliament but by other bodies to whom Parliament had delegated the power to legislate.

Explain:

(a) the reasons for this delegation;   (8 marks)
(b) the forms that delegated legislation may take;   (4 marks)
(c) the ways in which this delegated power is controlled.   (8 marks)

4   **CRIMINAL LAW AND CIVIL LAW (20 marks)**

Explain the difference between criminal law and civil law.

5   **REID (20 marks)**

(a) Acceptance of an offer completes a contract and normally the acceptance must be communicated to the other party. However, there are two exceptions to this general rule when an express acceptance may not be received by the party making the offer.

Describe these exceptions.

(b) Reid receives an unsolicited book by post with a note which says that unless the book is returned within fourteen days it will be assumed that the recipient has bought the book for £10.

What advice would you give to Reid?

6 SIDNEY (20 marks)

Explain, with reasons, whether a valid contract has been formed between Sidney and Brian in each of the following situations.

(a) Sidney agrees to sell goods to Brian 'on the usual terms'.

(b) Sidney offers to sell goods to Brian for £500. Brian says he will pay £400 but Sidney refuses to reduce his price. Brian then says he will pay £500.

(c) Sidney agrees to deliver goods to Brian on the condition that Tom pays him £200.

(d) Sidney offers to sell goods to Brian and gives him ten days to decide whether he wishes to buy them. After five days Sidney sells the goods elsewhere. Two days later, Brian says that he accepts the offer.

7 TYPES OF CONSIDERATION (20 marks)

State, with reasons, whether or not the following constitute consideration under the law of contract for a promise by A to pay £1,000 to B.

(a) B's promise to transfer his, B's, car to A. The car is worth £750.   (4 marks)

(b) B's previous performance of certain services from which A has benefited. (5 marks)

(c) B's undertaking to carry out a contract he has entered into with C but which he has yet to perform.   (4 marks)

(d) B's promise that he will make a payment of £2,000 to D.   (4 marks)

(e) B promises to steal certain goods from E.   (3 marks)

8 PRINCIPLE AND THE EXCEPTIONS (20 marks)

It is a fundamental principle of law that only the parties to a contract may sue or be sued for its breach but, as with so many such principles, a number of exceptions have arisen.

Explain both this principle and the exceptions that have arisen.

9 EXPRESS TERMS (12 marks)

When parties enter into a contract it is virtually impossible for them to include express terms to cover every eventuality. If a dispute arises it may then be necessary for terms to be implied into the contract.

Explain when these implied terms will be introduced:
(a) by the courts, and
(b) by statute.

10   NO LIABILITY (20 marks)

(a) Many contractual clauses purport to exclude liability for injury, loss or damage. Explain the general rules which determine the effectiveness of such clauses.   (10 marks)

(b) Discuss the effectiveness of the following statements.

(i)   A notice in a car park which reads 'No liability is accepted for any cars parked marks here'.   (5 marks)

(ii)   A sign in a shop window which states 'Goods bought in the sale will not be exchanged'.   (5 marks)

11   MISTAKE (20 marks)

Explain when and how mistake will affect a contract.

12   MORT (20 marks)

(a) What is misrepresentation and what effect will it have upon the formation of a contract?   (12 marks)

(b) Mort completed a proposal form for a life assurance policy. In answer to a question asking what other such proposals he had made he stated that one had been accepted. This was correct, but he omitted to mention that three other proposals had been turned down. Mort has now died and his widow is claiming on the policy. To what extent is she likely to succeed?   (8 marks)

13   RESTRAINT OF TRADE (20 marks)

Explain the main types of contract in restraint of trade which may exist, stating in each case the rules determining validity.

14   COTTON (20 marks)

Cotton, a clothing manufacturer, is in financial difficulties and is looking for short-term remedies which might help him. He has an order from Bernard for delivery on a fixed date and he writes to Bernard saying that he cannot guarantee that delivery unless Bernard promises to pay an additional sum to cover overtime working; Bernard makes that promise.

Cotton next approaches David, a debtor, and says that if David immediately pays 50% of the outstanding debt he will forget the balance; David makes that payment. Cotton also agrees to sell some of his stock to Eric for a ridiculously low price.

You are required to explain whether Cotton may

(a) recover the additional sum promised by Bernard;   (7 marks)

(b) recover the balance of the debt from David;   (6 marks)

(c) refuse to deliver the goods to Eric.   (7 marks)

15 PERFORMANCE (20 marks)

It is a basic rule that each party to a contract must perform completely and precisely what he has contracted to do.

(a) Explain this statement.

(b) What are the legally acceptable reasons which would justify non-performance?

16 SUBSEQUENT IMPOSSIBILITY (20 marks)

(a) Under what circumstances will a contract be brought to an end by subsequent impossibility of performance? (12 marks)

(b) How are the rights and duties of the parties adjusted when a contract becomes impossible to carry out? (8 marks)

17 LAGGARD (20 marks)

Laggard agreed to make and supply to Abel a piece of machinery by a certain date and in accordance with certain specifications. Delivery was late and the specifications were not followed.

Laggard pleads that the delay was caused by a shortage of labour. An outbreak of food poisoning at his works canteen had led to many employees being ill and this had then been followed by a strike. He also pleads that new safety regulations had made the machines more expensive to manufacture and that he had been obliged to economise by using cheaper materials.

Explain any remedies which may be available to Abel.

18 REMEDIES FOR BREACH (20 marks)

Every breach of contract gives a right to the injured party to claim damages but sometimes such an award may be neither adequate nor appropriate.

Describe the other remedies which may be available for breach and the circumstances when they are likely to be used.

19 SANDY (20 marks)

Sandy, a tour operator, sells package holidays through travel agents, one of whom is Jake. Ivan books one of these holidays through Jake who tells him that certain of the details contained in the travel brochure have been changed. This information later proves to be incorrect.

Partly as a result of this misinformation and partly for other reasons, Ivan is very disappointed with his holiday which falls far short of what he had been led to expect.

Advise Ivan:
(a) as to whether he has a claim for compensation; (4 marks)
(b) against whom such a claim may be made; (10 marks)
(c) the basis upon which any compensation may be awarded. (6 marks)

20 DAMAGES (20 marks)

Explain the principles which apply to determine:

(a) the validity of a contractual clause providing for damages payable in the event of breach; and

(b) the amount of damages awarded by a court following a breach of contract.

21 PROFFITT (20 marks)

(a) Under what circumstances may a professional person be held liable for statements made in the course of his practice? What steps may be taken to guard against such liability arising?   (12 marks)

(b) Proffitt, an accountancy lecturer, is explaining the principles of investment to his students and mentions, as an example, a company which he believes to have great potential for expansion. Frank, one of the students, tells Rustick, his friend, of this and they both invest their savings in the company. The company fails and the money is lost.

Advise Proffitt of his possible liability.   (8 marks)

22 MANUFACTURER'S RESPONSIBILITY (20 marks)

Martin, a manufacturer, produced what was described as a new medicine for influenza. The labels on the bottles containing the medicine clearly stated that, whilst the mixture was harmless, there had been little experience of its use and the manufacturer therefore took no responsibility if it was ineffective or unsuitable for any reason. Leonard bought a number of bottles for resale in his retail shop.

Because of impurities in the mixture a number of customers who bought and made use of it have become seriously ill. Leonard's small son cut himself badly when the rather fragile bottle broke in his hand. Discuss the legal position of Leonard.

23 CHEAPO LTD (20 marks)

Jean, the manager of Cheapo Ltd, a department store, engages Maurice to repair an escalator which has broken down. Maurice carries out the work badly and injures himself when he later turns on the escalator to test its operation. At the same time, injuries are caused to Mrs Smythe, a customer, and to Alan, a boy aged nine who has entered the store to play on the escalator.

Discuss the rights and liabilities of the parties involved.

24 DENNIS AND SAM (20 marks)

Some scaffolding collapses during the course of building operations and a number of employees are injured. Their injuries would have been greater if a shouted warning had not enabled them to scramble partially clear. However, two employees receive more serious injuries: Dennis is deaf and did not hear the warning and Sam, contrary to instructions, was not wearing a safety helmet.

(a) What must the injured employees prove in order to succeed in a claim for damages against their employer? What defences may the employer put forward?   (12 marks)

(b) What special considerations will apply to the claims of Dennis and Sam?   (8 marks)

25 WALTER (20 marks)

(a) An occupier owes a common duty of care to lawful visitors who enter his premises. Explain this statement.   (12 marks)

(b) Walter, the owner of a warehouse, spreads rat poison on slices of bread with the intention of putting it down to attract and destroy vermin.

Simple, an employee of low mentality, who has forgotten his lunch, finds the bread and eats a slice, as does Young, a small boy who has wandered into the warehouse.

Both Simple and Young become seriously ill.

Discuss the possible liabilities of Walter.   (8 marks)

26 DEFENCES AND REMEDIES (20 marks)

(a) Explain the meaning and effect of the following defences which may be put forward to an action in tort.
   (i)   consent;   (4 marks)
   (ii) contributory negligence; and   (4 marks)
   (iii) statutory authority.   (4 marks)

(b) What remedies may follow a successful tort action?   (8 marks)

27 GOOD FAITH (20 marks)

(a) An agent is said to owe a duty of good faith towards his principal.

What obligations does this impose upon the agent?   (12 marks)

(b) What remedies are available to the principal if this duty is broken?   (8 marks)

28 JACK AND JILL (20 marks)

(a) In what ways may an agent acquire authority to bind his principal?   (12 marks)

(b) Jack and Jill are partners and have a small garage where they sell petrol and carry out minor repairs and servicing of cars. They have expressly agreed that they will not buy and sell cars. One day, Jill, without Jack's knowledge, buys an expensive car on credit, sells the car for cash, and disappears with the proceeds.

Explain whether Jack may be held liable to pay for the car.   (8 marks)

29   CHARLES   (20 marks)

You have been asked to advise Charles of his legal position in the following situations.

(a)   He has entered into a contract with David, the agent of Eric. Eric is now denying liability under the contract on the ground that David has exceeded his authority as Eric's agent.
(6 marks)

(b)   He has entered into a contract with a firm of engineers through Nigel, a partner in the firm. The other partners in the firm are denying liability under the contract on the ground that the partnership agreement specifically restricts Nigel's authority in this regard.
(7 marks)

(c)   He has entered into a contract with the board of directors of a registered company. The company has gone into liquidation and the liquidator is refusing to honour the contract on the ground that it is 'ultra vires' the company.
(7 marks)

30   BRIGHT   (20 marks)

(a)   In what ways may the authority of an agent come to an end?   (12 marks)

(b)   Bright, a partner in a firm of consultants, intends to retire in the near future. Advise him of the extent to which he may still be liable for the firm's debts after retirement and of any measure he may take to avoid this liability.   (8 marks)

31   SAMSON AND DELILAH   (20 marks)

(a)   As a general rule an agent's power to bind his principal in a transaction is limited by the authority previously given to him by the principal.

In what exceptional situations may a principal be bound without the agent having prior authority?   (12 marks)

(b)   Andy is a partner of a firm of accountants. Without consulting the other partners he engages Delilah, a new typist, and agrees to buy on credit from Samson a very expensive word processor for her use.

He also agrees to sell to John the firm's only computer in an effort to induce his fellow partners to buy something better.

Under what circumstances, if at all, would the partnership be liable for Andy's actions?
(8 marks)

BUSINESS LAW
SUGGESTED SOLUTIONS

1 PRECEDENT

Tutorial note: it is not sufficient in answering this question to state merely that there is a hierarchy of courts and that the doctrine of precedent relies on *ratio decidendi* and *obiter dicta:* you must *explain* what is meant by the terms and *describe* the hierarchy. Note that the history of the doctrine of precedent is wholly irrelevant and the examiner awarded no marks for a description of it.

The doctrine of precedent is a necessary basis of the judge-made law in English courts. Every decision of a higher court is an application of principles of law to the facts of the case. In theory, the principles so applied are deduced from reports of earlier cases and the same principles should be applied in any subsequent case to which they are relevant.

The object of the system is to achieve consistency, expressed in the Latin maxim *stare decisis*, to conform to previous decisions. The judge does not make the law; he extracts it from earlier precedents and applies it afresh.

However, every judicial decision is in some measure related to the particular facts of the case. It is only the underlying legal principles of the decision which become precedents for subsequent application. Any such principle is called the *ratio decidendi* (the reason for the decision) of the particular case.

In his analysis of the case before him, the judge may discuss other points. In particular, to emphasise the reason for his decision he may say that if one fact (or several) were different he would reach a different conclusion. These are passing remarks (*obiter dicta*) which do not form part of the reason for the decision in that particular case.

If in some later case the alternative situation which had been envisaged in the earlier case is the actual circumstance now before the court, the court is not obliged to follow the *obiter dictum* pronounced on it in the earlier case. It is not a principle which has actually been applied in a previous decision; as such it cannot be a binding precedent. However, an *obiter dictum*, especially if formulated by a distinguished judge, may be treated as a persuasive precedent. In the latter case the court will take account of it but need not follow it.

There are two grounds upon which a judge may refuse to follow an earlier decision.

(a) *Status of court*

The position of a deciding court in the hierarchy of the court system determines whether the precedent set by another court is binding on it. Each court is only bound by precedents laid down by higher courts or (with the exception of the House of Lords) by the same court. However, a High Court judge sitting alone is not bound to follow a precedent established by another single High Court judge and a Divisional Court of the High Court (usually two judges sitting together) is not bound by decisions of the Criminal Division of the Court of Appeal since there is a right of appeal direct from the Divisional Court to the House of Lords. County and Crown Courts and magistrates' courts are not 'courts of record' and their decisions are not binding precedents on any later occasion.

(b) *Other reasons*

If the precedent is binding because of the status of the court which laid it down in relation to the court which is asked to follow it, the latter court may find reasons for not doing so. It may decline to follow a precedent where:

(1) it 'distinguishes' the earlier facts, asserting that in some material respect the earlier case differs from the one now under consideration;

(2) it finds the earlier decision obscure. This is most likely to occur when the earlier decision was given in an appeal court in the form of judgements by three or even five judges. In *Bell v Lever Bros 1932*, for example, the five members of the Judicial Committee of the House of Lords were unanimous in rejecting the employer's claim for repayment of money which it had paid. But some members of the court considered that a mistake as to a quality of the subject matter could never make a contract void and others thought that it might do so if the mistake related to a more significant fact than in the case before them. The latter view is not generally followed;

(3) it considers the previous decision to be in conflict with a fundamental principle of law, or the result of failure to consider some relevant principle or statute. Such an earlier decision is said to be reached *per incuriam:* 'without due attention to the law'. Lord Denning MR once dissented from one of his own earlier decisions on this ground;

(4) it considers an earlier precedent to be too wide. Thus the important decision of the House of Lords in *Donoghue v Stevenson 1932* on the nature of negligence has been refined and narrowed down in its application to a variety of different circumstances; or

(5) it has subsequently been overruled by a higher court than the one which first established it, or by statute.

2 INTERPRETATION OF STATUTES

> *Tutorial note:* when answering this question you would be wise to indicate clearly that you are aware of the distinction between interpretation *rules* and presumptions which assist interpretation. The latter 'fill in the gaps' where a statute is silent while the former assist the judges in interpreting ambiguities and resolving specific difficulties of applying the law to the facts of a case. Be careful too not to get sidetracked into sources which help judges to interpret words - such as the Interpretation Act 1978 - since these are neither rules nor presumptions but merely sources of assistance.

Statute is the supreme source of law in the United Kingdom but it is necessarily expressed in fairly general terms. Often the meaning, extent and applicability of a statute is very clear, but circumstances do arise in which judges must interpret a statute to see whether and, if so, how a statute applies to particular events or acts.

Where the meaning of the statute's words is unclear judges are assisted by certain rules of interpretation which they can apply. Where the application of the statute is unclear there are certain canons or presumptions (which can be rebutted) as to the statute's intention and scope.

(a) *Rules of interpretation*

   (i) *The mischief rule*

      If the words used are ambiguous the judge may use this rule to go beyond or behind the words and discover the 'mischief' or problem which the statute was intended to remedy. The judge will then adopt the meaning for the words which best gives effect to what it was that the statute intended to achieve.

It is a well-established, broad and flexible rule, dating from the sixteenth century. Following *Heydon's case 1584*, the judge should consider.

1. The state of the common law before the statute was passed and the particular mischief with which the statute was intended to deal.

2. The remedy for that mischief which Parliament indicated and the reasons for it.

Note that the judge can only look at the intention of Parliament as a whole, not at the intention of, say, the Government spokesman who introduced the statute as a bill. Since Parliament's intention can only really be gleaned from the words of the statute it passed, it can be difficult to apply the mischief rule.

An example of the mischief rule in operation is *Gardiner v Sevenoaks UDC 1950*. Regulations provided for the safe storage of inflammable film on 'premises'. A notice was served on G, who stored such film in a cave, that he should comply with the regulation. The case concerned whether a cave could be construed as being covered by the word 'premises'. It was held that the Act under which the regulations were made was intended to protect the safety of persons working in all places where film was stored. A cave was such a place and so G had to comply with the regulations.

(ii) *The literal rule*

This rule states that, where there is any difficulty in interpretation, words should be construed in their ordinary grammatical sense and, literally, with their ordinary meaning. This is so even if the result is one not intended by the statute. There can be said, therefore, to be some conflict between the literal and the mischief rules.

An oft-quoted example of the literal rule is *Fisher v Bell 1961*. The Restriction of Offensive Weapons 1959 prohibited persons from offering weapons for sale. A shopkeeper was prosecuted for exhibiting a flick-knife in his shop-window, but he was not convicted because such an exhibition was 'an invitation to treat' and not 'an offer for sale' (such an offer is usually made by the customer who offers to buy the item by tendering money).

(iii) *The golden rule*

Where a statute is capable of being construed in more than one way and with more than one result, the golden rule states that it should be construed so as to avoid a manifest absurdity or contradiction within itself.

The case of *Re Sigsworth 1935* demonstrates this rule. A man murdered his mother, who had not left a will. Under the rules of intestacy as set out in the Administration of Estates Act 1925 he was her only heir. The judge applied the golden rule to prevent the manifest absurdity of a murderer benefiting from his crime in this way.

A number of subsidiary rules exist which deal with the close textual interpretation of statutes. It is frequently argued, however, that the rules are themselves ambiguous, limited and unpredictable and that there should be substantial reform.

(b) Where a statute is express in what it covers or achieves then only the rules of interpretation of words need to be applied. Where a statute is silent certain presumptions exist as to what it is about. Obviously these presumptions - often called the 'canons of statutory interpretation'- can be rebutted. Equally often they can come into conflict with each other and with the rules of interpretation discussed above. In addition, it is difficult to predict which of the many presumptions the judges will favour. Again, therefore, there is strong grounds for reform of the law or at least for greater clarity of draftsmanship.

Unless a statute contains express words to the contrary the following presumptions are made:

(i) it does not alter existing common law nor repeal existing statutes;

(ii) it does not deprive a person of his property (say by nationalisation) without affording him compensation;

(iii) it does not seek to impose criminal liability without proof of fault. This means that, unless the statute states otherwise, there is no strict liability for criminal offences - so there must be an element of intention to commit an offence or, at least, lack of innocence. This presumption can be, and often is, rebutted by the statute. Well-known modern examples of strict criminal liability include dangerous driving under the Road Traffic Acts;

(iv) any point on which the statute leaves a gap or omission is outside its scope;

(v) it does not have retrospective effect to a date earlier than its becoming law;

(vi) it does not bind the Crown;

(vii) it does not have any application outside the United Kingdom; and

(viii) it does not operate counter to international law and should be interpreted to coincide with international legal obligations.

3 DELEGATED POWER

(a) In the recent past there has been an explosion of legislation to cope with the social, economic and political changes of the twentieth century. Parliament, which makes these laws, has not changed concurrently in size, duration nor expertise, since its members change at least every five years. As a result, Acts tend to be passed as a framework of rules, the full construction to be completed by Parliament's delegates who are normally ministers, government commissions or local authorities.

Due to lack of time and technical expertise therefore there has been an increase in delegated legislation. Distinct advantages exist for detailed rules to be made outside the Chamber.

(i) The subjects are often highly complex due to rapid changes in technology, so that details are beyond the ken of MPs, but can be dealt with competently by external experts.

(ii) Delegating rule-making leads to greater flexibility and better timing. For instance, the law to enforce the wearing of seat-belts can be tightened if advances in research show that safer seat-belts can be made, without passing a whole new Act. These revised rules, however, may be held in abeyance to give manufactures time to fit the belts.

(iii) Delegated legislation allows for local knowledge and custom. This 'sectional' argument applies both to areas of the country - regulations on road-width, for instance would vary greatly between Northumberland and the Home Counties - and to professional or trade divisions.

(b) Delegated legislation originates in an Act of Parliament which expressly gives power to a minister or public body, such as a local authority, to make laws for specified purposes. Most often, these laws take the form of 'statutory instruments' made under the procedure established by the Statutory Instruments Act 1946 and available from the Stationery Office.

Sub-categories of statutory instrument include 'Orders in Council', which are made by the Queen with the advice of the Privy Council; 'Proclamations', which are notices given by the Queen to her subjects; and 'Regulations', 'Rules', 'Orders', 'Schemes', 'Warrants' and, occasionally, 'Directions'.

An important form of delegated legislation, to be distinguished from statutory instruments, are byelaws made under the Local Government Act 1972. Section 236 states that byelaws cannot take effect until:

(i) the relevant minister has confirmed them;
(ii) public notice has been given no less than one month in advance of confirmation being applied for;
(iii) a copy of the proposed byelaw is available for inspection; and
(iv) the byelaw will come into effect one month after it is confirmed unless a different date has been fixed by the confirming authority.

(c) In a democracy, law-making is meant to be the exclusive preserve of the legislature. Consequently, it is not surprising that the modern upsurge in delegated legislation has at times provoked disquiet. The law apparently may be changed without reference to Parliament and without interested parties, normally Joe Public, knowing anything about it.

However, Parliament does exert control over delegated legislation by providing for statutory instruments to be laid before Parliament, and for them to cease to have effect if within forty days either House of Parliament so resolves.

There is an alternative system (reserved for particularly important subjects) by which the regulations are laid before Parliament in draft and must be affirmatively approved if they are to take effect at all.

In addition, there are standing Scrutiny Committees of both Houses of Parliament whose duty it is to examine statutory instruments with a view to raising objections if necessary.

The courts can also restrain the wrongful use of power to make delegated legislation. The power is given for defined purposes only. If it is alleged that delegated legislation exceeds the powers given, it is possible that the court will declare that it is *ultra vires* and therefore void.

4 CRIMINAL LAW AND CIVIL LAW

A crime is a public offence and as such will normally be prosecuted by the public authorities – the immediate victim of a crime (someone who has been assaulted, for instance) will usually have little say in whether criminal proceedings are begun and will not generally benefit when there is a conviction. The increasingly used right of private prosecution is a legacy of the nineteenth century and earlier when the main responsibility for prosecuting crime lay with private citizens – strictly as a *public* duty. Attention is always therefore focused on the wrongdoer.

The civil law, by contrast, exists to uphold private rights and to resolve disputes between private citizens. For instance, the law of negligence may enable the victim of an accident to sue for compensation from the person who caused his injuries, or contract law may help someone to enforce an agreement that he has made with another party. Attention is directed at the wronged.

Because of the distinctions between the objects of the law, in criminal cases the state (ie the Queen) is a party to the case as prosecutor (*R v Smith*). In a civil case, the wronged is the plaintiff and the case is stated as being between two persons (*Jones v Smith*). One act or wrong may easily give rise to both a criminal and civil action – for example, causing death by drunken driving may lead to a manslaughter conviction (criminal) and a demand for compensation for the victim's family (civil).

When a convicted criminal is sentenced – usually by way of a fine or a term in prison – the object is to punish him for the wrong that he has done and to deter him and others from committing the same crime in the future. The civil law, on the other hand, has nothing to do with punishment, only compensation. For example, before the law will interest itself in a person's negligence, someone must suffer injury as a result of it – the law is not concerned about negligence *per se*; on the same principle, the quantum of damages is assessed according to the plaintiff's loss – anything more than what would compensate the plaintiff would constitute punishment of the other party.

It will be gathered that, in a sense, crimes are more serious than civil offences. This is reflected in the different procedures in the criminal and civil courts. Thus rules of evidence are stricter in criminal cases, numerous high hurdles – such as the 'Judges' Rules' – having to be surmounted by the Prosecution before its evidence can be admitted. Similarly the standard of proof in criminal cases is higher than in civil, 'guilty beyond reasonable doubt' and proof 'upon the balance of probabilities' being the respective requirements.

5 REID

> *Tutorial note:* this question allows you to launch straight into a description of the two occasions when communication of acceptance is *not* required because it states the usual rule of communication in the title itself. Do not be tricked, therefore, into repeating the question. Such a straightforward bookwork question as part (a) allows you to demonstrate your knowledge of principles and of important case-law. Part (a) relates directly to part (b) so do not repeat yourself in part (b). Instead you should concentrate on applying the principles to the facts. It helps to be very clear as to 'who's who' – Reid is the offeree because it is open to him to accept; this makes the sender the offeror. This should highlight to you the ways in which the principles in part (a) do not apply to Reid in part (b).

(a) There are two recognised exceptions to the general rule that acceptance of an offer must be communicated to the offeror: where the offeror dispenses with the need and where the postal service is used as agent of the offeror.

Dispensing with communication

The offeror may in a 'unilateral' contract (one where the consideration is performance of an act) provide that due performance of the act shall constitute acceptance without need of communication to him. That was the main point of *Carlill v Carbolic Smokeball Co 1892*, where an advertiser undertook to make a payment to anyone who bought and used his product if it did not afford the immunity which he asserted it would. Mrs Carlill was entitled to say that she had accepted the offer by buying and using the medicine; it was immaterial that she did not at the time inform the advertiser that she was doing so.

The need for communication of acceptance is also waived where a person advertises that a reward is on offer for the return of lost property. A person does not have to communicate his acceptance of the offer of reward before he starts looking, but he will obviously not be able to enforce the agreement unless he provides consideration in the form of finding the article subject to the reward. Difficulties can arise in reward cases to do with communication of the *offer*, not the acceptance; if A offers a reward and B, in ignorance of the offer, finds the article or whatever, B cannot be said to have accepted the offer and provided consideration because the offer had not been communicated to him: *R v Clarke 1927*.

Use of the post

The offeror, expressly or by implication, may indicate that he expects to receive acceptance of his offer by the posting of a letter of acceptance. Even if not stated, this intention may be implied from the mere fact of making an offer by post *(Household Fire and Carriage Accident Insurance Co v Grant 1879)* unless other circumstances negate any such presumed intention: *Holwell Securities Ltd v Hughes 1973*.

Where acceptance by post is intended, acceptance is effected when a letter, properly addressed and stamped, is put in the post, even though it may subsequently be delayed or lost entirely in the post: *Adams v Lindsell 1818*.

(b) For an agreement to be valid there must be an offer and an acceptance, and both (usually) must be communicated to the other party. Although the offeror (the person who sent the book to Reid in this case) can dispense with the need for communication of acceptance if he chooses, he cannot impose this dispensation on the offeree (Reid). Reid may tacitly accept by adopting the contract in reading the book, but this is a quite separate issue from the offeror's attempt to force him to accept.

This situation is loosely based on that in *Felthouse v Bindley 1862* where the offeror offered to buy a horse at a certain price and stated that 'if I hear no more about him, I consider the horse mine at that price'. It was held that there could be no acceptance by silence in these circumstances - the offeror could not impose acceptance merely because the offeree does not reject the offer. There must be some act on the part of the offeree to indicate acceptance.

Goods which are sent to a person who did not request them are not 'accepted' merely because he does not return them to the sender. His silence is not acceptance of them, even if the sender includes a statement that he is deemed to have agreed to buy and/or pay unless he rejects them: Unsolicited Goods and Services Act 1971. Indeed, provided it was sent with a view to his acquiring it otherwise than for a trade or business, and he has not agreed to pay for or to return it, Reid may treat the book as an unsolicited gift. However if, within six months, the sender tries to repossess it or Reid unreasonably prevents repossession the book is not deemed to be his.

6   SIDNEY

> *Tutorial note:* This question requires a solid knowledge of the basic principles of contract law, and shows that you must be able to define and explain underlying concepts as well as the more abstruse and technical points to deal with this section of the paper effectively.

(a)   One of the most important principles of the law of contract is that the agreement between the parties, if it is intended to be a binding contract, must be clear and precise, enough to establish the rights and duties of the parties. If this precision is lacking from the agreement it may be that the courts will infer that there was no contract.

An agreement phrased to be 'on the usual terms' may be too vague to form a contract. In *Scammell v Ouston 1941*, an agreement on 'hire purchase terms' was held not to be a binding contract as the terms were too vague.

If, however, there is enough evidence to deduce the terms of the contract the courts will allow it to stand. The terms may be deduced form former dealings (*Hillas v Arcos 1932*) or from standard forms; if the meaningless words are part of a standard form and are inappropriate for the deal in question the courts will usually ignore them: *Nicolene v Simmonds 1953*.

Hence Sydney and Brian will have a binding contract only if they can show some way of giving this phrase a real meaning.

(b)   Another key factor of the creation of a contract is the existence of a valid offer and acceptance. In this case, Sydney has made his offer to sell and Brian has responded. To form a contract, however, Brian must respond with an unqalified acceptance. Introduction of new terms is a counter offer and not an acceptance: *Neale v Merritt 1930*. It is open for Sydney to accept this counter-offer, thus creating a contract, but he does not. This must be distinguished from an acceptance with an inquiry as to whether the exact terms of the contract could be varied, as in *Stevenson v MacLean 1880*.

The original offer by Sydney has been answered by Brian's counter offer; that first offer has lapsed and it is not open to Brian to accept it: *Hyde v Wrench 1840*. Thus there is no contract.

(c)   The third element necessary in a binding contract is consideration. This is the payment for the promise; in this case, it is the price payable for delivery of the goods. There are numerous rules surrounding the payment of consideration, one of which is that the consideration must move from the promisee - the parties themselves must pay the price.

In *Tweddle v Atkinson 1861*, a promise by two parties that each would pay a sum to a third party was not enforceable by that third party. This illustrates the rule that consideration moves *from* the parties - it is not necessary that the parties themselves should be recipients of the benefit. It also demonstrates the doctrine of privity of contract - only those parties who give consideration may enforce the contract (except in limited circumstances): *Dunlop v Selfridge 1915*.

Here the contract, if any, is between Sydney and Tom. Tom gives consideration for Sydney's promise to deliver the goods to Brian. Brian gives nothing and thus there is no contract between himself and Sydney. If Sydney fails to deliver the goods, it is for Tom to enforce the promise, not Brian.

(d) Sydney's offer to Brian will not stay open indefinitely. It is in fact open to Sydney to revoke it at any time before acceptance: *Routledge v Grant 1828*. This is because Brian has provided no consideration for Sydney's promise to keep the offer open for ten days.

However, Sydney must show that his revocation is valid. Sale of the goods to another party is clearly an implied revocation of his offer but it is not valid until notice of it is actually received by Brian: *Byrne v Van Tienhoven 1880*. It is not necessary that Sydney should inform Brian personally; notice to Brian by a reliable third party will suffice: *Dickinson v Dodds 1876*.

If Brian does not know of the sale, his acceptance within the time limit is capable of forming a binding contract - which Sydney will be unable to perform as he has sold the goods elsewhere and is thus in breach.

7 TYPES OF CONSIDERATION

Tutorial note: this question covers many of the more rarefied aspects of consideration. It is wide-ranging, and to answer it you need to be sure of your facts. A 'common-sense' approach is not enough.

(a) Consideration is essential to a valid contract. It is the price given by one party for the promise or performance of another. There are certain conditions attached to consideration; not every 'price' given for the contractual promise constitutes good consideration.

A promises to give £1,000 in return for B's car, which is worth only £750. The law requires only that the consideration given has sufficient but not adequate value; it does not necessarily have to be of a value equal to the benefit received: *Thomas v Thomas 1842*. Furthermore as long as there is some value in the consideration from the parties' point of view, it may suffice: in *Chappell and Co v Nestle Co 1959*, chocolate wrappers were sufficient consideration for a promise to supply a record made by the chocolate manufacturer.

Applying these principles to A and B's contract, there is valuable consideration even if the bargain is unequal, and thus there is a valid contract.

(b) Here the money is to be paid in respect of a performance of services which has already taken place. As a general rule, B's consideration is not adequate because it is past consideration; it was not given in return for the contractual promise. In *Re McArdle 1951*, improvements were made to a house, and the future owners later agreed to pay for those improvements. It was held that this promise of payment was not binding as it was made after the improvements were made.

However there are certain exceptions to this rule. It may be that B performed these actions beneficial to A at A's request. If so, there was an implication that A was ready to pay B for his actions: *Lampleigh v Braithwaite 1615*. In this case, it may be possible to infer that A made such a promise to B if he asked him to perform these services, and the contract would then be binding.

(c) B has not yet entered into his contract with C nor performed any obligations, so there is no question of past consideration. The performance of an obligation incurred under a contract with another policy is capable of being good consideration: *Shadwell v Shadwell 1860*. This is because, by being assured that B will contract with C, A will have received a benefit to which he had no previous right, and B will have assumed an additional obligation to perform the contract. Thus in this case, B's promise is good consideration for A's promise of payment.

(d) The consideration for A's promise of £1,000 in this case is B's promise to make payment of £2,000 to D. It is irrelevant that there is a discrepancy in the amounts involved and the consideration is sufficient even though the payment is made to D rather than to A. There is a valid contract between A and B which means that D cannot enforce it, even though he is the person who benefits from B's promise: *Tweddle v Atkinson 1861*.

(e) There is a principle that contracts for illegal or immoral purposes are void on the grounds of public policy. B's promise to steal from E in return for £1,000 is not a contract.

8   PRINCIPLE AND THE EXCEPTIONS

> *Tutorial note:* this is a question on a very particular point of law – privity of contract – and you are required to confine yourself to this point and not to get involved in 'extraneous material'. In addition, you are asked to *explain* both the principle and its exceptions – a list of exceptions, for instance, is inadequate. This shows once again how important it is to READ THE QUESTION and SATISFY THE REQUIREMENTS.

The basic principle of the law of contract that only the parties to the contract may enforce that contract is known as the doctrine of privity of contract.

The leading case on privity is *Dunlop v Selfridge 1915*, where D contracted with X that it would supply tyres to X which would then be supplied to retailers. The contract between the retailers and X provided that the tyres must be resold at a minimum price and that if the retailer sold the tyres at less than this price, it would have to make a payment to D. S, a retailer, sold tyres supplied by X at less than this price and D sued for the payment. D failed in its claim; the promise was made as part of the contract between S and X and only they could enforce that contract even though the actual benefit was for D.

The principle has also been explained in terms of consideration: a promise may only be enforced by the person who has provided consideration for it: *Tweddle v Atkinson 1861*. Thus the benefit of a contract may be for a third party, but it is only the actual parties who can enforce it. It follows that the party who does not receive the benefit of the contract will only receive nominal damages on breach.

A slight difference arises where one party acts in a representative capacity, say as agent or trustee, for one of the parties to the contract. For instance a widow entitled to an annuity under a contract made by her husband enforced the contract as his personal representative and obtained a decree of specific performance: *Beswick v Beswick 1968*.

Some exceptions have arisen to the privity rule. The most obvious is where the *benefit* of the contract has been assigned to a third party. A legal assignment must be in writing with notice to the other party, and the assignee can have no better rights under the contract than the assignor had. Rights of action and personal rights cannot be assigned *(Kemp v Baerselmann 1906)* and nor can the *burden* of contractual obligations, as opposed to the *benefits*. A party may delegate actual performance of contractual obligations to a third party but is still liable under the contract.

Where a contract is made by an *agent*, the undisclosed principal of that agent may adopt the contract. The principal will then be party to the contract. Other exceptions to the doctrine of privity arise through specific statutory provisions, for instance the Road Traffic Act 1972 allows a person injured in a motor accident to sue the other party's insurers.

9 EXPRESS TERMS

> *Tutorial note:* the distinction between express and implied terms in a contract is very important, and may well come up in a straight contract question such as this. Be careful then to distinguish between statutory and common law implied terms.

(a) The terms of a contract are generally decided by agreement between the parties and as a rule a court will look no further than those terms when settling disputes. In certain cases, however, some terms will be treated as part of the contract even though there is no express agreement to this effect; at other times the court will seek to clarify and supply an unclear express clause.

Custom may dictate that, in certain contracts, a particular term is included. Express agreement to the contrary will rebut this: *Les Affreteurs v Walford 1919*.

There are also common law rules which imply terms into particular contracts. The most common example of this approach is the contract of employment. As well as various statutory requirements there are a series of implied terms concerned with the rights and duties of both parties. The employee is bound to carry out his duties in a reasonably careful and skilful manner, and in good faith (*Boston Deep Sea Fishing & Ice Co v Ansell 1888*), and the employer is bound to ensure that he has a safe work environment and safe work colleagues.

The purpose of such an approach is to maintain a degree of equality in the contractual relationship, inserting implied terms where the weaker party may not be able to insist upon as express terms.

Provided there is a sufficient degree of agreement to establish that there is a contract, the courts will be ready to imply the inclusion of such terms which are so obvious that they are not expressly stated. The test is that of the 'officious bystander' who, had he been present when the contract was made, would have pointed out the necessity of this type of term to the parties. They would then reply that the inclusion of this term was self-evident: *The Moorcock 1889*. 'Business efficacy' is the reason for this practice; the contract should not fail for the parties' lack of express terms when their intention was obvious.

(b) The common law principle of implied terms has been carried into statute law. Again these implied terms help adjust the 'balance of power' within a contract but also help to clarify the terms which are to be implied.

146

In some cases such terms were already established by common law (eg the Sale of Goods Act 1979). By that Act, every contract of sale (within the definition of s2) includes a number of terms. Furthermore, these terms are classified as conditions or warranties; this classification determines whether breach of the term will lead to repudiation and damages (condition) or damages only (warranties). Examples of conditions are the seller's right to sell the goods (s12) and that goods correspond with the contract description (s13).

Although the distinction between conditions and warranties is obviously an important one, some statutes only imply a 'term'. It is then up to the court to decide whether the 'term' is a warranty or condition (eg Supply of Goods and Services Act 1982).

Other terms are introduced to correct inequalities which have arisen (eg by the Consumer Credit Act 1974 and some of the employment legislation). For example, under the Employment Protection (Consolidation) Act 1978 s27, trade union officials are permitted to take time off for union activities. Part III of that Act gives female employees who have completed at least two years continuous employment a right to maternity leave and pay.

10 NO LIABILITY

(a) The effectiveness of an exclusion clause may be governed by statute law or case law. The relevant *statute* is the Unfair Contract Terms Act 1977. If the clause is void under this statute then it has no effect at all. Clauses purporting to exclude liability for death or personal injury are always void (s2), as are clauses in a contract for the sale of goods which attempt to exclude the implied condition that the seller has title to the goods. Certain clauses in consumer contracts which deal with other forms of damage or loss are valid only insofar as they are reasonable. Reasonableness is judged according to the criteria set out in s11 and Sch 2 of the 1977 Act.

The requirement for reasonableness is applied to any clause restricting liability for negligence (provided this does not result in death or injury), certain clauses in standard term consumer contracts and indemnity clauses in consumer contracts. In consumer contracts no clause can restrict or exclude liability for loss or damage caused by defects in the goods, nor can the clauses as to description, quality, fitness for the purpose and sample implied into sale of goods contracts be excluded.

An exclusion clause will also be assessed following rules of *case-law*. Generally a clause cannot be disputed if it is contained in a document which the party aggrieved has signed: *L'Estrange v Glaucob 1934* (although it may still be if its meaning was misrepresented: *Curtis v Chemical Cleaning Co 1951*). But in order to be treated as a part of the contract it must be put forward as a term *before* the contract is made (*Olley v Marlborough Court 1949*), and its effects must have been made known to the person affected by it at the time of agreement: *Churchhill v Barry UDC 1940*.

Total failure to perform the contract will not of itself prevent reliance on any valid exclusion clause in that contract: *Photo Productions v Securicor 1980*.

(b) (i) Assuming there is a contract for the use of the car park (which there will be if payment of some kind is made) the validity of the clause will firstly depend on whether it can be treated as part of the contract. Such a notice may be inadequate if not seen until after the contract was entered into: *Olley v Marlborough Court 1949*. However an analogy may be drawn with the printing of conditions on a railway ticket in *Thompson v LMS Railway 1930*; the ticket was given at the time the contract was made and, if the notice was visible at the same time, it is likely that the notice is part of the contract. If the ticket contained reference to the notice, as in *Thompson v LMS Railway 1930*, the notice may still be binding on the customer although this is more likely to be so if the customer had used the car park previously and so had constructive and/or actual notice of it.

An interesting case which actually concerns a car park is *Thornton v Shoe Lane Parking Ltd 1972*. Here it was held that a contract was formed *before* the plaintiff received the car park ticket: the 'parking' sign was an offer and his act of parking was acceptance. A notice disclaiming liability for damage to cars which was on display inside the car park after the ticket was received was therefore found not to be validly included in the contract.

As the term covers damage to property it must be decided whether it is reasonable within the 1977 Act: s2. This will depend on the criteria of Sch 2: the relative strength of the parties, the offer of inducements to enter into the contract, awareness of the effect of the contract and so on.

If there is no contract because the parking is free, the notice must still satisfy the requirements of reasonableness if it is to exclude liability in tort for any loss caused to visitors by the negligence of the car park occupier. The notice may help to form the defence of *volenti non fit injuria* - that in parking there, the car owner voluntarily assumed any risks.

(ii) The notice here is clearly displayed in the shop window and until 1977 it would have been part of the sale contract. However, the 1977 Act specifically deals with attempts to exclude some of the terms of the Sale of Goods Act 1979 from consumer contracts for the sale of goods. S6 of that Act prevents the exclusion of ss12-15 of the 1979 Act from any contract for the sale of goods where one party is a consumer. These terms cover fitness for purpose, quality, description and sample. This restriction applies even to special 'sale' contracts; the standards of quality and fitness may be judged in relation to the lower price, but this does not mean that the terms do not apply at all.

The right to exchange goods is outside the scope of the Sale of Goods Act 1979. Any exclusion of the right must still, however, satisfy the condition of reasonableness of the 1977 Act since a shop sale is a sale to a consumer and s3 UCTA makes any exclusion clause in a contract where one person deals as a consumer subject to the reasonableness requirement; the fact that there is a sale may be of some relevance here.

11 MISTAKE

As a general rule a party to a contract may not escape his obligations under that contract on the grounds that he is mistaken as to its terms or the general circumstances. A view is taken that parties who have reached a bargain should not be allowed to withdraw from their obligations merely because one of them has, for example, miscalculated the profit he will make, or misunderstood the extent of his obligations.

The exception to this rule is operative mistake, which will in certain cases allow a person not to fulfil his obligations, although the effect of such a mistake will depend on the type of operative mistake in question.

Common mistake arises where both parties unknowingly make a contract concerning non-existent or perished subject matter: *Couturier v Hastie 1852*. In this case the contract is void from the start and is of no effect. The principle has been extended to cover those cases where one party tried to buy something he already owns: *Cochrane v Willis 1865*. The doctrine would appear to apply only where there is a mistake as to the substantive existence of the subject, not its quality: *Bell v Lever Bros 1932*.

Mutual mistake arises where the parties are at cross-purposes as to the terms of the contract. Where the mutual misunderstanding amounts to a failure to agree at all, the contract is void: *Raffles v Wichelhaus 1864*. Again the doctrine applies where there is a material mistake as to the subject-matter itself *(Scriven Bros v Hindley 1913)* and not merely to its quality: *Smith v Hughes 1871*. In most cases the mistake can be resolved by the terms of the contract which will usually favour one party's view: *Tamplin v James 1880*.

Unilateral mistake arises where there is a mistake by one party. The case-law tends to feature mistakes as to identity and illustrates the distinction between those contracts rendered void by the mistake and those which are merely voidable (of legal effect unless and until action is taken to rescind the contract).

(a) Where a person intends to sell to a particular person, the contract will be void if the sale is made to a person impersonating that intended buyer: *Cundy v Lindsay 1878*.

(b) If the mistake really relates to some attribute of the buyer rather than the identity *(Kings Norton Metal v Edridge Merrett 1897)*, then the mistake will not be operative to render the contract void *ab initio*. This is usually the reason why, in cases where the seller and buyer actually meet *(Phillips v Brooks 1919)* it is difficult to show that there was no intention to sell to that person. In these cases, the contracts are voidable because of the misrepresentation which induced the mistake. The party deceived may rescind the contract and claim damages. He will not be able to reclaim the goods sold if they have been sold on to a third party who bought them in good faith.

Equity provides some other kinds of relief where the contract is voidable. If the contract is written and does not reflect the parties' intention it may be rectified: *Joscelyne v Nissen 1970*. The court may impose a compromise solution as in *Solle v Butcher 1950*. The court may also refuse to make an order for specific performance against a party making a mistake of which the other party was aware even if there was no misrepresentation: *Webster v Cecil 1861*. There is also the principle of law called *non est factum*, which allows a person to repudiate a signed document if he can show that he understood its effect to be fundamentally different to the actual case and that this misunderstanding did not arise from his own carelessness: *Saunders v Anglia Building Society 1971*.

12 MORT

> *Tutorial note:* be careful when answering a question such as this to use legal terms correctly. Misrepresentation is *not* the same as mistake, and a *voidable* contract is very different to a *void* one. With misrepresentation the common law remedy is rescission, because the contract is voidable, but damages under common law and statute (the Misrepresentation Act 1967) may also be available. It is worth your while to remember that any mention of insurance (or life assurance) in an exam question should ring alarm bells in your mind as to *uberrima fides* - extreme good faith.

(a) A misrepresentation is an untrue statement of fact, made in the preliminary course of negotiating a contract, by one party to the contract to the other in order to induce the other party to enter into that contract. It does not itself become part of the contract. To be actionable it must actually have induced that person to enter the contract. The misled party may be able to sue for damages and/or rescind the contract as a result.

The statement must be a statement of fact. If it is no more than a statement of opinion it is not a misrepresentation *(Bisset v Wilkinson 1927)* although, in judging this, the knowledge of the party making the statement will be taken into account: *Smith v Land and House Property Corporation 1884*. Silence is not usually a representation, unless there is a special duty of extreme good faith, or the undisclosed facts are enough to make those given misleading and untrue: *R v Kylsant 1931*. There is a duty to correct a statement which becomes false before the contract is made: *With v O'Flanagan 1936*.

The statement must have been made by one party to the other to induce that other party to enter into the contract. This principle covers misstatements made to the public at large (eg in an advertisement), and also covers a statement made to one person in the knowledge that it will be passed on to the person making the contract: *Pilmore v Hood 1873*. The recipient is not expected to make further investigations into the truth of the statement: *Redgrave v Hurd 1881*. Because the statement must have induced the party to enter into the contract, it must be shown that he knew of the statement, allowed it to influence his judgement and was unaware of its untruth. It need not be the only reason for making the contract, however, provided the influence is shown: *Edgington v Fitzmaurice 1885*.

If a contract has been made as a result of a misrepresentation it is voidable. This means that the party misled may bring the contract to an end (rescission) and refuse to perform his part of it. If the misrepresentation is a fraudulent one (made with the knowledge of its falsity, or in the belief that it was false, or careless of whether it was true or false) the common law also gives a right to claim damages. Rescission is also a remedy for a negligent misrepresentation (where there is no reasonable ground for the maker's belief in its truth) or innocent misrepresentation (where there are such grounds). The Misrepresentation Act 1967 gives a right to claim damages for loss suffered in a negligent misrepresentation, but not an innocent one.

The right to rescission is not absolute. Under the 1967 Act, damages may be awarded *instead* of rescission for innocent or negligent misrepresentation if this is considered a fairer result. However, this is not possible if the right to rescind has been lost for other reasons. If the misled party affirms the contract expressly or implicitly after discovering the facts, the right is lost. Lapse of time may also act as a bar in the case of innocent misrepresentation: *Leaf v International Galleries 1950*. Finally, the right is lost if it would affect the rights of innocent third parties or if it has become impossible to restore the party misled to his or her pre-contract position: *Clark v Dickson 1858*.

(b) Mort has made a statement which contains only part of the facts. Although there is no general duty to disclose all facts, silence may cause a misleading interpretation to be given to a statement already made: *R v Kylsant 1931*. In this case, the fact that he has had a policy application accepted looks rather different when the three policies turned down are revealed. This would appear to be sufficient to turn the statement made into a misrepresentation.

Furthermore this is a contract for insurance and as such is a contract of extreme good faith *(uberrimae fidei)*. In this case, there *is* a duty to disclose all material facts. Clearly Mort has not done so here. In the circumstances, the insurance company would be able to rescind the contract and Mrs Mort would be unable to claim on it.

13 RESTRAINT OF TRADE

A contract which purports to restrict the ways in which a person may carry on his trade is *prima facie* void as contrary to public policy: *Nordenfelt v Maxim Nordenfelt Guns & Ammunition Co 1894*. It may be valid, however, if the person imposing the restriction has a legitimate interest to protect and if the restraint is reasonable both as between the parties and as seen objectively.

The most common category of restraint of trade contract is that imposing restrictions on employees once they have left the service of their employer. A restriction may be reasonable if the employee has secret information acquired from his employment *(Forster & Sons v Suggett 1918)* but this does not extend to restrictions on the use of personal skills: *Morris v Saxelby 1916*.

An employer may prevent the employee from dealing with the employer's customers; this would be upheld where there is much personal contact by the employee with customers (such as a solicitor's clerk: *Fitch v Dewes 1921*) but not otherwise (contact by phone: *Strange v Mann 1965*).

Restrictive agreements by groups of employers not connected directly with the employee may be declared void if the employee's interests are affected: *Greig v Insole 1978*.

The restriction must be no wider than is necessary to protect the employer's interest. The modern tendency is to be very strict; restrictions aimed at covering a wider area than the employer's catchment area are usually void, as are unlimited time restrictions: *Attwood v Lamont 1920*. The restriction must also be limited to the employer's type of business. Thus a milkman could not be barred from the sale of all dairy produce as well as milk: *Home Counties Dairies v Skilton 1970*.

When presented with a contract of employment which appears to be in restraint of trade, the courts will attempt to reach a reasonable agreement. This may involve the 'blue pencil' rule - the court will strike out that part of the agreement which is excessive whilst retaining the rest of the restraint, as in *Skilton's Case*. In *Littlewoods Organisation v Harris 1977* the court went so far as to rewrite the agreement totally, but this procedure was not applied in *Mason v Provident Clothing Company 1919* and this earlier rule is probably the better one.

Other types of contract may be in restraint of trade. A buyer of a business is entitled to protect his interest in its goodwill by preventing the seller from dealing with the customers but this must not go beyond the scope of that business: *British Concrete Co v Schelff 1921*. The courts are quite sympathetic to such restraints, particularly where the parties are of similar standing and consideration has been given in respect of the restraint: *Allied Dunbar (Frank Weisinger) Ltd v Frank Weisinger 1987*.

Solus agreements whereby a retailer agrees to deal with only one supplier are often carefully scrutinised by the courts. They are particularly seen in petrol retailing whereby the small garage owner agrees to take all his oil supplies from a single supplier; the scope for abuse of power by the large supplier is obvious. If an agreement is for an unduly long period it will be void even if it is attached to a lease or mortgage: *Esso Petroleum v Harpers Garage 1969*. Where the owner sells his garage to the oil company and then leases it back with a supply agreement, the restriction may be void if the company's main consideration is monopoly rather than land use.

A restraint of trade contract may be void if the restrictions are such as to make the benefit of the contract fall on one party only: *Schroder Music Publishing v Macauley 1974*. This has been seen especially in the entertainment industry, where the *prima facie* reasonableness of a restraint has been overridden by the undue influence of the more powerful party.

Contracts in restraint of trade are also dealt with to some extent by statute. The Fair Trading Act 1976 and the Restrictive Trade Practices Act 1976 promote trade and competition and restrict attempts to distort this. The latter requires that arrangements between manufacturers and traders designed to fix prices or regulate the supply of goods must be registered with the Director General of Fair Trading. They will be void unless the Restrictive Practices Court is satisfied that they are in the public interest.

The Resale Prices Act 1976 makes a term imposing a minimum resale price by the manufacturer void, unless the Court exempts it (which it has only done in the cases of books and certain medicines).

The EEC also has many rules prohibiting the establishment of monopolies and the restriction of competition between member states. The most important of these rules are contained in Articles 85 and 86.

14   COTTON

(a)   Cotton may only recover the extra payment from B if B has agreed to make that payment under an enforceable contract. An enforceable contract requires an offer, an acceptance and the payment of consideration for the promise(s) given under the contract. The original agreement appears to fulfil that criteria; C has agreed to supply clothing in return for payment from B. B is therefore providing consideration for C's promise of delivery.

It is a principle of the law of contract that the promise of extra remuneration for the performance of the contract will only be enforceable if consideration is given for that extra payment, such as the performance of some task over and above that already provided for in the contract: *Hartley v Ponsonby 1857*.

Performance of the original contractual obligation is not enough: *Stilk v Myrick 1809*. In this case, the obligation is to make delivery of the goods on time and there is no extra obligation undertaken that might serve as consideration for B's extra payment. The overtime working is not part of the contractual obligation. In addition, it is arguable that C has applied 'economic duress' to B in his allusions to the possibility of delivery being late unless extra payment is promised.

(b)   The basic necessity for further consideration to support a new or additional promise is reflected in D's case. C allows D to pay a fraction of his outstanding debt and D does so. However D must provide consideration for C's promise to waive his existing rights to full payment or C's promise will not be binding and he may go on to claim the full amount: *Foakes v Beer 1884*. In order for the lesser payment to provide consideration in itself it must be something different from the consideration first envisaged: *Pinnel's Case 1602*. Payment of a cheque as opposed to cash is not sufficiently different: *D & C Builders v Rees 1966*.

D may seek to claim the benefit of promissory estoppel. This doctrine, first formulated in *Central London Property Trust v High Trees House 1947*, would prevent a claim for full payment by C even if that promise is unsupported by consideration if the intention is that D would act on that promise (in some way other than the mere payment of the reduced sum) and D does so act. There is no evidence of such an intention in this case. Furthermore, if C's acceptance of part payment is motivated by economic pressure (by D taking advantage of its cash flow problems) the doctrine will not apply: *D & C Builders v Rees*.

(c) E and C have a binding contract for the sale of the goods if there is consideration and if that consideration is sufficient. 'Sufficient' is not judged on a commercial basis; it is enough that it has some value even if there is a gross discrepancy between the actual value of the promise and the consideration offered. In *Chappell v Nestlé 1959*, chocolate wrappers were held to be adequate consideration for a record. The court will enforce a properly made contractual bargain even if commercially unsound.

The result might be different if C could show that he was induced to enter into the contract by the undue influence of E. it is very difficult to prove this sort of influence in an ordinary commercial relationship: *National Westminster Bank v Morgan 1985*. Establishment of a special relationship between the two, with evidence of C's previously justifiable trust in E might allow this claim to succeed: *Goldsworthy v Brickell 1987*. Alternatively, if C can show that E induced him to enter the contract by a fraudulent misrepresentation (perhaps regarding the value of the goods), C would be able to rescind the contract and possibly claim damages.

15 PERFORMANCE

> *Tutorial note:* this is a very specific question which asks you to *explain* performance as a method of discharging a contract. Do not simply state the rule again, without any explanation, or discuss the *formation* of a contract – which is the wrong end of the stick entirely!

(a) It would be fair to say that persons contract in order that something may or may not happen. If this basic object is fulfilled then 'performance' has occurred and the contract is at an end.

Since persons are supposed to have freely contracted (although in practice this may be unrealistic, particularly where standard forms are used) they must perform exactly what they originally intended. Once a contract has fulfilled the requirements of offer, acceptance, consideration, capacity and intention it is then only reasonable that the contract's terms be followed through.

As a general rule, if one party fails to perform completely and precisely what he agreed to do, he is in breach of contract. In some circumstances it may not be the fault of the party in breach, as where liability is strict and no defences are available.

If the other party prevents performance, then the person threatened with his own breach must 'tender' performance, such as offer to deliver goods where the customer has renounced the contract. Failure to do this may lead to effective breach of contract.

Partial or incorrect performance may lead to a party being in breach: *Moore v Landauer 1921*. There is then no right to partial payment for partial performance: *Cutter v Powell 1795*.

Time is often an important factor in complete and precise performance. For some contracts, time is of the essence, so that late performance is no performance. In other cases, time may be a subsidiary consideration, so that lateness will not nullify performance.

Any doubts about whether performance has discharged the contract as formulated should be resolved by reference to the terms of the contract itself. These may reveal, for instance, that time is not 'of the essence', that a small defect in performance is not central to the whole thing, or that performance in the given manner would be unacceptable or illegal. In these cases, then, the deficient performer may be relieved of his liability in breach.

Courts normally will not enforce performance by issuing a decree for specific performance, since in many cases they cannot monitor compliance. The remedy for non-performance constituting a breach is usually that of damages.

(b) Non-performance of the terms of a contract may be legally justified as follows.

    (i) *Frustration* - performance is rendered impossible or futile. Instances are:

       1 where the subject-matter is destroyed or never existed;
       2 where personal incapacity prevents performance;
       3 where performance becomes illegal subsequent to the agreement.

    However the doctrine is applied very strictly.

    (ii) *Prevention of performance* - one party prevents performance by the other. The other party must at least manifest a willingness to perform his obligations. Where these obligations are to pay money, willingness must be shown by the payment of money into court. A breach of contract by one party will give the other the option of repudiating the contract; where a breach is foreseeable, the other party may anticipate that breach and treat the contract as terminated: *Hochster v de la Tour 1853*.

    (iii) *Agreement* - the parties may agree to discharge the contract regardless of performance. This may depend on a condition subsequent or precedent - for instance, the contract may not come into effect at all until a certain event occurs.

    If there is partial or complete performance on one side, the other party will have to provide consideration for the discharge by agreement, unless it is a release by deed. Alternatively, the old contract may be replaced by a new one, in which case the new contract provides consideration for the cancellation of the old (novation of the contract).

    The parties may also agree to accept less than the original standard of performance, so long as there is 'accord and satisfaction', that is some new consideration. Where this latter does not occur the lesser performance may still stand under the doctrine of equitable estoppel: *Central London Property Trust v High Trees House 1947*.

    (iv) *Invalidity* - where the contract is invalid through, for instance, misrepresentation, non-performance is justified if the contract is rescinded.

    (v) *Exclusion clause* - different performance or non-performance may be allowed by the terms of the contract where these contain exclusion clauses. These are theoretically used for varying performance in a reasonable manner but, since they have often been abused, they are now subject to the Unfair Contract and Terms Act 1977. Some are void *ab initio* while others are subjected to a test of reasonableness. A party's claim to be entitled to render substantially different performance or no performance at all will only be upheld in a standard form consumer contract if it is reasonable.

16 SUBSEQUENT IMPOSSIBILITY

(a) The law generally holds that a person is bound to perform a contractual promise on the grounds that the parties should make provision for any difficulties which may arise under the contract itself. However if circumstances so change that the performance as originally intended by both parties is no longer possible, the contract will be terminated under the doctrine of frustration or subsequent impossibility.

Impossibility of performance is judged strictly. The contract may be so frustrated where the subject matter has been destroyed (such as a contract to let a concert hall frustrated by destruction of that hall: *Taylor v Caldwell 1863*). A contract to perform personal services may be frustrated by subsequent personal incapacity or death: *Condor v Barron Knights 1966*.

If a party to the contract has accepted the risk that he may not be able to perform his part of it, he will be unable to claim frustration: *Budget v Binnington 1981*. Supervening illegality or government intervention may also frustrate the contract (as when goods sold under contract are requisitioned: *Re Shipton, Anderson & Co 1915*). However, where there is a degree of choice regarding the effect of these official actions there may not be frustration. In *Maritime National Fish v Ocean Trawlers 1935*, a contract for the hire of an extra trawler was not frustrated because too few licences were granted, as the hirers had chosen to allocate these licences to their own trawlers.

Non-occurrence of an event may be frustration provided that event was the only reason for the contract. Two cases, involving the cancelled coronation of Edward VII, illustrate this. A contract for the hire of a room from which to watch the procession was frustrated by it (*Krell v Henry 1903*), whereas a contract to hire a steamboat to tour a naval review was not: *Herne Bay Steamship v Hutton 1903*. In the former case, there was no other reason to rent the room, whereas in the latter, the tour of the assembled ships was still possible.

An interruption which prevents performance in the way intended by the parties may be a case for frustration but only in some circumstances. The test is whether the interruption so interferes with the contract as to alter fundamentally the basic nature of the contract. In *Jackson v Union Marine Insurance 1874*, a ship chartered for immediate use had to go into dock for lengthy repairs; this was frustration of the charter as it was no longer possible to perform the contract in the commercial sense. This may be compared with *Tsakiroglou v Noblee Thorl 1962*, where closure of the Suez Canal meant delivery had to be made by a longer, more expensive route. As delivery was still possible, the closure of one route was not sufficient to frustrate the contract.

If performance simply becomes more expensive this is not impossibility: *Davis Contractors v Fareham UDC 1956*.

(b) The rights and liabilities of the parties to a frustrated contract are now largely governed by the Law Reform (Frustrated Contracts) Act 1943. As a rule, any money already paid under the contract by one party is to be repaid: any sums still due cease to be payable.

Where the person who has received payment, or is due to receive it, has already incurred expense, the harshness of the rule is mitigated. The court has a discretion to allow him to keep or to claim sufficient money to cover those expenses incurred up to the time of the discharge. This will only extend as far as those sums are actually paid or due to be paid at the time of the discharge. Any excessive expenses cannot be claimed.

The Act also covers those cases where something other than money passes under the contract. Where one party receives something of value such as goods under a contract of sale, but the contract is frustrated before payment is made, the court has the power to order that party to pay the other all or some of the value of those goods.

The Act does not cover all types of contract. Contracts for the carriage of goods by sea, contracts for the sale of perishable goods where frustration is caused by their perishing, and contracts of insurance are all outside its ambit - special rules apply to each type.

Many commercial contracts contain express provisions to handle the situation where frustration occurs to prevent performance. Reference should first of all be made to these before considering the 1943 Act. Such provisions are known as 'force majeure' clauses.

17   LAGGARD

> *Tutorial note:* be careful, when answering problem questions, that you have fully appreciated the situation with which you are presented. The surface impression here, of actionable contractual breach, gives way on closer examination to a discussion of the doctrine of frustration.

At first sight it would appear that Abel may have an action for breach of contract against Laggard. Laggard fulfils his contract but he does so imperfectly, with late delivery of substandard products. Breach of these contractual specifications is a breach of both an express term of the contract and of s13 Sale of Goods Act 1979 (goods to correspond with contract description). Partial performance is not full performance *(Moore v Landauer 1921)* and, as a general rule, time is of the essence in commercial contracts: *Elmdore v Keech 1969.*

It would appear then that Abel has access to all the usual remedies for breach of contract. However Laggard may be able to show that the contract has actually become impossible to perform and thus has been discharged by frustration, and not by breach. The essence of this doctrine is that the underlying fundamental assumptions of the parties when making the contract have not materialised and thus the contract is now fundamentally different in its nature. A contract is also discharged by frustration if the parties assumed that certain underlying conditions would continue and those assumptions prove to be false.

Being an exception to the general rule that parties are bound by their contractual promises, the doctrine is limited in scope and Laggard will have to show that the events preventing performance are sufficient to amount to frustration.

The shortage of labour due to illness and the strike may be sufficient to frustrate the contract, if Laggard can demonstrate that the contract relied heavily on personal skills exercised by the absent members of the workforce: *Condor v Barron Knights 1966.* He would have to show that it was not possible to make up the lost time in some way. However if Laggard has diverted workers away from Abel's work to fulfil other contracts this positive choice will mean that he cannot plead frustration on this ground: *Maritime National Fish v Ocean Trawlers 1935.*

Laggard may claim that the strike interrrupted performance in such a way that it prevented performance. The test to be applied is whether the interruption is such that the contract can no longer be performed in the way envisaged by the parties: *Jackson v Union Marine Insurance 1874.*

The strike may well be regarded as an event which was within Laggard's power to avoid, and thus be declared not relevant to the issue of frustration.

Laggard may also point to the new regulations and the consequent added expense as causing frustration. A change in the law rendering performance impossible will certainly be a frustrating event: *Re Shipton, Anderson & Co 1915*. The important point here is impossibility; if Laggard is still capable of performing the contract in some other way there is no frustration *(Tsakiroglou v Noblee Thorl 1962)* even if the alternative involves him in additional expense: *Davis Contractors v Fareham UDC 1956*.

Laggard is likely to fail in his plea of frustration, and Abel will seek damages to compensate him for his losses. However, if Laggard succeeds, the terms of the contract may provide for a solution in the event of subsequent impossibility. If they do not do so, the Law Reform (Frustrated Contracts) Act 1943 will apply to determine the respective rights and obligations of the parties. Money paid by Abel to Laggard must be repaid by Laggard, although the court may allow Laggard to retain or recover expenses incurred up to the time of discharge (up to the amount due from Laggard at the time of frustration). The court may also order Abel to pay Laggard the value of the benefit received under the contract, that is the machinery.

18   REMEDIES FOR BREACH

> *Tutorial note:* when answering this question you should be careful not to be distracted into a discussion of damages. This is expressly *not* required. Instead you should concentrate on the range of equitable remedies available for breach of contract. A common mistake is to confuse rescission with repudiation - the former is an action which may be taken when a contract is voidable (say for misrepresentation or undue influence), while the latter is the right to cancel obligations when the other party has indicated that he will not perform his obligations.

Damages are a common law remedy for breach of contract which arise as of right; provided a person has suffered loss and has proved the other person to be liable to compensate him for this loss the award of damages is available without exercise of discretion by the court. In some cases, however, damages are an inadequate award. It is then open to the court to order a variety of equitable remedies. The wronged party may also exercise the right of repudiation.

Equitable remedies

Specific performance and injunction are equitable remedies for breach of contract which are granted only when damages provide inadequate relief.

A decree of *specific performance* directs a defendant to carry out a contractual promise. The order will rarely be made in respect of a contract for the sale of goods, since damages are almost always deemed adequate compensation. Specific performance may be granted where the goods are clearly unique, but it is in the area of 'real' property that the order is most often made on these grounds.

Contracts which require constant supervision are not 'specifically enforceable' and the specific performance remedy is therefore not available, and nor will it be ordered of personal service contracts since no one should ordinarily be compelled to work for or to employ another person. Lastly, specific performance must in general satisfy the requirements of 'mutuality': namely, an order will not be made in favour of one party unless, in principle, it could be ordered against him.

General principles of equity will guide the decision and, in particular, ensure that it reflects fairness: 'he who seeks equity must do equity' and 'he who comes to equity must come with clean hands'. Thus the equitable remedy of specific performance might be withheld:

(a) from a plaintiff who provokes repudiation (see below) by failing to perform a promise which induced the defendant to enter the contract but which is unenforceable for one reason or another;

(b) where the plaintiff takes unfair advantage of the defendant's condition - he may be ignorant or drunk - as a means of inducing the contract;

(c) where the defendant will otherwise suffer severe hardship - for example, where the cost of (specific) performance it out of all proportion to the benefit that it will confer on the plaintiff.

An *injunction* is a decree by the court directing a person not to do something; it can be used therefore to prevent a breach of contract.

It will not be granted if its effect is to compel - even indirectly - the defendant to do acts which he could not have been ordered to do by a decree of specific performance. Thus an employee cannot normally be prevented from breaching his contractual duty to do certain work, since that would be equivalent to specific enforcement of a contract of service: *Whitwood Chemical Co v Hardman 1891*.

As a remedy, an injunction is most effective when applied to a negative contractual obligation, for instance, a restriction placed upon permissible land use or a restriction in an employee's contract preventing that employee from working for someone else: *Warner Brothers Pictures Incorporated v Nelson 1937*.

Interlocutory injunctions are sometimes awarded in order to restrain a defendant from doing something until such time as the case is resolved in court. Because the plaintiff may not ultimately be successful in the trial he must give an undertaking to pay damages to the defendant if he fails in his case. This is to compensate the defendant for the prejudice caused by the interlocutory injunction.

In some circumstances a *quantum meruit* award may be made for breach of contract on the basis of 'how much is it worth': it is a restitutory award which aims to restore the plaintiff to the position in which he would have been had the contract never been made. It is likely to be sought when one party has already performed part of his obligations and the other party then repudiates the contract by anticipatory breach (that is, he states that he has no intention of fulfilling his obligations). The former party may claim a reasonable amount for the work he has done: *De Bernardy v Harding 1853*. In most cases, a *quantum meruit* claim is involved where one party has unjustifiably prevented performance by the other: *Planche v Coburn 1831*.

Whether these equitable remedies are awarded depends very much on the nature of the contract (particularly regarding decrees for specific performance) and the extent of the breach. It is a matter for the court's discretion.

Repudiation

Another remedy which may be available but is not always a matter for the court's discretion is that of repudiation. This means that the wronged party can refuse to carry out his obligations and treat the contract as terminated, and he may seek damages in addition. The remedy often arises when there has been anticipatory breach by the other party – that is, that party intimates expressly or by conduct that he does not intend to perform his side of the agreement (he repudiates it): *Hochster v de la Tour 1853*. The wronged party may elect to repudiate the contract immediately on the other party's repudiation, even though the time of performance has not yet arrived, or he may elect to treat the contract as still being in force. If he adopts the latter course he runs the risk of an event terminating the contract by frustration, so that he loses his right to repudiate and seek damages: *Avery v Bowden 1855*.

Whether the wronged party has a right to repudiate the contract depends upon the seriousness of the other party's breach; if a 'condition' is violated, then he has this right – he can regard himself as discharged from his obligations under the contract and also sue for damages: *Poussard v Spiers 1876*. Violation of a warranty limits his relief to damages: *Bettini v Gye 1876*.

Breach of an 'innominate term', which is neither a condition nor a warranty, entails a right to repudiate only when the consequences of the breach are sufficiently serious: *Cehave v Bremer 1975*.

19 SANDY

> *Tutorial note:* deciding whether Ivan has grounds for a claim for compensation first of all requires us to consider whether that claim would be for breach of contract or for misrepresentation. The latter gives rise to different remedies depending on the type of misrepresentation at issue.

(a) Ivan is likely to have a claim for compensation on two counts. Firstly, he may have an action for misrepresentation against Jake. This will be the case if he can show that the incorrect information given by Jake induced him to enter into the contract for the holiday; it would have to be assumed that the changes which Jake suggests had been made to the brochure were generally 'improvements' on the original deal (which Sandy ended up getting). He will also have an action in contract against Sandy for the failure of the holiday to match its contract description.

To succeed in the first case, Ivan would have to show that the remarks were representations of fact as opposed to sales talk: *Bisset v Wilkinson 1927*. To succeed against Sandy, Ivan would have to show that the difference between the contract terms and the reality of the holiday was sufficient to amount to a breach of contract.

(b) As Jake acts as Sandy's agent, Ivan would bring his case against Sandy as principal; it is Sandy with whom he has made this contract. The contract will be binding on Sandy only if it was made by Jake within the limits of his authority.

An agent may have different types of authority. As a travel agent, Jake obviously had express authority to make a contract for a holiday. The question is whether he also had authority when he made the representations to Ivan. As agent, Jake would have implied authority to do anything within he normal powers of one in his position: *Waugh v Clifford 1982*. If it is considered normal practice in the travel agency profession for an agent to modify brochure details in this way then the agent will have implied authority to do that:

Howard v Sheward 1866. Provided Jake was acting within the usual authority of an estate agent he creates contractual liability for Sandy even if he has abused his power: *Panorama Developments Ltd v Fidelis Furnishing Fabrics Ltd 1971.*

Apparent authority is similar in that it is the authority which the principal represents that he has given to his agent, by virtue of usual practice and by his conduct; the principal may imply that he has given the agent the power to do certain things by failing to restrain him. If Sandy has allowed Jake to make similar representations to customers in the past, that may amount to authority for him to make contracts on these terms and Sandy will be bound by them.

As Jake acted for a disclosed principal he has no direct liability under the contract. If, however, it is decided that he has acted outside his actual and apparent authority (and thus Sandy is not bound by the contract), Ivan may have an action for breach of the warranty that he had the authority to make this contract on these terms: *Yonge v Toynbee 1910.*

Sandy may also have an action against him for breach of the agency agreement if he, as principal, has to pay damages to Ivan. Jake had a duty to act with care and skill which he would appear to have breached.

(c) Contractual damages would be awarded on the principles set out in *Hadley v Baxendale 1854*; they are given for the loss arising naturally from the breach of conduct or for those losses which the parties may have reasonably expected at the time the contract was made. The first part of the rule covers those losses arising 'in the normal course of things': *Victoria Laundry (Windsor) Ltd v Newman Industries 1949.* The measure of the damages awarded is the amount needed to put the plaintiff back in his original position - it is largely concerned with actual financial loss: *Lazenby Garages v Write 1976.* This principle of restoration also applies to damages for misrepresentation.

Ivan has lost the price of the holiday including travel arrangements; possibly he had to incur extra expenditure in order to obtain some enjoyment. In *Jarvis v Swan Tours 1973*, the court awarded a disappointed holidaymaker damages for loss of anticipated enjoyment. This now seems to be a well-established head of damages, and so Ivan should be able to claim for this too.

Similarly, damages would be the most appropriate remedy for the misrepresentation; although the usual remedy is rescission of the contract in a case where the contract has been performed (albeit badly), this is not really feasible in the case of a holiday and hence the alternative remedy of damages (available under the Misrepresentation Act 1967) would be given instead.

If Sandy can show that Ivan had a reasonable opportunity to mitigate his losses (say by returning home early), he may be able to reduce the damages which he has to pay: *Payzu v Saunders 1919.*

20 DAMAGES

Tutorial note: part (a) of this question fooled many candidates when it was set in a CIMA Stage 1 paper; it relates to liquidated damages and penalty clauses, *not* to exclusion clauses.

(a) Measuring damages in a case of breach of contract can be complicated but is based on the principle that the plaintiff should be put in the position he would have been in had the contract been performed. Compensation is for actual financial loss: *Lazenby Garages v Wright 1976.*

In some cases the parties themselves may put a provision into the contract which purports to deal with the measure of damages by specifying a formula with reference to which the damages are to be calculated. This is known as a liquidated damages clause. A typical example is that often found in building contracts by which a percentage of the price payable is forfeited for every week by which work overruns the period specified for completion, subject to an overall limit.

These clauses are valid if they are considered to be genuine pre-estimates of loss. Provided the formula chosen is an honest attempt to quantify damages the clause will be upheld, even if in reality it is virtually impossible to predict accurately the level of damage suffered: *Dunlop v New Garage & Motor Co 1915.* If it is onerous the formula should be highlighted: *Interfoto Picture Library Ltd v Stiletto Visual Programmes Ltd 1988.*

The clause will not be enforced if it appears to be a penalty clause, designed to discourage breach by setting too high a level of damages. In this case, the court will disregard the penalty clause, treating it as void, and damages will be measured in the usual way, the plaintiff having to prove actual loss.

(b) The award of damages is intended to restore the plaintiff to the position in which he would have been had the contract been completed.

The first issue in determining the amount is the remoteness of damage - how far was the damage suffered a result of the breach? The rules for remoteness of damage were first established in *Hadley v Baxendale 1854;* damages may be awarded only in respect of loss which flows naturally from the breach or which the parties might reasonably be supposed to have foreseen as the probable result of a breach at the time of making the contract. A loss which is outside these limbs of the test will be compensated only if it arises from special circumstances which are within the defendant's actual or constructive knowledge. Thus in *Victoria Laundries (Windsor) v Newman Industries 1949* the defendants were late in delivering a boiler; the plaintiffs succeeded in their claim for normal business losses but not for special losses caused by the loss of lucrative 'dyeing contracts', of which the defendants knew nothing.

The question of foreseeability has been developed by the courts. Where the loss is one which would obviously occur if breach were to happen, damages can be claimed (for example, fluctuation in commodity prices would obviously cause loss on a late delivery of sugar: *The Heron II 1969*). Provided the type of loss is not too remote, damages for the full loss can be claimed even if this is more serious than could be contemplated (eg mouldy pig food caused foreseeable illness to pigs but owner was also allowed claim for consequent death: *Parsons v Uttley Ingham 1978*).

The measure of damages is intended to put the plaintiff in the same position as if the contract had been performed. Where there is a clear financial loss, this is the measure and, in general, only the actual loss can be claimed: *Lazenby Garages v Wright 1976.* Damages are given only for some forms of non-financial loss (eg disappointment in inferior holiday facilities: *Jarvis v Swan Tours 1973*). In any case, the plaintiff has a duty to mitigate his losses as far as is reasonable: *Payzu v Saunders 1919.* But he is not required to take discreditable or risky measures since these are not reasonable.

21 PROFFITT

> *Tutorial note:* professional negligence is a topic which is currently of great significance to accountants and is going though considerable changes following the 1990 decision in the *Caparo* case. This question is specifically concerned with the tort of negligence although you would also be given marks for an understanding of the contractual side of the question. In part (b) there is a difference between the claims of Frank, who heard Proffitt's statement, and Rustick, to whom it was reported. It is fair to assume in these 'problem-type' questions that each 'character' has a particular role to play and is differently affected in law. You should keep your eyes open, therefore, for probable distinctions of this kind.

(a) In certain circumstances there is a duty of care not to cause financial loss by negligent misstatement. The duty applies in particular to the professional person acting in his capacity as a professional adviser. In *Hedley Byrne v Heller & Partners 1964* it was established that where there was a 'special relationship' between the person making the statement and the recipient, that person would be liable for loss if it was foreseeable that the recipient of the negligently-given advice would rely on it.

Subsequent decisions have shown that this special relationship is assumed when the adviser is acting in his professional capacity *(Esso Petroleum v Mardon 1976)* and it is also assumed that the person advised will take his advice. The principle will apply therefore to a lawyer or accountant advising a client on a legal or financial matter.

It is established that the duty may extend beyond the recipient to a third party if the maker foresaw or should have had foreseen that the third party would rely on the statement: *Twomak Ltd and Goode v Davidson, Macfarlane & Robinson 1983*. For example, a beneficiary may be owed a duty of care when a solicitor is advising a testator: *Ross v Caunters 1980*.

The duty applies to persons who profess to a particular expertise and are acting in the course of their business: *Esso Petrol v Mardon 1976*. The duty does not extend to casual remarks made on a social occasion, say at a party, but it may extend to a personal relationship if there is a business aspect: *Chaudry v Prabhakar 1989*.

Recent developments in case-law have defined more clearly the circumstances in which a professional person can be held liable for loss arising out of advice given or statements made in the course of business. There must be a 'special relationship' in which the professional person knew of the nature of the transactions which the plaintiff had in mind, knew that the advice or information would be communicated to the plaintiff and knew that it was likely that the plaintiff would rely on the advice or information when deciding whether to go ahead with the transaction in mind: *Caparo Industries plc v Touche Ross & Co, Dickman and Others 1990*.

In assessing the standard of care to be taken in fulfilment of the duty of care the courts will look to current professional practice and the level of risk to the plaintiff. The former may be judged by existing guidelines (eg the Standard Statements of Accounting Practice for accountants). Furthermore the professional will not be expected to anticipate future developments: *Roe v Minister of Health 1954*. The court will also be careful to distinguish between an error of judgement and negligence: *Whitehouse v Jordan 1981*.

If the professional fails to reach the required standard of care then he is in breach of his duty of care and may be liable for financial or economic loss thereby arising.

Negligence is a tort but it must also be remembered that there can be liability in contract for negligent misrepresentation. A person induced to enter a contract by a negligent misrepresentation may rescind the contract and claim damages under the Misrepresentation Act 1967. The professional may also be liable for breach of the contractual term, implied by the Supply of Goods and Services Act 1982, that he will perform his duties with skill and care. But this will only apply where the plaintiff has a contractual relationship with the professional.

A professional adviser may seek to limit his liability by including an exclusion clause or disclaimer of liability clause. This saved the defendants from liability in the *Hedley Byrne* case. However, the freedom of a person to make such disclaimers is now severely restricted by the Unfair Contract Terms Act 1977. This Act requires the defendant to show that the disclaimer is reasonable in the circumstances and forbids any disclaimer which purports to limit or prevent liability in the case of personal injury or death arising from negligence.

The most practical way to avoid the harsh effects of liability for negligent misstatement is to have appropriate professional indemnity insurance.

(b) Quite apart from any question as to whether Proffitt could possibly be said to be making a negligent statement in citing a company as an example in his lecture, it does not appear that the necessary 'special relationship' is established. Here Proffitt is acting as a lecturer rather than a professional adviser and is thus unlikely to have established the necessary business relationship with his students which could give rise to any question of liability for his erroneous statements. Even if Proffitt also acts as a professional adviser, he does not act in that capacity here.

Furthermore although it may be foreseeable that a person at the lecture (Frank) would act on the lecturer's words, it is not foreseeable that a third party would do so. It is therefore highly unlikely that Proffitt would be liable to either Rustick or Frank.

22 MANUFACTURER'S RESPONSIBILITY

Tutorial note: careful analysis of this question reveals that a number of issues are at stake: the liability of Leonard to his customers and his chances of claiming from the manufacturer; the relative importance of liability in contract and in tort; the position of Leonard's son; and the attempt at a disclaimer by the manufacturer. Careful planning and structuring of your answer should allow you to cover each of these issues.

As a supplier of goods to his customers Leonard is likely to be liable to them for breach of conditions implied by the Sale of Goods Act 1979 s14.

As purchaser of the goods from the manufacturer (Martin) Leonard is probably entitled to the protection of the same conditions, including a claim made on behalf of his son.

The effectiveness of the disclaimer on the label has to be considered under the provisions of the Unfair Contract Terms Act 1977.

(a) The medicine is described as 'for influenza'. In spite of the impurities it does apparently satisfy that description. Hence there is no breach of condition under s13 of the 1979 Act, the goods being in accordance with the description.

S14 of the 1979 Act provides that in a sale of goods in the course of a business (Leonard is a trader) there are two implied conditions, namely

(i) the goods are to be of merchantable quality (subject to certain limitations which do not apply here). They must be reasonably suitable for the purpose or purposes for which they are commonly bought; and

(ii) where the buyer makes known the purpose for which he requires the goods in circumstances where he relies on the seller's skill and judgement the goods must be reasonably suitable for that purpose (again there are exclusions which do not apply here).

This is a strict liability - it is no defence for the seller to show that he took reasonable care to avoid a breach: *Frost v Aylesbury Dairy Co Ltd 1905*. If goods have only one purpose the buyer discloses his purpose in asking for goods of that type: *Priest v Last 1903* (purchase of a hot-water bottle).

The presence of the noxious impurities makes the medicine unsuitable for use and so there is a breach of both the conditions mentioned above. The disclaimer on the label is no protection to Leonard since his customers are 'dealing as consumers'. Moreover s2 of the 1977 Act overrides any disclaimer of liability for causing personal injury; the medicine has caused serious illness.

The customers will have a right of action against Martin as manufacturer under the Consumer Protection Act 1987. It does not matter that they had no contract with him since liability is strict, and he may be sued instead of Leonard at their choice. Martin's most likely defence would be that of 'development risk' - that the state of knowledge at the time of manufacture and supply of the influenza remedy was such that no manufacturer could have been expected to detect the fault. But since the purported disclaimer expressly states that the medicine has not been tested it is unlikely that Martin could claim that he is a reasonable manufacturer.

(b) Leonard in turn can claim against Martin the manufacturer. Here however the disclaimer is not automatically overridden since Leonard is not 'dealing as a consumer'; he is a trader buying for resale. But the disclaimer is only valid if it satisfies tests of reasonableness laid down in Schedule 2 of the Unfair Contract Terms Act 1977.

In other circumstances where the buyer is well able to understand the effect of a disclaimer and to take appropriate measures the courts have shown some unwillingness to treat as unreasonable such clauses in a contract between businesses: *Photo Productions Ltd v Securicor Transport Ltd 1980*. But in the present case, despite the warning given on the label, the court would probably not hold that so general a disclaimer by a manufacturer, who knows what his product contains, against a retailer who does not, should be upheld as reasonable.

Leonard would claim against Martin for the amount of his liability to his customers plus any loss which he may suffer by damage to the goodwill, and sales turnover, of his business. He would argue that this was loss and damage covered by the first part of the rule in *Hadley v Baxendale 1854*, that is, it was the natural and therefore foreseeable result of supplying medicine containing impurities to a retail chemist for resale to his customers. S50(2) of the 1979 Act brings this test into the law on sale of goods.

(c) The claim in respect of the 'rather fragile' bottle would be that goods supplied in an unsuitable container are unmerchantable on that account, apart from other defects.

The injury is to a member of Leonard's family, his small son, who does not have a contract with Martin on which to act. Leonard may bring an action in contract on his behalf, or the son may bring an action for the tort of negligence, as he is owed a duty of care by his neighbour: *Donoghue v Stevenson 1932*.

In addition, as user of defective goods (a definition which expressly includes containers) the son has an action against Martin under the Consumer Protection Act 1987. Martin's only defence would be that the defect did not exist at the time of supply - which could not hold.

23 CHEAPO LTD

> *Tutorial note:* this is a question which requires careful analysis of relationships and liabilities and an outline plan is a good idea in order for it to have structure and clarity. In addition, you should be careful to take both common law and statute into account.

The rights and liabilities of the parties in this case are governed by the law of tort. Two of the persons injured, Mrs Smythe and Alan, may be able to make a claim against Maurice, Jean or Cheapo Ltd.

Jean (or, as is more likely, Cheapo Ltd) may be liable to Mrs Smythe and Alan under the statutes governing occupiers' liability. Mrs Smythe is protected by the Occupier's Liability Act 1957 which imposes a duty of care on the occupier towards all lawful visitors to premises. As a customer, Mrs Smythe has the implied, if not express, authority of Jean to enter the store. Jean is in breach of her statutory duty in failing to ensure that the premises are reasonably safe by keeping lawful visitors away from the testing of the escalator.

Alan is a trespasser in that he has entered the store without permission; there is presumably no implied invitation for visitors to play on the store's equipment. However the Occupiers' Liability Act 1984 imposes a duty of care on the occupier towards certain foreseeable trespassers. This duty arises where there is a risk of injury, where it is foreseeable that the trespasser may enter the premises and where the hazard is one against which it is reasonable to offer protection. If Jean was aware that children might enter the store, she is negligent in failing to take precautions to keep them away.

If Jean has provided some sort of warning (a notice for example) this may go some way towards diminishing her liability to Mrs Smythe (there may be contributory negligence if Mrs Smythe ignored a warning) but is unlikely to have much effect on Alan's case against her; the standards of care expected from adults and children differ: *British Railways Board v Herrington 1972*.

The common law may make Maurice liable for damage to Alan and Mrs Smythe if its can be shown that he was negligent. There is a duty of care owed to anyone who may reasonably be foreseen to suffer as a consequence of negligence *(Donoghue v Stevenson 1932)*, and that duty is breached if there is a failure to take reasonable care.

Here Maurice is negligent in his repair work and it is foreseeable that this neglect might lead to injury to the visitors of the store. There must be a sufficient link between Maurice's actions and the injury suffered: if the type of injury is one caused by something too remote from the faulty escalator, there will be no liability for those injuries: *The Wagon Mound 1961*.

Alan and Mrs Smythe may choose to bring their cases against Cheapo Ltd. As Jean's employer, Cheapo Ltd will be liable for any tort committed by her in the course of her employment under the principle of vicarious liability. An argument by Cheapo Ltd that it left it to Jean to manage the store and is therefore not liable is likely to fail on the grounds that it assigned those managerial duties to her: *Cassidy v Minister of Health 1951*.

Cheapo Ltd may not be liable for the faults of Maurice as he is an independent contractor rather than an employee; it may however be liable on the grounds that it failed in its duty to ensure that a competent contractor was employed. Liability for the wrongs of independant contractors also exists where the operation is of a particularly dangerous nature *(Honeywill & Stein v Larkin Bros 1934)*, although it is unclear whether the work here would fall into that category.

Maurice also suffered injury, but it is unlikely that his case against Jean or Cheapo Ltd would succeed; an occupier's liability does not extend to a lawful visitor called in to exercise his specialist skills if the damage is caused by his negligent exercise of those skills: *Roles v Nathan 1963*.

Thus it would seem that Mrs Smythe and Alan have a case against Maurice, Jean and Cheapo Ltd. It is possible that the defendants may be able to prove contributory negligence, that is the plaintiff's own actions contributed in some way to the injury suffered, under the Law Reform-(Contributory Negligence) Act 1945.

If Cheapo Ltd is liable it may seek indemnity from Jean under an implied term in the employment contract that she will reimburse the company for loss to it caused by her personal negligence: *Lister v Ice and Cold Storage Ltd 1957*.

24 DENNIS AND SAM

> *Tutorial note:* you should remember to treat common law and statutory provisions separately in this question - indeed, such is a good procedure to follow in a great number of business law situations. You need to be careful to restrict your answer in part (a) so that you still have material with which to answer part (b).

(a) To claim compensation from their employer the injured employees must demonstrate that the employer is liable either under common law or for breach of statutory duty.

Common law

At common law the employer has a duty to do what is reasonably necessary to provide a safe place of work; this includes suitable plant, machinery, tools and scaffolding, maintained in proper condition, and also probably an adequate warning or alarm system: *Smith v Charles Baker & Son Ltd 1891*. He also has duties to employ reasonably competent workers and to operate a safe system generally.

The employer would appear to be in breach of these requirements and so to be liable to the employees for the tort of negligence - that is, it owed a duty of care, it breached that duty and the injuries suffered by the employees arose from that breach. In order to show that the employer breached the duty of care the employees must show that he did not meet a sufficient standard of care - which is that of a reasonably competent and safe employer, taking into account the costs of safety procedures, the foreseeability of the accident and the experience of the employees.

BUSINESS LAW: SUGGESTED SOLUTIONS

Statute

The employees may also seek to claim against the employer for the latter's breach of statutory duty under safety at work legislation - notably the Health and Safety at Work Act 1974 and the Factories Act 1961.

These duties are very specific and the employees will have to show that a statutory provision, or a piece of delegated legislation, can be said to refer to the accident that occurred. It may be, however, that the employer has strict liability which requires an absolute standard of care so that, unlike the common law action, the employer may not defend himself by saying he met a certain standard of care.

Employer's defences

The employer's defences will probably be that the statute does not apply or that the accident did not arise from a cause covered by the statute.

It may also claim that the injured employees consented to the known risk, a defence rarely available in common law and never for breach of statutory duty. It would only be a successful claim where the employees were highly trained and knowledgeable, and had statutory duties themselves: *ICI v Shatwell 1963*. An employee who continues in a job does not consent to abnormal or necessary risks created by the employer merely because he is aware of them: *Smith v Charles Baker & Sons 1891*.

It is more likely that the employer would be liable but a deduction would be made for contributory negligence.

(b) *Dennis*

The standard of care owed by the employer to Dennis is higher because he has an infirmity, even if he did not previously make the infirmity known: *Paris v Stepney Borough Council 1951* (the 'thin skull' principle). However, if he did not make clear his inability to hear shouted warnings he may have a reduced award because of contributory negligence.

Sam

Unless he is claiming under the employer's strict liability for breach of statutory duty Sam may find that the employer raises against him the defence in negligence of *volenti non fit injuria*, that is consent. This may be effective since, in failing to wear the hat which he was instructed to wear, Sam has consented to the risk of suffering additional avoidable injury. The employer may also claim a reduction in damages for contributory negligence.

The court will look at the circumstances, taking into account Sam's experience and training, the clarity of instruction and the extent of supervision and enforcement of instructions. It may find that simply providing hats and instructing use is not sufficient if Sam is a known defaulter or if he was engaged in a task where hats were known to 'get in the way'.

25 WALTER

(a) The occupier of premises is the person who has control or possession of the property, and this person is not necessarily the owner. The occupier owes a duty of care to all visitors to the premises; the extent of this duty is set out in the Occupiers' Liability Act 1957, the Act which codified the existing common law.

167

Visitors include those persons who enter the premises with the express or implied permission of the occupier or at his invitation. Those who enter the premises to do business with the occupier are also visitors; in this case the duty extends to casual callers such as salesmen. They also include persons with a legal right to enter the premises.

The duty of care only exists while the visitor stays within the bounds of his legitimate purpose; if he strays into other areas he is trespassing (although the Occupiers' Liability Act 1984 does contain some provisions to protect trespassers).

The standard of care will vary with the visitor. A specialist visitor is taken to be aware of any risks associated with his particular task (for example, a sweep is deemed to be aware of poisonous fumes in a boiler: *Roles v Nathan 1963*). Conversely, the care owed to a child is particularly high.

The duty of care is discharged if the occupier takes reasonable steps to see that the premises are safe for the purposes for which the visitor enters them. If a hazard requires specialist attention, he will not be liable for work done badly, although he should make efforts to check it and to employ competent contractors. He will be liable if the task is relatively simple (such as clearing icy surfaces). He should also give warnings where necessary but again the adequacy may depend on the visitor (a 'keep out' sign may be insufficient for a small child for example). The provisions of the Unfair Contract Terms Act 1977 should be borne in mind; it is not possible to exclude liability for death or personal injury arising from negligence and other notices are effective only insofar as they are 'reasonable'.

(b) As Walter owns the warehouse he is liable as the occupier; as Simple is his employee he is clearly a lawful visitor. Walter's liability to Simple will be determined by the 1957 Act.

Walter has had the poisoned bread put down in the premises and is thus liable if visitors are injured by it unless he has taken reasonable steps to avoid this. It is not clear whether there were any warnings about the bread; in any case, they would be ineffective against a claim for personal injury if it was shown that Walter was in breach of his duty of care - that is, was negligent.

The court may also consider Simple's behaviour; in eating the bread he has contributed to his own injury and any claim against Walter would be duly reduced to reflect this, although it is not clear how Simple's acknowledged lack of intelligence would effect this.

Young's is a different case. He is not a lawful visitor but a trespasser. Walter's liability to him is governed by the Occupiers' Liability Act 1984. The duty of care owed to a trespasser is established if the occupier knew of a hazard, knew or should have known that a person may come into the vicinity of that hazard and it is reasonable to expect him to offer that person protection against the hazard. The duty may be discharged by warnings and can only apply to personal injury. The important point here is that Young is only a child. The courts impose a very stringent duty of care towards child trespassers: *Herrington v BRB 1972*. It is unlikely that Walter would have been judged to have discharged this duty against Young.

26   DEFENCES AND REMEDIES

> *Tutorial note:* specific questions concerning remedies can arise, as this question shows, but remedies form an element of almost all tort problems and are therefore an almost constantly recurring subject. You would be well advised to know them thoroughly.

(a) (i) Consent as a defence in tort is summed up by the latin phrase *'volenti non fit injuria'* - no wrong is done to one who consents to it. It must be a true consent, freely given, and not mere knowledge of the risk.

Voluntary acceptance of a risk of injury may suffice. In *ICI v Shatwell 1965*, workmen who failed to observe safety procedures of which they were well aware were held to have no claim against their employer. Consent may be implied where the plaintiff has undertaken a dangerous pastime, even where injury is exceptional (eg a broken leg caused by a fair tackle during rugby: *Simms v Leigh RFC 1969*). However, awareness of risk is not of itself consent to abnormal or unnecessary risks created by a person's negligence: *Smith v Baker & Sons 1891*. Consent and knowledge are to be decided on the facts of each case: *Dann v Hamilton 1939*.

Where the damage is as a result of the plaintiff making a rescue attempt, he will succeed in defeating the defence of consent only if he is impelled to help in order to prevent danger to others and the defendant is to blame for the accident. In *Haynes v Harwood 1935* the successful plaintiff acted to save others, whereas in *Cutler v United Dairies 1933* there was no such risk to other people and his claim failed. If a person creates a hazard through his own negligence and a rescuer is injured, there need not be an exceptional risk over and above the inherent risks of rescue for that person to be liable and consent to be an ineffective defence: *Ogwo v Taylor 1987*.

The Unfair Contract Terms Act 1977 invalidates notices seeking to disclaim liability for death or personal injury. A defence of 'implied consent' where there is such a notice is therefore not available. Other statutes which impose strict liability for wrongs also prevent the defence being raised, such as the Health and Safety at Work Act 1974 and the Road Traffic Act 1972.

(ii) If the damage was partly caused by the plaintiff then his claim is reduced in proportion to his contributory negligence: Law Reform (Contributory Negligence) Act 1945. The test is: what was the cause of the damage? If the answer to this is at least partly the failure of the plaintiff to take account of a foreseeable risk, then there is contributory negligence and the plaintiff receives less damages in recognition of his fault.

In *O'Connell v Jackson 1971* the plaintiff motor cyclist was held to have suffered avoidable hurt in his failure to wear a safety helmet. Whether the risk was foreseeable is to be determined with reference to all the circumstances - for instance children may be too young to appreciate a risk: *Yachuk v Oliver Blais 1949*. The contributory negligence of an adult who accompanies a child is not a defence to an action by the child.

(iii) If an action is authorised or required by statute, there is no liability incurred in its due performance. If a statute merely permits an action it must be done in a manner least likely to cause harm. Thus if the action is performed negligently, or causes a nuisance beyond any envisaged by the statute, then the defence will not apply.

Often the deleterious effects on individuals of this defence is mitigated in the Act itself, which may provide for compensation to be paid.

(b) The usual remedy for a successful action in tort is an award of damages. Here the court seeks to compensate the plaintiff for the wrong done by ordering the defendant to pay an amount of money which will adequately reflect the loss suffered by the plaintiff.

Ordinary damages are awarded as compensation for the damage suffered in general. Where particular items of damage can be identified - to specific items of property, for example - *special* damages will be awarded, based on that actual loss. Where there is no real injury done, say in a case of harmless trespass onto land, the damages awarded will be *nominal*, a token recognition that there has been a breach of the defendant's rights but no real harm has been caused.

However, some damages go beyond compensation. *Aggravated* or *exemplary* damages are punitive, indicating strong disapproval of the actions of the defendant and aimed at discouraging similar actions by others. Exemplary damages can only be awarded where the defendant calculated to make more money from the tort than he would have to pay in damages, where a government official acts oppressively, arbitrarily or unconstitutionally, or where statute permits.

Contemptuous damages are awarded where the court finds for the plaintiff but has no sympathy for his case, and awards a suitably tiny sum.

Alternatively, the court may award an injunction, which will prevent the defendant from doing certain things which are causing, or may cause, damage to the plaintiff. Interlocutory injunctions are granted before a court hearing to preserve the status quo, so that the case may be heard later in full. Perpetual injunctions are permanent (or operate until revoked by the court) and are awarded after a full hearing. If the defendant fails to comply with the injunction he will be in contempt of court and may be fined or even imprisoned until he agrees to obey the order.

Before an interlocutory injunction will be granted the plaintiff must undertake to compensate the defendant for any loss arising out of its grant.

27 GOOD FAITH

> *Tutorial note:* candidates often write all-they-know-about-agency without considering the actual question being asked. You should be careful to focus particularly on the duty of good faith which is owed *by* the agent *to* the principal and then *explain* (not simply list) the remedies available to the principal where the duty is breached.

(a) An agent carries out acts and assumes legal obligations on behalf of his principal. In acting on the principal's behalf, the agent owes a general duty of good faith, which imposes certain obligations on the agent.

If the agent receives payment for his services, he is contractually bound to carry out his agreed task: *Turpin v Bilton 1843*. He is not bound if there is no consideration for his acting as agent. Even if paid, he is not bound to carry out any task which amounts to an illegal act.

The paid agent must exercise a certain degree of skill in completing his task. A higher standard is expected of a professionally qualified, paid agent than of a gratuitous agent who does not profess any particular skill. The latter type of agent is only expected to show the same skill as an ordinary person displays in managing his own affairs. A professional agent is expected to show the skill and care of a reasonably competent fellow-professional.

Personal performance is usually required of the agent although he may delegate in special circumstances, for example if specialist skill is required.

Other instances of good faith concern the financial obligations of the agent. He must not benefit from his actions without the principal's consent, although he may retain any profit if the principal gives his permission. Secret profits are not allowed, even if the principal's own financial interests are not prejudiced.

The agent owes a duty to avoid a conflict between his interests and those of the principal. Thus an agent cannot sell his property to the principal even at a fair market price: *Armstrong v Jackson 1917*. Furthermore, he owes a duty to keep his principal fully informed of transactions and he must account for all moneys arising.

The agent's duties to the principal clearly mean that any act of bad faith will be breach of them. For instance, acceptance of any financial inducements to carry out his work so as to favour a particular third party will clearly be a breach: *Boston Deep Sea Fishing Co v Ansell 1888*.

(b) The principal has redress against the agent if the duty of good faith is breached. In the case of bribery of the agent by a third party, the principal may dismiss the agent, withhold payment of remuneration and recover the amount of the bribe from the agent. This may also apply to any other profit wrongfully received by the agent. It is open to the principal to sue the third party for damages if loss has resulted: *Salford Corporation v Lever 1891*. There is the possibility of prosecution of agent and/or the third party under the Prevention of Corruption Act 1916.

In other cases, the agent's breach of duty may give rise to an action for damages by the principal. The principal is entitled to repudiate the agency contract on discovery of the breach. Any sums earned by the agent from the breach may be recovered by the principal.

28   JACK AND JILL

> *Tutorial note:* note that, in part (b), Jack's liability depends upon whether Jill had apparent authority to buy such a car, and not on the express agreement to the contrary made between Jack and Jill.

(a) The acquisition of authority to act as an agent hinges upon the creation of an agency relationship and the consequential powers that gives. Agency may be specifically created by the appointment of one person to act on another's behalf. It may also arise by implication; for example, a wife is the implied agent of her husband, and an employee who makes contracts on his employer's behalf is the implied agent of his employer in that capacity.

The *actual authority* of the agent may be expressly given (say to make certain contracts on the principal's behalf) or it may be implied from the nature of the agent's duties. In the latter case, the agent is assumed to have the authority to do those things incidental to his job; a company secretary, for instance, has the implied authority to hire cars for the company: *Panorama Developments v Fidelis Furnishing Fabrics 1971*. If restrictions are put on the agent's actual authority they must be communicated to the third party to be effective: *Watteau v Fenwick 1893.*

Furthermore, the agent may bind his principal on matters which are within his *apparent authority* or ostensible authority. This is similar to implied authority, but it is not restricted to those tasks which are usual to one in the agent's position. It extends to that authority which the principal, by words or deed, appears to confer on the agent. If, for example, the principal allows the agent to act beyond his implied powers he will have represented to third parties that the agent has this extra authority and will be bound: *Waugh v Clifford 1982.*

The agency relationship may be created in other ways. The law implies an agency of necessity in certain very specific circumstances. This arises when the 'agent' is entrusted with the principal's goods, an emergency arises which imperils these goods and the agent, unable to contact the principal, takes action to protect the principal's interests. In this case, the principal becomes liable for the agent's actions: *Great Northern Railway v Swaffield 1874*. If the agent acts for his own convenience, there is no agency: *Sachs v Miklos 1948*. Under agency of necessity, the agent has acquired authority to do those things necessary to protect the principal's interests.

Another manner in which the agency relationship arises is by ratification. The agent acts as agent (so the principal must be identified as a party to the contract: *Keighley Maxstead v Durant 1900)* without authority to do so, but the principal subsequently ratifies the contract, accepting the role of principal. The ratification must be made clearly, expressly or implicitly, and must be made within a reasonable time of the contract being made. The whole contract must be ratified and the principal must be aware of its terms or be prepared to ratify whatever has been decided. Here then the agent's authority depends on the principal's willingness to ratify the contract.

Finally, agency may be created by estoppel. Under this doctrine, the 'principal' leads a third party to believe that his 'agent' has authority to act, and the third party contracts with the 'agent' on that basis: *Freeman & Lockyer v Buckhurst Park Properties (Mangal) Ltd 1964*. Agency by estoppel does not arise where it is the 'agent' who holds himself out as such: *Armagos v Mundagas, The Ocean Frost 1986*. The authority of an agent by estoppel is that which is usual.

(b) A partnership is not an independent entity with a legal personality distinct from that of its members. However the law imposes some sort of group responsibility in that under the Partnership Act 1890 one partner acts as agent for all the others (in most circumstances).

Each partner has implied authority to bind the partnership regarding matters carried on in the ordinary course of its business. A restriction on that authority is effective against third parties only in as far as the restriction is made known to them.

It may be assumed that a partner who runs a garage has the implied authority to buy a car on behalf of the partnership if it is within the ordinary scope of the garage's business. In judging this, normal trade practice will be taken into account: *Howard v Sheward 1866*. The knowledge of the car sellers as to Jill's actual powers and the expensive nature of the car may also be important.

It appears that Jack may be liable as Jill would appear to have had implied authority to act as she did. The remedy of a suit against Jill for breaching her warranty of authority exists but is of little practical use since she has absconded.

29 CHARLES

> *Tutorial note:* part (c) of this question is affected by the Companies Act 1989, which overhauls the *ultra vires* rule, inserts a new s35 into the 1985 Act, and changes the rules on constructive notice. You should make yourself aware of these changes.

(a) The contract made by David, purportedly as Eric's agent, will be binding on Eric only if David is acting within the bounds of his actual or apparent authority.

Actual authority is that given to David by Eric to enter into legal relations on Eric's behalf. It may be given expressly or it may be implied from what is the usual authority of agents of this type. David carried with him the authority to make the type of contracts associated with his position: *Howard v Sheward 1866*. An express restriction or withdrawal of David's powers will only invalidate the contract if Charles knew of that restriction: *Watteau v Fenwick 1893*.

Alternatively, David may have apparent authority - Eric, by his words or behaviour, may have implied that David has authority to make this particular type of contract, even though it is a function outside the usual ambit of one in David's position.

Charles should be able to enforce his contract with Eric, unless it can be shown that David lacked authority. This would be the case if Charles knew of his limited authority, or if the contract is beyond the normal scope of David's duties and Eric had not indicated that there was any special authority in this case.

(b) The Partnership Act 1890 s5 sets out the circumstances in which a partner may bind the firm as agent; a partner is, then, agent and principal at one and the same time.

The engineering firm will be bound if the act done is in the way of carrying on business of a type usual to the firm. However there is an exception if the act is beyond the authority of the partner and the other party either knows of this, or does not know or believe that the partner is in fact a partner of the firm. Charles is thus only bound by restrictions on Nigel's authority in the partnership agreement if he is actually aware of them *(Mercantile Credit v Garrod 1962)* or if he did not believe Nigel to be a partner in the firm.

So if the contract was of a type normally made by engineering firms and Charles was unaware of this restriction on Nigel's powers, the contract will be enforceable against the partnership.

(c) If the contract is *ultra vires* the company then it is one which was beyond the powers of the company to make. A company has its aims and objects set out in its memorandum of association; it cannot do anything outside these powers and any such contract is void: *Ashbury Railway Carriage & Iron Co v Riche 1875*. The officers of the company, such as its directors, cannot do anything in the name of the company which goes beyond these powers: *Rolled Steel Products v British Steel Corporation 1985*.

Charles may seek the protection of s35(1) Companies Act 1985 which states that the validity of an act done by a company shall not be called into question on the grounds of lack of capacity by reason of anything in the company's memorandum. In addition, provided Charles is acting in good faith the power of the directors to bind the company to him is unlimited: s35A.

Charles shall not be treated as acting in bad faith even if he knows the company's directors are exceeding their powers unless the contrary is proven; it is unclear whether there must be total honest ignorance of the restriction for good faith to apply. As the contract is made with the board, it probably satisfies the criterion of a transaction decided on by the directors. Thus it appears that Charles may be able to enforce his contract, even though it is *ultra vires*.

30 BRIGHT

Tutorial note: this question examines two popular subjects: agent's authority and partnership liability, and you should ensure that you are clear in your knowledge of this area.

(a) An agent is a person who acts on behalf of another (his principal), usually in a business capacity. The relationship is created by mutual agreement, for general or specific purposes. The agent may create legal and binding obligations for the principal on his behalf.

Agency may come to an end (and authority be revoked) by the express action of the parties involved. An agent engaged for a specific function will cease to act in that capacity when the transaction is complete. It may also end by mutual agreement or by one party giving notice to the other of his intention to withdraw from the relationship.

There are some exceptions to this.

(i) The principal may not give notice of revocation where the agent has begun to act and has incurred liabilities.

(ii) An authority coupled with a financial interest cannot be ended by notice; this arises where the agent has an interest in the transaction (for example a creditor appointed as agent to sell the debtor's goods).

(iii) Certain statutory agency powers are difficult to revoke, for instance under the Enduring Powers of Attorney Act 1985.

Third parties who are not informed of the termination of the agency may be able to continue to rely on it.

Some agency agreements end by operation of law. It is thought that insanity of the principal ends an agency, but the law is confused; in *Drew v Nunn 1879* the principal continued to be liable but in *Yonge v Toynbee 1910* he did not. Only formal powers of attorney executed under the Enduring Powers of Attorney Act 1985 may continue through a period of insanity. Death of the principal ends the agreement, and bankruptcy of either party may end the agreement but, in the case of the agent, this is the case only if the agent is thereby prevented from carrying out his duties. Frustration of the agency contract (say because of supervening illegality) will also terminate it.

(b) As a partner Bright will have been in the position of agent to the firm of partners as a whole. This means that he would have been able to make contracts and so on which would bind the entire firm, provided that they were within the usual scope of a partner's authority.

When he retires this relationship is broken with the other partners, but third parties are still entitled to treat Bright as a partner and thus an agent of the firm (which would be bound) until they are informed of the change of circumstances. In addition Bright would be bound by contracts made by the firm until it was made clear that he was no longer a partner. It would not matter that they were made after actual retirement if it was not known that he had retired and the firm continued to hold him out as a partner.

Bright would be advised to inform known customers of his retirement directly and to make some sort of general announcement, perhaps in a trade publication or in the London Gazette (s36 Partnership Act 1890). To ensure that he is no longer held out as a partner he should have his name removed from letterheads.

31   SAMSON AND DELILAH

> *Tutorial note:* there is a particular tendency in students when answering agency questions to 'write all they know about agency'. This is *not* what is being looked for and you should be careful to *read the question* and talk about only what is required. To some extent the principles outlined in part (a) are applied in part (b). Do not repeat yourself in part (b) as it is perfectly all right to refer back to part (a).

(a)   In most agency situations the authority of the agent to act for the principal extends only as far as the actual authority granted to him by that principal. However as the third party cannot always be expected to know the extent of this authority there are certain conventions by which an agent is recognised as having authority beyond the scope of that expressly granted.

Implied actual authority is given to an agent by virtue of his position. If the agent is employed in a certain capacity by the principal he carries all the powers implied by that status. Thus contracts made within the ambit of these powers will be valid unless the third party had notice of any express restriction on them: *Watteau v Fenwick 1893*

In rare cases, an agency of necessity may arise. The agent has possession of goods (usually for transportation), some emergency arises and it is not possible to contact the principal. Provided action taken is in the interests of the principal and not merely for his own convenience, the agent may bind the principal as a consequence of that necessary action. Thus a claim for the upkeep of a horse which the owner had failed to collect succeeded: *Great Northern Railway v Swaffield 1874*. Conversely, sale of stored furniture after the owner failed to collect it was not an action of necessity but was in the agent's interest: *Sachs v Miklos 1948*. It is necessary in these cases to show that an agency relationship already existed.

More common is the case where an agent claims to act for his principal after his authority has been terminated or even without authority. If the principal is aware of this but fails to notify the third party, he will be estopped (denied) from disclaiming liability under the contracts. In *Freeman & Lockyer v Buckhurst Park Properties (Mangal) Ltd 1964*, a director made contracts on behalf of a company; his fellow directors were bound as they took no steps to bring his lack of authority to the attention of the third party.

Authority may be given retrospectively, whereby the principal adopts a contract made by his agent but without his authority. This is agency by ratification. It may be used only in strict circumstances. The agent must make it clear that he is acting for the principal (*Keighley Maxstead v Durant 1900*) and the principal must be ascertainable and in existence when the contract is made. A new company, therefore, cannot ratify contracts made on its behalf before incorporation: *Kelner v Baxter 1866*. Ratification must be within a reasonable time of the contract being made, and it must be ratified in full. The principal must be aware of the terms (or ready to ratify whatever has been agreed by the agent) and the intention to ratify must be made clear.

(b)   The Partnership Act 1890 makes it clear that a partner acts as agent for the firm as a whole. This is subject to any express restriction imposed by the partnership agreement. Since Andy carries the usual authority to do any acts within the usual ambit of the powers of a partner, in the absence of notice of any restrictions the validity of these acts as binding on the partnership is to be judged on the basis of agency.

Engagement of staff and sale and purchase of property are all acts likely to be within the usual authority of the partner and are *prima facie* binding on the partnership, unless Samson and John were not acting in good faith in that they should have been put on notice to enquire whether Andy's usual authority was co-extensive with his actual authority.

In the cases of the sale of the computer and purchase of the word processor, the circumstances are slightly unusual, particularly in the former case. It is a question of fact whether these circumstances should have alerted John and Samson. It may be open to these parties to show that the other partners implicitly allowed these contracts (agency by estoppel), that similar contracts had been made before, or that such conditions were usual in this type of trade: *Howard v Sheward 1866*.

These are questions for the courts to decide; in particular, they will look to see if Andy had any personal motive in entering those contracts. Even so, if the contracts themselves were within his apparent authority they will be binding notwithstanding a personal interest: *Panorama Developments Ltd v Fidelis Furnishing Fabrics Ltd 1971*.

If the partners are successful in denying liability for the sale and purchase contracts, John and Samson may sue Andy on the grounds that he has warranted that he had authority to enter into these contracts and has breached that warranty of authority, provided they can each prove that they were unaware of any constraints on his power: *Yonge v Toynbee 1910*. If the partnership is bound by the contracts they may seek indemnities from Andy for the loss suffered.

As for the contract for employment of Delilah, this appears to be within his authority as partner and there are no suspicious circumstances by which she should have been alerted to the fact that Andy had limited authority. It would appear to be binding on the partnership.

BUSINESS LAW
OBJECTIVE TEST

1   In its historical origin the law on negotiable instruments is derived mainly from

    A   common law
    B   European community law
    C   Roman law
    D   mercantile custom

2   Which one of the following sources of law is defined as a subsidiary source?

    A   Common law
    B   Mercantile law
    C   Judicial precedent
    D   Custom

3   Which one of the following is a remedy at common law for an action in contract?

    A   Damages
    B   A decree of specific performance
    C   Injunction
    D   Rescission

4   Which one of the following most correctly describes the golden rule of statutory interpretation?

    A   A rule to avoid unpleasantness
    B   A rule to avoid absurdity
    C   A rule to avoid mischief
    D   A rule which should be used by reference to the context of the words

5   Which one of the following is seen in a civil case before a court?

    A   The plaintiff
    B   The accused
    C   The prosecution
    D   The sentence

6   What is the aim of the criminal law?

    A   Compensation of injured parties
    B   Recovery of property taken from its true owner
    C   The enforcement of legal obligations
    D   Punishment of wrongdoers

7   In accepting an offer (and thus creating a binding contract) the offeree must always

    A   personally communicate his acceptance to the offeror
    B   take some action by way of acceptance
    C   accept the offer within a defined period
    D   reply by post to an offer received through the post

8   One of the following is *not* a means by which an offer to enter into a contract is terminated. Which one?

   A   The offer is expressed to be kept open for a limited time which expires without acceptance
   B   The offeror tells the offeree, who has not yet accepted, that the offer is withdrawn
   C   The offeree requests further information
   D   The offeror withdraws the offer

9   In *Carlill v Carbolic Smokeball Co 1893* the manufacturer's intention to create legal relations was implied from

   A   the manufacturer's advertisement
   B   Mrs Carlill's purchase of the medicine
   C   Mrs Carlill's notification of claim
   D   the manufacturer's deposit of £100 at a bank

10   Consideration must be

   A   adequate only
   B   sufficient only
   C   sufficient *and* adequate
   D   adequate but not necessarily sufficient

11   Which one of the following constitutes the rule that only the parties who actually make the contract are able to enforce the rights and obligations arising under it?

   A   Promissory estoppel
   B   Privity of contract
   C   *Nemo dat quod non habet*
   D   Part performance

12   An agreement under which Sam, aged 17½, agrees to purchase a personal computer for use in his videogame programme company is

   A   valid
   B   voidable
   C   unenforceable
   D   void

13   A share purchase contract entered into by an infant is

   A   valid
   B   voidable
   C   unenforceable
   D   void

14   What is the significance of a contractual term being a condition?

   A   Its breach automatically entitles the injured party to claim damages
   B   Its breach automatically entitles the injured party to a decree of specific performance
   C   Its inclusion predetermines the amount of damages payable on its breach
   D   Its inclusion signifies that the parties intended to enter into legal relations

15 In *The Moorcock 1889* a term was implied into a contract on the grounds that the parties obviously meant it to be included in the contract but did not bother to express it. This is known as

A   promissory estoppel
B   privity of contract
C   the *contra proferentem* rule
D   the officious bystander rule

16 What is an exclusion clause?

A   It is a contractual warranty that the terms of the contract will be performed
B   It is a clause excluding the rights of persons other than the contracting parties to sue for breach of contract
C   It is a clause which limits the contractual capacity of one of the parties
D   It is a clause which limits a person's liability for breach of contract

17 In *Tamplin v James 1880* the defendant went to an auction and bid for property which he believed comprised a public house and an adjoining field occupied with it. The written auction particulars however made it plain that only the public house was offered for sale in that lot. In the categories of mistake which may affect a contract this mistake should be categorised as

A   mutual mistake
B   unilateral mistake
C   common mistake
D   operative mistake

18 If a contract contains an operative mistake it is

A   void
B   voidable
C   valid
D   unenforceable

19 The remedies for negligent misrepresentation are

A   rescission of contract, refusal to perform obligations, damages for tort of deceit only
B   rescission or damages in contract, refusal to perform obligations only
C   rescission or damages in contract, refusal to perform obligations, damages under the Misrepresentation Act 1967 only
D   rescission or damages in contract, refusal to perform obligations, damages under the Misrepresentation Act 1967, damages for the tort of deceit

20 The 'blue pencil test' is used in connection with

A   mistake
B   misrepresentation
C   contracts in restraint of trade
D   undue influence

21 Where there has been anticipatory breach of contract the injured party is entitled to sue

    A   after a reasonable time
    B   from the moment the other party is in actual breach of contract
    C   from the moment the other party indicates he does not intend to be bound
    D   from the moment the other party indicates he does not intend to be bound *provided* the injured party has already completed his own obligation

22 An award of basic damages for breach of contract aims

    A   to ensure that the injured party receives payment for acts performed
    B   to ensure that the injured party is in the same position as he would have been had the contract been performed
    C   to ensure that the defaulting party does not profit from his breach
    D   to ensure that the defaulting party is penalised so that the breach will not recur

23 A contract is entered into for the supply of 100 books. The market price is £2.50, the contract price is £2.00 and the onward selling price, known to all parties, is £4. The contract is breached by the supplier. What is payable in damages to the buyer?

    A   £50
    B   £150
    C   £200
    D   £250

24 In tort the rule that there must be a relationship of cause and effect between the wrong (*injuria*) and the damage (*damnum*) means that

    A   a person will be liable for loss arising out of his wrongful act or omission if *damnum* is not too remote from *injuria*
    B   a person who commits an *injuria* with the intention of causing *damnum* will only be liable if the latter is not too remote
    C   a person will never be liable for *damnum* arising out of another person's intervention in his *injuria* so as to break the chain of causation
    D   a person can never be vicariously liable for another person's *injuria* when the *damnum* is not its immediate effect

25 Smokestack Industries plc operate a factory. The factory emits noxious fumes. Bernard and Fenella and the other residents of nearby Greenpeace Crescent have complained to Smokestack Industries but without success. They now wish to take legal action against the company to restrain the emission of fumes. What is their most appropriate course of action?

    A   Public nuisance
    B   Private nuisance
    C   *Rylands v Fletcher* liability
    D   Trespass

26 Since the decision in *The Wagon Mound 1961* the test for the recoverability of damages in general tort is that

    A   the loss or damage was reasonably foreseeable by the defendant only
    B   the loss or damage was reasonably foreseeable by both plaintiff and defendant
    C   the loss or damage was the direct and natural consequence of the defendant's breach of duty
    D   the loss or damage caused by something under the defendant's control was of a kind which would not have been suffered but for the defendant's negligence

27 Peter's wife, Jane, has in the past without his consent purchased expensive items of jewellery from Gems Ltd. Peter paid the bills to avoid embarrassment. However, the marriage has now broken down and Jane has left the matrimonial home. She then returned to Gems Ltd and bought a brooch, saying that 'It was an absolute necessity and my husband will pay for it'. The bill has now reached Peter. He is liable to pay it because

    A   Jane is his wife

    B   Jane bought the brooch as his 'agent of necessity'

    C   his previous payments prevent him from denying that on this occasion Jane had his authority to make the purchase

    D   his previous payments amount to ratification of Jane's authority in making the latest purchase

28 What is ostensible authority?

    A   The authority given expressly by a principal to an agent to enter into a particular transaction

    B   The authority given to an agent by virtue of the office he holds

    C   The authority which the principal represents to other persons has been given to the agent

    D   The authority vested in an agent of necessity

29 Which one of the following persons is a partner by holding out?

    A   A person who has been led by others to believe that he is a partner

    B   A person who offers to make someone a partner

    C   A person who is represented to others by someone else as a partner

    D   A person who has only limited rights to share in the partnership profits

30 Tim and Gerry are the sole directors and shareholders of Timgo Ltd, which runs a garage for car repairs. Bob is suing for damage inflicted on his car while it was at the garage: (i) how will the garage appear in the court listings and (ii) who will be liable to Bob?

	(i)	(ii)
A	Timgo Ltd, plaintiff	Timgo Ltd, Tim and Gerry jointly
B	Timgo Ltd, defendant	Timgo Ltd
C	Tim & Gerry, plaintiff	Timgo Ltd, Tim and Gerry jointly
D	Tim & Gerry, defendant	Tim and Gerry jointly

1.	D	16.	D
2.	B	17.	A
3.	A	18.	A
4.	B	19.	C
5.	A	20.	C
6.	D	21.	C
7.	B	22.	B
8.	C	23.	C
9.	D	24.	A
10.	B	25.	A
11.	B	26.	A
12.	C	27.	C
13.	B	28.	C
14.	A	29.	C
15.	D	30.	B

ECONOMICS

ECONOMICS
QUESTIONS

1   OPPORTUNITY COST (15 marks)

(a) Define 'opportunity cost'.

(b) Explain briefly how this concept applies to:

    (i)   an individual in spending his income;
    (ii)   an individual in allocating his time to different activities;
    (iii) a firm in choosing which goods to produce;
    (iv)   the state in relation to public spending.

2   THE STUDY OF WEALTH (20 marks)

Economics has been described as the study of wealth. Discuss the adequacy of this definition, making clear the nature and scope of the subject.

3   THE PRICE MECHANISM (20 marks)

How efficient is the price mechanism in allocating the resources of a free enterprise economy?

4   MARKET CONDITIONS (20 marks)

What is a market? State the conditions necessary for a perfect market and describe the factors which cause imperfections.

5   ECONOMIC WEALTH AND WELFARE (20 marks)

Describe the nature and characteristics of economic wealth, and explain its relationship with economic welfare.

6   COMMAND ECONOMY (20 marks)

(a) Outline the advantages and disadvantages of a command economy.
(b) What justification would you advance for government intervention in a free market system?

7   THE STANDARD OF LIVING (20 marks)

Explain the term 'standard of living'. Outline the factors which determine the standard of living in an industrialised country.

8   SMALL FIRMS (20 marks)

The number of small firms in the United Kingdom has considerably increased in the last decade. Give reasons for this increase and assess the contribution of small firms to the UK economy.

9 HIGHER REAL COSTS (20 marks)

Comment on the assertion that Government intervention in the location of industry causes an efficiency loss in the form of higher real costs of production.

10 ENTREPRENEUR'S REWARD (20 marks)

Describe the function of the entrepreneur and explain in detail the complex nature of his reward.

11 RETAILER (20 marks)

You are required to:

(a) state the economic functions of the retailer;   (8 marks)
(b) describe the forms of retail outlet and the factors which have caused them to change in the past thirty years.   (12 marks)

12 COOPERATIVE ENTERPRISES (20 marks)

What characteristics distinguish co-operative enterprises from other forms of business organisation?

13 ECONOMIC FACTORS (20 marks)

What economic factors might a manufacturing company take into account in deciding whether or not to move to a new location?

14 PRICE TAKERS AND PRICE MAKERS (15 marks)

Distinguish the market conditions in which a company is:

(a) a 'price taker';
(b) a 'price maker'.

Illustrate each with a diagram, and compare the prices, output and profits of the two types.

15 PRICE DISCRIMINATION (20 marks)

What market conditions are necessary to enable a company to practise price discrimination? How may it do so?

16 PRICE ELASTICITY OF DEMAND (20 marks)

Explain the concept of price elasticity of demand. How is it measured and by what factors is it determined?

17 ELASTICITY OF SUPPLY (20 marks)

Show how the elasticity of supply is influenced by (a) time, and (b) costs.

18 SHORT RUN AND LONG RUN COSTS (20 marks)

How does the determination of short-run costs differ from that of costs in the long run?

19 DISECONOMIES OF SCALE (20 marks)

What diseconomies and consequent problems may be associated with large-scale production?

20 PRECISE RELATIONSHIP (20 marks)

Explain the precise relationship between utility, value and price.

21 OLIGOPOLY (20 marks)

You are required to:

(a) describe the market conditions known as oligopoly; (6 marks)
(b) show how the firms involved in these conditions may behave in order to obtain maximum benefit. (14 marks)

22 CHARACTERISTICS (20 marks)

You are required to distinguish between a cartel, a merger, and a holding company, describing the main characteristics of each.

23 VARIOUS TYPES (15 marks)

(a) Define inflation, distinguishing between the various types.
(b) How is inflation measured?

24 IMPORTANCE OF MONEY (20 marks)

You are required to explain the economic importance of money, making clear the ways in which it facilitates the working of an economy.

25 THE BANK OF ENGLAND (20 marks)

What are the functions of the Bank of England?

26 DEPOSIT CREATION (20 marks)

'Bank deposits ... are largely created by the commercial banks themselves.' (Hanson).

Explain this statement, and describe how the power of the banks to create deposits is limited.

27 CONFLICTING AIMS (20 marks)

A commercial bank distributes its assets so as to reconcile the conflicting aims of liquidity, profitability and security. Explain this statement by an analysis of the bank's assets.

28 NBFIs (20 marks)

"The activities of the non-bank financial intermediaries (NBFIs) are important to the long-term financial market." (Hanson)

Who are the NBFIs, and what services do they provide, both as a group and as individual institutions?

29 FORMS OF BUSINESS CREDIT (20 marks)

What forms of credit are available to a business and why are these important?

30 COMPANY FINANCE (20 marks)

Describe the ways in which a public limited company may finance its activities.

ECONOMICS
SUGGESTED SOLUTIONS

1   OPPORTUNITY COST

(a)   The opportunity cost of an action is its cost measured in terms of the alternative actions foregone. (The concept of opportunity cost arises because resources are scarce. In choosing which goods to produce from scarce resources, society is forced to do without those goods which might otherwise be produced. In choosing what to produce the next best alternative foregone or sacrificed is referred to as the opportunity cost of what is produced).

(b)   (i)   The income of the individual restricts the range of goods and services he is able to consume and he is thus forced to choose between alternatives. In choosing to buy a textbook, for example, a student may forgo a meal in a restaurant. The meal is therefore the opportunity cost of the textbook. The individual's income is such that he can have one or the other but not both.

(ii)   Time, as well as income, is a scarce resource for the individual. If a student decides to spend an evening at home revising for an economics examination, for example, the opportunity cost of such revision could be the time not spent revising for an accountancy examination.

(iii)   At the level of the firm, the concept of opportunity cost may be illustrated with reference to Figure 1, which shows a production possibility curve. We assume that the firm only produces two goods, X and Y.

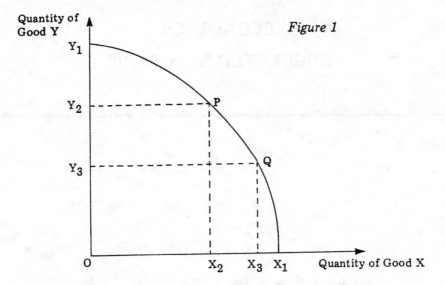

The production possibility curve shows the maximum output the firm can produce when all of its resources, in the form of labour, capital, land and raw material inputs are being fully used.

Given the resources available to the firm it may decide to produce either Y_1 units of good Y (for example washing machines) or X_1 units of good X (for example refrigerators), or some combination of the two, shown by points along the production possibility curve.

If the firm decides to produce X_1 refrigerators and no washing machines the opportunity cost in output terms of producing X_1 refrigerators is Y_1 washing machines. In other words, Y_1 washing machines represents the forgone output of the firm's decision to manufacture X_1 refrigerators.

If the firm is currently producing at point P on the production possibility curve, producing Y_2 units of Y and X_2 units of X, and subsequently moves to point Q, then production of Y will fall to Y_3, while the production of X will increase to X_3. In order that the firm may increase the output of X from X_2 to X_3 it is necessary to reduce the output of Y from Y_2 to Y_3. Thus the opportunity cost of increasing the output of X from X_2 to X_3 is $Y_2 - Y_3$ of Y.

In devoting resources to the increased production of good X, the firm is sacrificing the profit opportunities that are available in producing good Y instead. The opportunity cost of the increased output for good X is the profit foregone on the reduction in output of good Y.

(iv) The concept of opportunity cost applies to the state when it decides between alternative spending programmes. If the decision is taken to undertake a new hospital building programme, the resources devoted to this cannot also be used in the road building programme. The opportunity cost of the additional hospital construction can be viewed as the road building which is forgone. The social benefits and costs of each must be considered.

The concept of opportunity cost also applies to the state in that state expenditure financed by taxation implies a reduction in private expenditure because after taxation individuals are left a lower level of disposable income with which they may purchase consumer goods. The opportunity cost of a pound's worth of public expenditure is a pound's worth of private expenditure taxpayers must go without.

2 THE STUDY OF WEALTH

Wealth can be defined as possessions of any kind that have exchange value. In economics, valuable possessions are identified as scarce resources, not just land and capital but also labour and entrepreneurship. A fundamental feature of economic analysis is that resources are scarce, and so there are not enough resources to go round without a system of allocation or rationing. In a free-market economy, this system of allocation is the price mechanism whereas in a centrally-planned economy, it is based on government decisions.

Since there are not enough resources for everyone to have as much as they might want, and since scarce resources must be rationed out, some individuals (and societies) will get a bigger share of what resources there are than others; hence they will be more wealthy.

Scarce resources have a price or value, and so an individual's wealth consists of the stock of goods he owns and also any services to which he has a claim (eg. membership of a club or society). In a modern society, individual wealth will also include money and financial wealth. These are items that we would associate with a 'popular' definition of wealth. However, in economics, the definition of wealth goes much further and includes:

(a) the capitalised value of any future earnings (since labour is a scarce resource with an exchange value);

(b) the value of claims to public services, such as state schools and hospitals, public transport, fire and police services etc.

A society's wealth is the sum of the wealth of its individual members.

To define economics as the study of wealth is therefore misleading unless the full definition of wealth is appreciated. It is also an inadequate definition because it fails to explain the dynamic nature of economics, and the significance of *choice* and *efficiency* in the use of resources.

Choice is necessary because resources are scarce. Consumers must choose what goods and services they will buy and firms must choose which goods to make. Choice involves a sacrifice because by using scarce resources in one way, there will be opportunities of using them in other ways that have to be foregone. Resources have an *opportunity cost* which is the value of the benefits foregone by not using them in an alternative way. The market price of a resource and its opportunity cost need not be the same value. Economics involves the study of how choices are made, and of how decisions are taken to use resources in one way instead of other ways, and so account must be taken of opportunity costs as well as market prices.

Resources might be used efficiently or inefficiently. The 'choice' about how to allocate resources might result in profit-maximisation for a firm or utility maximisation for individuals. In terms of a national economy, all scarce resources might be utilised or there might be inefficiency in the form of unused resources. Economics involves the study of how resources can be utilised most efficiently so as to maximise wealth.

Economics is concerned with decisions and choices by individual households and firms (microeconomics) and also with the combined effects of all of these individual choices on a national economy (macroeconomics).

The study of economics attempts to be objective and 'scientific', but because human behaviour and attitudes are involved in decisions about resource allocation, the science is a 'social' science which cannot be exact in a true objective sense.

In summary, the definition of economics as the study of wealth is accurate provided that the meaning of wealth is properly understood. But it is too narow a definition to be full and satisfactory, ignoring as it does the 'scientific' approach to study, the full scope of the subject and the dynamic nature of economic decisions which involve choice and efficiency.

3   THE PRICE MECHANISM

Tutorial note: the essential point to discuss in this question is the *efficiency* of the price mechanism. Since it works imperfectly, as your solution should go on to explain, there is some need for state intervention/regulation - ie. a mixed economy.

Suggested solution

The basic economic problems in a market economy is that of how to allocate scarce resources amongst the many possible ways of using them to meet people's needs and wants. The potential demand for resources (goods and services for the consumer, and factors of production for firms) exceeds the available supply, and some system of resource allocation is essential. The price mechanism is an effective means of allocating scarce resources, but it cannot always be relied upon to provide a fair and socially acceptable allocation.

The price mechanism operates through the interaction of supply and demand. The higher the price of a good, the greater will be the amount of the good that firms are willing to supply. Firms must earn enough to cover their costs, including an amount for 'normal' profit. If prices go up, they will be able to produce more and still earn the required profit, even if the other unit costs of producing the extra output go up. If prices go down, firms that are not making a sufficient profit (ie. whose economic costs of production exceed the price of the good) will eventually leave the market.

The price mechanism works through demand as well as supply. At higher prices, consumers will demand less of a good, partly because they cannot afford to buy as much and partly because they can switch to buying other goods. (At higher prices, the marginal utility obtained from buying extra units of the product will be less.) The implication of the price mechanism for consumers is that unless they have the money to pay for goods, they will not be able to afford even the basic necessities of life, such as food and clothing. Whereas some sections of a community might be wealthy and live in luxury, another section might live in poverty and a state of deprivation.

The criticisms of the price mechanism arise because the allocation of resources that results from it might be unsatisfactory for social reasons. The uneven distribution of wealth, resulting perhaps in a section of the community living in destitution, is just one criticism of the potential consequences of the price mechanism. Other criticisms are:

(a) some services must be shared by the community - for example, the armed forces and government - and the price mechanism does not provide a way in which such shared services can be paid for;

(b) arguably, some goods should not be allowed for sale, even if there are customers willing to pay for them. These include socially harmful goods such as drugs and weapons. With an unrestricted price mechanism, such goods would be made available for sale;

(c) firms that enjoy a monopoly in a market, or a position in a market where there is oligopoly or monpolistic competition, can, in the absence of regulation, usually control the market supply and price of their goods, so as to earn supernormal profits. This means that they can exploit the price mechanism, because of their position in the market, so as to obtain a high return for their owners and so an 'unfair' allocation of resources;

(d) in some markets, the interaction of demand and supply can produce sudden and unforeseen changes in price, so that the price mechanism creates uncertainty and loss of confidence for traders in the market. Examples are the commodity markets and foreign exchange markets. To overcome the uncertainty and risk of trading in them, futures and forward exchange contracts have been developed, government intervention may be used to dampen exchange rate fluctuations. These fluctuations could cause inefficiency;

(f) the price mechanism does not seem to be effective at solving the problems of wages and employment. In theory, firms should be willing to pay a wage rate equal to the marginal revenue product of labour, and if wage levels rise above this, firms must reduce output (to reduce unit costs or as a consequence of having to raise the selling price of its products). If there is unemployment, labour ought to be willing to accept lower wages just to get a job, since firms will employ more people if wages costs are lower. In practice, this does not appear to work:

(i)   organised labour can resist reductions in wages;
(ii) reducing wages can result in a fall in aggregate demand in the economy, because consumers earn less money for the purchase of goods. An economic recession would suggest that resources are being under-utilised, so that the price mechanism would not be operating effectively.

Because the price mechanism can operate unfairly and inefficiently, the government intervenes in the economy, for example in providing shared services, running certain industries itself, and providing income to the unemployed, old and needy. Progressive direct taxation may be used to mitigate the effects of unequal income distribution which would be caused by the free action of the price mechanism in the labour market. A *mixed* economy of some form is necessary to allow the price mechanism to operate within certain constraints that preserve an acceptable society. Just what is acceptable is however a political and ethical issue rather than an economic one.

4 MARKET CONDITIONS

Tutorial note: this is a wide-ranging question, and it is important not to deviate or 'wander' from the question asked. Monopoly influences can be important in causing imperfections, but you should not spend time describing imperfect market types such as duopoly or oligopoly.

Suggested solution

The word 'market' originally designated a place where certain things were bought and sold, for example, Billingsgate market (the former London fish market). The modern usage of the word is in terms of a medium through which buyers and sellers negotiate the exchange of a well defined commodity. Hence the word market refers to the totality of buyers and sellers (both actual and potential) of a particular good or service. Hence it is possible to discuss the market for cabbages, the housing market, and the equity market. It is not necessary for markets to have a physical existence. For example, the foreign exchange market does not constitute a physical place but is a system of communications between those who wish to buy and those who wish to sell foreign currencies.

A market is thus an exchange mechanism that brings together sellers and buyers of a product, a financial security or a factor of production. Economists define a market as a group of products which consumers view as being substitutes for one another. A free market economy is one in which the allocation of resources is determined by production, sales and purchase decisions taken by firms and households. At the opposite extreme is a centrally controlled economy, in which all the decisions about the allocation of resources are taken by the central authorities.

The theory of markets distinguishes between markets according to their various structural characteristics. A perfect market is one that contains the following characteristics:

(i) All units of the commodity are exactly the same, ie there are homogenous products, with one unit of the good being exactly like another. If this is the case then buyers will be completely indifferent as to which seller they purchase the commodity from.

(ii) There are a large number of sellers and a large number of buyers in the market. Each seller and each buyer constitutes so small a part of the whole market that the behaviour of the individual buyer or seller will have no significant influence on the market price. For example, an individual seller may significantly change the volume of the commodity that he brings to the market. Although this represents considerable change in his quantity of output, the total market supply will change by only a very small amount and hence will have no perceptible impact on market price.

(iii) There is assumed to be perfect knowledge on the part of sellers and buyers. Sellers are fully aware of the activities of buyers and other sellers. Buyers are fully informed as to the strength of demand from other buyers and of the intentions of sellers. Should a particular seller raise his price above the prevailing market price, for example, buyers will immediately recognise that other sellers are supplying exactly the same good at a lower price and hence the demand for the seller's product would fall to zero.

(iv) There are no barriers to entry or exit from the market. If abnormal profit is being earned in the market this will encourage entrepreneurs to move into the market, thus increasing supply and causing price to fall until only normal profit is earned. The reverse process will occur if firms are making losses in the perfect market.

All of these conditions mean that the focus of competition in a perfect market is *price* competition. In a perfect market there will be one, and only one, market price, and this price will be beyond the influence of any one buyer or seller. Many buyers and sellers ensures that individual buyers and sellers have no market power. The assumption of perfect knowledge ensures that buyers will not pay different prices, while homogenity of product ensures that preferences will not arise which might be converted into price differences. Finally, the assumption of free entry to and exit from the market ensures that factors of production will move to eliminate any price differentials which might tend to arise.

Imperfections occur where the underlying assumptions associated with perfect markets do not apply. The clearest example of this is the market situation of monopoly. This is a type of market structure characterised by:

(i) one firm, ie the market is comprised of a single supplier. This means that the market demand curve is the monopolist firms' demand curve. Given that the market demand curve is downward sloping this provides the monopolist with some discretion over the setting of price. The monopolist could for instance set a high price and accept a low volume of sales, or conversely, produce a high volume of output and accept a lower price for his product.

(ii) The monopolist is in part able to do this because of a lack of substitute products, ie there are no close substitutes for the monopolist's product. In other types of markets imperfections may occur because of differentiated products, that is, the products offered by competing firms are differentiated from each other in one or more respects. These differences may be of a physical nature, involving functional features, or may be purely 'imaginary' in the sense that artificial differences are created through advertising and sales promotion. The less well informed buyers are of the qualities of competing brands, the more susceptible they are likely to be to persuasive advertising.

The purpose of such differentiating activity is to secure an initial demand for the firm's products and to cultivate brand loyalties to ensure that sales are increased. Product differentiation is significant in that it widens the dimensions of competitive actions, with firms competing against each other in quality, advertising, product features and so on, rather than on price alone. Although product differentiation is an aspect of market imperfection, this does not imply that heterogeneity of products is bad. Genuine differences among products imply greater diversity and therefore greater choice for consumers.

(iii) A third characteristic of monopoly is that of blocked entry, ie there are barriers to entry which make it impossible for new firms to enter the market. These obstacles may arise in a number of ways. For example, lower cost advantages of established firms from the possession of substantial market shares and the benefits of economies of large scale production; strong consumer preferences for the products of established firms resulting from product differentiation, as discussed above; large capital outlays required by new entrants to set up production; the control of raw materials, technology and distribution channels by established firms either through direct ownership or through patents and exclusive dealing contracts.

Barriers to entry are significant in that by blocking entry to markets by new firms they enable established firms to earn abnormal (ie above normal) profits and prevent the allocation of factor resources in line with patterns of consumer demand.

5 ECONOMIC WEALTH AND WELFARE

Tutorial note: the first part of this question is looking for, firstly, a *definition* of economic wealth, and, secondly, a *description* of its essential characteristics. The Stage 1 examiner commented that in candidates answers to this question 'wealth was frequently considered in purely monetary terms as cash, bank deposits, bonds and other securities. Confusion arose between wealth as a stock of resources and the factors of production which combine to create forms of wealth. Few candidates described the four characteristics – scarcity, utility, transferability and money value – adequately'.

The approach suggested by the examiner was:

(1) Define wealth – actual and potential.
(2) Describe the characteristics of wealth and comment on forms of ownership.
(3) Define welfare and briefly discuss its relationship with wealth.

Suggested solution

Economic wealth can be viewed as the stock of net assets owned by households, firms and the State. Another way to consider economic wealth is in terms of the total stock of goods of a society at a given time. Four qualities can be specified in order to define the nature of such goods.

1. They must possess utility – that is, they must be capable of yielding satisfaction.

2. In order for goods to be considered as wealth they must have a money value.

3. They must be limited in supply. Goods are scarce in the sense that the resources available to society are insufficient to meet all wants to the level of complete satiety. Given their relative scarcity in relation to demand, 'scarce' goods will have a price or 'money value'. Few goods are in fact so abundant that nobody will give anything for them. Air is perhaps one of the few exceptions, although a consumer may put a value on being able to consume clean air in preference to polluted air.

4. The ownership of such goods must be capable of being transferred from one person to another. This implies that all wealth is owned by someone.

But this definition of wealth would exclude intangible things such as acquired skills. A craftsman, such as a carpenter, would count his tools as part of his personal stock of wealth, but would exclude his skill in using them, as skills are not transferrable in the sense of point 4 above. In speaking of a nation's wealth, however, it would be legitimate to include the quality of the labour as represented by the stock of human capital where maintenance is determined in part by the level of education and training. And so we can define economic wealth as the total stock of tangible and intangible possessions.

It is possible to distinguish three classes of ownership of wealth.

1. *Personal wealth*

    This comprises personal belongings such as clothes, cars, books, washing machines, compact disc players and other consumer durables. It would also include houses, land, paintings, jewellery and other property owned by individuals. All these things presumably give satisfaction to their owner, or we may suggest that they would not have been acquired; all have a money value, all are limited in supply, and in general, ownership is transferrable from one person to another.

2. *Business wealth*

    This comprises such things as factory buildings, machinery, raw materials, stocks of finished goods etc. These things also possess all the attributes of wealth, although they do not yield satisfaction for their own sake. They are derived merely to assist the production of other things and, as an agent of production, are usually termed capital.

3. *Social wealth*

    This consists of wealth owned collectively and includes all property owned by the national government and local authorities, for example the nationalised industries, roads, schools, public libraries and museums. It is possible to transfer wealth from the private sector to the social sector and vice versa. So, for instance, the coal mines, railways, gas and electricity concerns were nationalised shortly after the second world war, while during the 1980s, gas, telecommunications, and other forms of wealth owned by the state have been transferred to the private sector under the Government's privatisation programme. Some social wealth (eg works of art) is similar to personal wealth, in being desirable for its own sake, but too expensive for most people individually to afford, while some of it is collectively owned business wealth used to enable other things of utility to individuals to be produced, eg railways and coal mines.

The form of ownership of wealth determines the form of the economic system. As indicated above, business wealth - or capital - can be owned by individuals or the state. Under private enterprise (a 'laissez faire' system) most wealth is owned by individuals, with a minimum being collectively owned. Under a communist system, although the individual might be allowed to own some personal possessions, most kinds of wealth would not be available for ownership by individuals. It is, however, primarily the ownership of business capital that has given rise to different economic and political systems. Under capitalism, business wealth is owned by individuals; under a command economy it is collectively owned by the state. In the UK there is a mixed system, with most business wealth being owned by private individuals but with the road systems, most health care and education facilities, together with a number of basic industries, including coal and the railways being in public or State ownership. As noted above, however, during the 1980s the number of basic industries owned by the State has been reduced in the UK.

Economic welfare may be defined as the satisfaction derived from the quantity of commodities (ie goods and services) available to citizens whereas economic wealth measures the stock of goods available, economic welfare is a measure of the satisfaction obtained from the consumption of a given stock of goods. Production increases material well-being - that is, the economic welfare of people. Economic welfare depends on the volume of production and consequently to expand the volume of production will generally increase economic welfare. It is also pertinent to consider the distribution of these goods and services across the population. Generally, the more nearly equal is their distribution, the greater will be the economic welfare of the community as a whole.

Although economic wealth may be measured in terms of 'marketable wealth', ie physical and financial assets which are relatively liquid, it does not follow that this measures economic welfare. Utility, ie the satisfaction derived from the consumption of goods and services, is not directly measurable: although it is possible to see differences in the utility of different goods or services to individuals through the preferences they reveal in the choices they make, it is difficult to quantify individuals' utility. It is still more problematic to make comparisons between the utility which one person derives from something with that which another person derives from it. It follows that the total of economic welfare for all individuals cannot be quantified meaningfully. Statements about welfare are essentially value judgements which will be influenced by the preferences and priorities of those making the judgement.

6 COMMAND ECONOMY

(a) There are three sorts of choices about allocating resources to be made in any economy. These are:

(i) what goods and services should be produced;
(ii) how they should be produced;
(iii) to whom the goods and services should be distributed.

In a command economy these choices are made by a central planning authority. The government fixes the nature and quantities of goods and services which are to be produced, decides how to produce them and determines on what basis the goods and services should be allocated. The government will thus make decisions as to how many resources should be employed in producing capital goods as opposed to consumer goods, the degree to which each worker should specialise and the price at which goods and services are to be distributed to the consumer. These decisions are not left to the forces of supply and demand.

For the consumer, the advantage is that, in return for a sacrifice of economic freedom, there may be greater security and greater social equality. Basic necessities should be available to all consumers since the government should be able to ensure that basic necessities are provided by the economy at a price attractive even to the poorest consumer.

But the efficiency and effectiveness of central control depends on the accuracy of the government's plan in forecasting society's wants and allocating resources to meet them. Frequently in practice the planned output mix is inefficient and wasteful incurring shortages and surpluses. There are a number of reasons for this:

(i) it is difficult to gauge consumer demand because the price mechanism is controlled;

(ii) the co-ordination and management of large-scale economic plans is difficult in practice simply because of the enormous scale of the undertaking;

(iii) planning requires a large labour force, and so can be considered wasteful of human resources.

In addition, command economies can be criticised on the grounds that central planning stifles individual initiative; as a result, productivity is lower than it might be under free-market conditions.

(b) In a wholly free market economy, the three choices discussed above are made not by a central authority but by the market forces of supply and demand in equilibrium.

(i) The choice as to what goods and services should be produced will be determined, unless the government intervenes, solely by what consumers are willing to pay and the price at which suppliers are willing to produce. However, the free-market economy may be reluctant to produce desirable goods which require extensive, long-term investment.

In addition, some goods and services by their nature are unsuitable for production in free-market conditions: it is difficult, for example, to visualise a firm which produced and 'sold' defence services to 'consumers'. The government can therefore be considered justified in encouraging the output of goods and services which the free-market economy is unwilling to provide and producing those goods and services that the free-market economy is unable to provide. On the other hand, the government may consider that some goods and services that may be produced in a wholly free market are undesirable: there are lucrative markets in narcotics, alcohol and tobacco, but most governments regard the consumption of these products as undesirable and so intervene to restrict the market or even to destroy the market altogether. Whether this is justifiable depends largely on one's attitude to freedom of choice for the individual.

(ii) The government may intervene to determine how goods and services should be produced. Many governments consider that goods and services should be produced with the least possible harm to the environment and so will intervene to control, for example, pollution. Some goods and services are produced by natural monopolies and thus supplied at a higher price and with a less efficient use of resources than might be the case were they produced by firms in perfect competition; the government may wish to intervene to control prices for the benefit of the consumer or to set a level of production that makes the most efficient use of resources. In the same way, the government may see itself as justified in intervening to break up cartels or to limit the extent of restrictive practices (as happened in the case of opticians).

(iii) Many governments regard the distribution of the resources of a free-market economy as undesirable. Health and education will be provided in all free-market economies, but would probably not be provided to the poorer members of society. As a result, the UK government has intervened to ensure that health and education are available at very low costs. More generally, there are many who argue that wealth is unfairly distributed and that it is the government's duty to ensure fairer shares of national wealth and national income.

But the justification for government intervention does not end with micro-economics, as described above. The government can be considered justified in intervening to ensure that there is full employment, price stability, economic growth and a healthy balance of payments. Government intervention can be useful in dampening the effects of trade cycles, in protecting declining industries and supporting infant industries.

7   THE STANDARD OF LIVING

The standard of living is based on a measure of the total goods and services produced in a country, ie gross domestic product (GDP). It is to be expected that as total output as measured by GDP rises then so will living standards. The situation is not as simple as this, however, and care must be taken when relating changes in GDP to changes in the standard of living.

First, it is necessary to measure the *real* level of output. Nominal GDP measures output at the prices currently prevailing when these goods and services are produced. If, for example, in successive years the same physical quantity of output is produced but all prices rise by 10% in the second year, then nominal GDP will be 10% higher than in the first year. However it cannot be claimed that the standard of living has risen because there has been no increase in the physical quantities of output available to the population, ie. real GDP is unchanged. Real GDP adjusts for inflation; it is the real changes in output that will affect living standards.

The total real GDP does not indicate, however, what is happening to the standard of living of a representative individual within a country. To obtain a simple measure of the standard of living enjoyed by a person in a particular country it is necessary to look at per capita real GDP, which is obtained by dividing real GDP by the total population. For a given level of real GDP, the larger the population the smaller will be the quantity of goods and services available for each individual. It is clearly necessary for the percentage growth rate of GDP to exceed the population percentage growth rate in order for the per capita GDP, and hence the standard of living, to rise.

Even per capita real GDP is only a wide indicator of the standard of living however. It is also necessary to take into account the distribution of income. Two countries may have a per capita GDP which is exactly the same. However, if in the first country income is very unevenly distributed, so that there are relatively few but extremely wealthy people, while a large proportion of the population is very poor, while in the second country income is fairly evenly distributed, the per capita real GDP figures will give a very misleading picture of the average standard of living in the first country. Also the more the income distribution is changing over time, the less reliable will be the change in per capita real GDP as an indicator of what is happening to the average standard of living.

There are other problems in measuring the standard of living from GDP figures because of the way in which the national income figures are calculated. There are many valuable goods and services which are excluded from GDP because they are not marketed and are therefore difficult to measure accurately, for example, DIY activities, household chores and activity in the 'black economy'. The greater the level of these unrecorded activities the higher will be the true standard of living in a country, but this will not be reflected in the official per capita real GDP measure.

Conversely, some forms of economic activity will detract from the standard of living of a country, and again this will not be reflected in official measures. Production and distribution of goods and services may create congestion and pollution. Economic activity therefore produces 'bads' as well as 'goods'. Subtracting from the traditional GDP measure an allowance for all the nuisance goods created during the production process would provide a better measure of the standard of living. This is not done, however, because it is difficult to quantify the costs such nuisance goods impose on society.

Measuring the standard of living in terms of per capita real GDP also makes no provision for the value people obtain from leisure time. Assume, for example, that people in country A value leisure more highly than people in Country B. Then, other things being equal, people in B will spend more time at work and produce a greater level of output, therefore B will have a higher measured GDP. It is not sensible to argue, however, that this establishes that people in A have a lower standard of living. By choosing to work fewer hours - ie. by consuming more leisure - they are revealing that the extra leisure is worth at least as much as the extra goods that could have been produced by working more hours. Despite such problems, per capital real GDP remains the best measure of the average standard of living.

There will be a number of factors that determine a country's standard of living. Where a country is particularly well endowed with natural resources, for example where a country has widespread mineral deposits, fertile soil, suitable climate for crops and coastal fisheries, then the standard of living will in general be high. The quantity and quality of the workforce will also be important. The greater the proportion of workers to the total population and the longer their working hours the higher will be the standard of living. Also the better trained and educated is the workforce the more productive and adaptable to change it will be and hence the higher the total output level. The amount of capital the labour force has to work with will be an important determinant of productivity. If the quantity of capital grows faster than the labour force this will improve productivity, increase total output and help ensure material progress.

The technical and organisational quality of management will also be an important determinant of output. The better the education and business training of management the more adept they should be at organising production and exploiting new markets. Where these skills allow one country to win markets from foreign competitors its standard of living will rise more quickly than it will abroad.

The political environment may cause variations in the standard of living. Where there is a stable government this will tend to produce confidence and encourage investment in new capital projects. This will therefore increase output and improve living standards.

There are a number of external factors which will also affect the standard of living. Changes in the terms of trade - ie. the rate at which nation's output exchanges against another nation's output - may be an important cause of living standard changes in a country very dependent on international trade. If the terms of trade move against a country this means that a greater quantity of exports must be exchanged for a given volume of imports. This occurs because the price of imports rises relative to the price of exports. This means that a smaller volume of production may be consumed at home simply because there has been an adverse movement in the terms of trade. Conversely, an improvement in the terms of trade will lead to an improvement in living standards.

The standard of living will be affected by foreign loans and investments. A country which lends and invests abroad will obtain income in the form of interest and profit which may be used to purchase goods or services from debtor countries without having to give goods and services in return. Conversely, where a country has borrowed from abroad, goods and services have to be exported to cover the interest payments. The standard of living determined by the real output available will clearly be affected by such factors. Finally, where a country obtains gifts or grants from abroad, especially for purposes of economic development or defence, these will have the effect of maintaining or improving its standard of living.

8   SMALL FIRMS

Tutorial note: this question calls for a discussion of an aspect of UK economic trends in recent years. Keeping up to date with the financial press will help you to write with confidence on a topic such as this.

Suggested solution

The large increase in the number of small firms which occurred during the 1980s can be seen as the result of various changes in the UK economy which occurred during the years in which the government was, at a political level, espousing the advantages of individual enterprise. Following the election of a Conservative government in 1979, much political emphasis was placed on what was called the 'enterprise culture'. This idea implied that opportunities should be widely available for individuals to become small scale entrepreneurs. It has often been remarked that many of the country's large and successful companies of today, such as Marks and Spencer and Tesco, had small beginnings.

With government support, the business environment was made more conducive to the establishment of successful small enterprises during the 1980s. Government agencies and local authorities assisted the development of numerous industrial estates containing small factory units. Low rents and rates were often offered as incentives for small firms to create employment opportunities in local areas.

Financial assistance was provided in the form of various business start-up schemes, which could provide allowances in the early stages of a business as well as capital. Loan guarantee schemes were also made available. The Business Expansion Scheme provided generous tax incentives for investors who were prepared to supply risk capital. The expansion of venture capital providers gave an additional funding option for some small and medium-sized firms. Smaller companies which were not able to meet the full listing requirements necessary to offer shares for sale on the Stock Exchange were provided with the alternative of the Unlisted Securities Market (USM), which was established in 1980.

The expansion of the number of small firms has been helped by a fast-changing technological environment. Advances in hardware and information technology have cut the costs of computer equipment and enabled small firms to reap the benefits in efficiency which computer systems can bring.

Changes in the labour market also played a part. The early 1980s saw large increases in unemployment. This change involved many skilled people being made redundant, and many of these people chose to set up small businesses, often making use of the redundancy payments they had received as capital for the business venture. Some people bought out the firm which had previously employed them.

The success of many small firms derives from the particular benefits which may be derived from small-scale operations. Innovation and entrepreneurship are often important ingredients of the success of the firm. The owners of the small firm are able to operate without the numerous levels of management necessary in a large organisation. The management of such firms is consequently often able to make decisions more quickly than the management of large firms, and may therefore be well suited to meeting frequent or rapid changes in demand.

Small firms are able to make a positive contribution to the economy and they play a particularly useful role at a local level. The improved environment now available for the growth of small firms enables many goods and services to be provided more widely and more efficiently than a large firm would be able or willing to do. Services which are very specialised in nature are often provided most effectively by small firms. The best products for small scale enterprise are those not requiring mass production or a lot of capital investment. The growth of small firms can be said to have widened consumer choice in many product areas and has encouraged innovation. The small firm also provides opportunities to those with initiative and drive who have a good product idea which has potential in the marketplace. In addition, some people may derive benefits from working as an employee for a small firm as compared with a larger organisation.

A negative aspect of the rapid expansion in the number of small firms set up during the 1980s is the high proportion of business failures which has followed. The reasons for failure are of course various, but often an inability to maintain a viable cash flow resulting from inadequate financial management will lead to the collapse of a business.

Many small businesses are relatively labour intensive, and it may be difficult for a business to meet wages costs at times when demand conditions or some unexpected event affects the market for the firm's products. Macroeconomic conditions also affect the rate of business failures. High interest rates early in the 1980s and in the period from 1988 to 1990 have contributed to the failure of many small businesses. Not only are firms' borrowing cost raised by higher interest rates; high credit costs lead to cutbacks in demand by consumers which can seriously affect levels of sales for many businesses. The economic slowdown of the late 1980s brought with it a slump in the housing market. Lower consumer confidence and a lower number of owner-occupiers moving home reduced spending on house-related goods and services. This particularly affected small businesses such as builders and plumbers.

9   HIGHER REAL COSTS

The assertion that government intervention in the location of industry (through regional policy) causes an efficiency loss would imply that regional policy should be abandoned. This case is founded on the belief that in the long run a perfectly competitive market will lead to the optimal allocation of resources and the optimal location of economic activity. Regional imbalances, whereby there are unemployed resources in one region and a shortage of resources in another region, would be corrected through the price mechanism. If resources are scarce, their price will rise, and if they are in excess supply their price will fall. Higher prices in one region than another will result in a movement of resources (labour) from the low price to the high price regions, until an equilibrium is achieved whereby all resources are located optimally. The optimal location of resources in a perfectly competitive market implies that output is produced at the minimum cost in the optimal place. Location is relevant to this situation, because of transport costs from the location of production to the location of markets (a spatial demand curve could be established for the quantity of demand at any price, allowing for transport costs).

This argument has certain drawbacks. In the first place, factor prices and in particular the cost of labour, will not necessarily reflect regional scarcities. National wage agreements might exist, so that wage levels are the same in regions with unemployment as they are in regions with job vacancies and so there would be no economic advantage to investing in an area of high unemployment. Furthermore, labour immobility might prevent the migration of individuals from a low wage region with unemployment to a high wage region with jobs to offer. Investment by entrepreneurs in low wage regions will not necessarily occur, if the owners and managers of the business prefer the 'quality of life' in high wage regions even if this means lower profits.

Given the immobility of labour and the imperfections in markets, it is not certain that without regional policy, the expected changes in location and resource allocation would occur and that a cost-minimising equilibrium would be achievable. Even if it were, the adjustments would probably take place over a very long time.

If this counter-argument is accepted, it should be concluded that regional policy might justifiably be aimed at providing investment into regions that would not otherwise occur in any other region, or where at least production costs would be no more expensive. The argument in favour of planning therefore depends on the belief that the government's planners should be able to devise a sensible policy for the regions which takes work to the workers without raising costs, because costs are very little affected by location. (There is a belief that costs should take account of the social costs of allowing regions to remain depressed, as well as economic costs, so that taking work to the workers would provide net benefits to society).

This argument in turn, although theoretically defensible, can be challenged on practical grounds. Regional policy might involve the payment of government grants to industries that invest in a depressed region, but such grants, if applied to all investments, would fail to distinguish between efficient and inefficient investments. High-cost producers might remain competitive because of government subsidies. When government assistance is selective, and bureaucrats or politicians are empowered to decide which investments should be given public money, and the consequences might be uneconomic investment decisions. There is no reason to suppose that civil servants or politicians can recognise an efficient investment in a suitable location. The experience of the wasted public funds in the de Lorean sports car firm in Northern Ireland testifies to the high-cost failures that might occur with arbitrary regional investment decisions. Even so, the government's regional development policy since 1984 has been one of selective assistance.

Regional policy might also take the form of tax incentives to firms that purchase new equipment. No matter whether assistance for regional investment is in the form of grants, tax incentives or any other measure (eg rent-free factories) it can also be argued that many firms taking advantage of the measures would have made their investment anyway. In such a situation, government money, by reducing costs, might affect the pricing and output decisions of firms.

In conclusion, it is suggested that the assertion should be challenged that in a perfectly competitive market the optimal cost-minimising location of industry will result from the free play of market resources, because this would not occur except over a long period of time. On the other hand, regional policy can still be inefficient, because firstly it might fail to create new investment and possibly cause a switch of some investment to less economic locations, but mainly because regional policy is bound to be arbitrary and clumsily-administered, so that assistance is given to uneconomic projects that will eventually collapse.

10   ENTREPRENEUR'S REWARD

Tutorial note: in answering a question requiring description and explanation, you need to be sure that you have interpreted the wording of the question carefully. The examiner made the following comment: 'A common error was the confusion of function with purpose, as in the statement that "the function of the entrepreneur is to make a profit". Making a profit is the purpose of object of the enterprise; its function is the activity undertaken to fulfil the purpose, ie the combination of the factors into a productive unit'.

Suggested solution

The term 'entrepreneur' is of French origin, meaning one who undertakes a project, a contractor or master builder. Economists have, however, found it difficult to determine what an entrepreneur is and what it is that he does. There are differing views of the main function of the entrepreneur. One such view is that the entrepreneur is the organiser or coordinator of economic resources. In order that economic activity may take place, someone must organise the factors of production, ie someone must combine the future inputs of labour, land and capital in such a way that consumer demands may be met. But the role of organisation may be regarded though as a managerial function, and management should be classified under the 'labour' heading. Viewing the organisation role in this way leaves the distinguishing feature of entrepreneurship as that of risk bearing, with the receipt of profit being seen as the reward for taking the risks of business.

Some of the risks a firm faces are calculable, in the sense that a statistician is able to calculate the probability of the event occurring, for example, the probability that the firm will suffer losses from such events as fire, theft or storm damage. Because such risks can be calculated it is possible for the firm to be insured against them. By paying a premium to an insurance company such risks are reduced to a normal cost and the firm is able to contract out of the risks involved.

There are certain other kinds of risks for which it is not possible to calculate the probability of the event occurring. For instance the risk of the demand for a product being different from that estimated by the entrepreneur cannot easily be reduced to a statistical probability. Such a risk cannot be insured against and consequently must be accepted by the entrepreneur. It is thus not possible for the entrepreneur to insure against commercial losses or business failure.

A fundamental problem for the entrepreneur is that production is usually undertaken in anticipation of demand. Entrepreneurs will seek to supply those goods and services which they believe will yield a profit, but entrepreneurs do not know that they will do so because the future is unknown. Moreover, production takes time. Decisions about what should be produced must be taken months or even years before the goods will actually appear on the market. These production decisions are being taken in anticipation of demand. There is no certainty that consumers will wish to purchase all that has been produced. Whether the entrepreneur recovers the cost of production will depend on the level of demand when the goods are available to sell. From the time the decision to produce has been taken to the time the finished goods are available for consumption there may have been a change in tastes away from the good; or the entrepreneur may simply produce a product which consumers do not particularly want. Another danger is that a rival producer may, in the time it takes the product to come on to the market, be selling a substitute good at a lower price, which he is able to do because he has developed a more effective technical process. Under such circumstances an anticipated profit may turn out to be an actual loss.

According to this view, the entrepreneur earns profit for facing the burden of decision-making under conditions of uncertainty. Although profit is the reward to the entrepreneur, the calculation of profit is not straightforward. To the economist profit arises when a firms total revenue exceeds its total cost. This concept of profit differs, though, from the accounting view of profit because the nature of costs differs between the two. The accounting concept of profit only considers explicit costs, while the economist takes into account both these and implicit costs.

Explicit costs are direct charges on the business - such as the payment of wages and salaries, interest payments on borrowed funds, rates and rent and the provision for the depreciation of capital stock. Some of these explicit costs will be fixed costs (those not varying with output) such as rent and rates, fixed interest payments, depreciation and other overhead charges. Other explicit costs will be variable costs (the level of costs varying as output varies); wage costs, for example, will rise if more labour is required to increase output; and similarly with raw materials, fuel and energy costs.

Implicit costs arise when the entrepreneur also provides his or her own labour, capital and land to a business. The opportunity cost to the entrepreneur of doing so must be taken into account. Opportunity cost is a measure of the economic cost of using resources in one line of production in terms of the alternative foregone. Implicit wage, rent and interest costs must be taken into account, therefore, when the entrepreneur could have obtained wages by working for someone else, earned interest by investing his capital in someone else's business, and obtained rent by hiring his land to another person.

Normal profit is the rate of profit which is just sufficient to ensure that a firm will continue to supply its existing good or service. The normal profit is the opportunity cost of the entrepreneur's services. Unless the entrepreneur obtains a reward equal to normal profit for undertaking activity in the present line of business he will leave one market and enter another where he believes the profit level earned will be at least the normal expected return.

Abnormal profit is the profit which is greater than those just sufficient to ensure that a firm will continue to supply its existing product, ie it is the return over and above opportunity cost payments and hence is the profit earned over normal profit. Abnormal profit can therefore be defined as a residual which is left after all explicit and implicit costs have been met, including the transfer earnings or opportunity cost of the entrepreneur. There are a number of synonyms for abnormal profit, the common ones being super-normal profit, monopoly profit and pure profit.

The uncertainty theory of profit (following on from the theory of the entrepreneur which assumes that the main entrepreneurial function is to bear uncertainty) views profit as the residual left for the entrepreneur after he has paid the contractual payments agreed for the factor inputs he hires. The entrepreneur is identified as being ultimately in control of the future and thus ultimately responsible for all costs and all revenues. The entrepreneur is thus subject to the uncertainty which surrounds the amount of the difference between total costs and total revenue. Profits cannot be positive unless there is a non-insurable uncertainty. The role of the entrepreneur is to shoulder the burden of uncertainty and therefore to take the reward of profit.

11   RETAILER

(a)   The retail trade is that part of commerce where goods are sold to the final consumer. The chief functions of the retailer are:

   (i)   *To provide a local supply of goods*
         Consumers require goods to be available for purchase relatively near to their homes. A local supply becomes particularly important when an item is purchased frequently, for example food-stuffs and petrol. Consumer durables are usually sold in town centres where the greater number of customers makes it worthwhile for retailers to offer a wide selection.

   (ii) *To break bulk*
         This means buying in large quantities and selling in smaller quantities. The word 'retail' is from the old French word 'retailler' - to cut again. This is a particularly important function of the retailer: to buy in large quantities and cut up into smaller quantities. An example is the butcher who buys whole carcasses of cattle, pigs and sheep and cuts them into various joints.

         Even if there is no actual cutting to do, the retailer will still break bulk in other ways. Mass production techniques mean that producers turn out large quantities of goods. Manufacturers will wish to clear the production lines quickly by disposing of these goods to large scale wholesalers. The bulk has to be broken down and the last link in the chain of supply is the retailer.

(iii) *To provide credit*
Retailers often provide credit in order that customers are able to obtain the goods now and pay for them over a period of time. Traditionally retailers have allowed customers to buy on 'hire purchase'. Today the provision of finance is seen in major stores accepting credit cards as a means of payment or else by issuing their own credit cards for exclusive use in the firm's stores.

(iv) *To act as a liaison between the consumer and the manufacturer*
By conveying information to the manufacturer about customer attitudes to particular goods, the retailer provides a key source of market research to producers. Such information often results in improvements in the design of a product, greater durability, greater safety and greater reliability.

(b) There are various forms of retail outlet.

(i) *Street market traders*
Market traders hire a stall in the market from the local council. Such 'markets' generally only take place on one or two days per week in most towns.

(ii) *Independent small traders*
Small shopkeepers in business on their own account, or in partnership, used to be the backbone of the retail trade in Britain. However the independents now only account for about 30% of total retail sales.

(iii) *Co-operative retail societies*
The co-operative movement is based on consumer ownership and control - the members of the society who have the voting and dividend rights are the customers. The number of co-operatives has been falling rapidly due to a series of mergers designed to achieve greater economies of scale. Co-operatives' sales are about 5% of total retail sales.

(iv) *Multiple shops*
These are large organisations run from a central head office and are usually public limited companies. Woolworth, Marks and Spencer and Boots are well known examples of multiple retailers in the UK. Multiples have over 55% of retail sales.

(v) *Department stores*
These provide the benefits of many shops under one roof, with each department selling a different range of goods. Probably the best known example of a department store in Britain is Harrods. Department stores have about 5% of total retail sales.

(vi) *Mail-order firms*
Many firms sell by mail-order presenting their goods in a catalogue which is distributed to potential customers. Not all mail-order firms issue catalogues, however. Some successful businesses have been set up using newspaper advertisements. Mail-order has about $3\frac{1}{2}$% of total retail sales by value.

The UK retail trade has changed dramatically over the last 30 years with the greatest changes in trading techniques occurring in the 1960s. While a number of factors have led to these innovations, many of the developments have been in response to increased competitive pressures, intensified in part by the abolition of resale price maintenance in 1964, which led to the closure of many small scale retailers.

The most significant change in the retail trade has been the growth in importance of multiple retailers. At the start of the 1960s independent retailers accounted for almost 55% of total retail trade but, thereafter, as competition intensified, the independents lost market share to the multiples who established a competitive edge through economies of scale. The multiples now occupy a commanding position with their market share doubling since the early 1960s whilst the share attributable to independent retailers has fallen by almost 25 percentage points.

During the 1950s, the co-operative societies pioneered the development of self-service stores and supermarkets. However, the co-operative movement began to lose ground towards the end of the 1950s, largely because of a lack of sufficient funds for investment and an inadequate product range. Today, their share of the retail trade is only about half that held in the early 1960s.

Despite their growing dominance in the market, the multiples are finding it extremely difficult to achieve further gains at the expense of the independents. Consequently, a number of different company strategies are being pursued. These include price discounting, geographical expansion, mergers and acquisitions, and diversification into other product areas. So, for example, several major food retailers now include clothing and electrical goods in their product range, whilst in addition to diversification into womenswear, some menswear retailers have begun to sell executive toys/accessories, and even soft furnishings. For some companies the object of diversification has been to build on success. For others, however, the strategy has been more defensive, aimed at creating a viable and broader market presence with which to fend off more aggressive rivals.

As the multiples have broadened their product range, there has also been a growing trend in favour of larger stores. Consequently, as many multiples have closed their smaller, uneconomic stores in favour of larger outlets and competitive pressures have continued to force many independent retailers out of business, the total number of retail outlets has declined. The move towards larger stores has been particularly noticeable in the food retailing sector. In the 1960s when planning permission was generally more difficult to obtain, the growth in the number of superstores was slow. However, the rate of growth in the number of superstores accelerated in the 1970s. Today there are hundreds of superstores in Great Britain, compared with only two in 1963. A most recent trend has been towards edge-of-town trading and competition for suitable sites is increasing. In contrast to this there has been the emergence of new specialist retail outlets, such as computer stores and video shops, which is stimulating more competition for traditional high street sites.

Retailing techniques are becoming more sophisticated, helped in part by the use of electronic point of sale (EPOS) systems and scanning equipment. This equipment is basically designed to help retailers monitor stock levels and sales more effectively and, therefore, to exert better cost control. Its usage is best established in the food retailing sector, where stock turnover is high and monitoring the flow of goods through the store is crucial. The concept now extends to electronic funds transfer at the point of sale (EFTPOS) or 'cashless' shopping.

As the UK retailing industry continues to mature and competition intensifies, greater attention is being paid to store design and store image. In this context, an increasing number of multiple retailers are beginning to aim at specific market segments - for example, the Next chain.

12 COOPERATIVE ENTERPRISES

Tutorial note: the examiner expected a description of the structure, divisions and characteristics of the co-operative movement. Although the question may appear to be fairly wide-ranging on a first reading, it is really about co-operative enterprises and other forms of business organisation should be brought in to your answer only by way of contrast or comparison with co-operatives. A good answer requires a knowledge of specific facts about the characteristics of co-operative enterprises.

Suggested solution

There are two main types of co-operatives, consumer co-operatives and worker or producer co-operatives. A co-operative enterprise differs from private enterprise and forms of public ownership in that consumers or producers belonging to the co-operative benefit according to the volume of its trade rather than through the amount of capital they have invested. Members' shares may be for a nominal amount, and members will have equal voting rights unlike the case of the joint stock company, in which voting rights are related to the number of shares held. Members of many co-operatives elect a management committee to run the organisation.

A consumer co-operative is a group of consumers who organise themselves into a collective group for the purpose of purchasing goods for consumption. A shop or chain of stores might be run as a co-operative whereby goods are purchased collectively in bulk by the co-operative and then resold to individual co-operative members. Any surplus could then be distributed to members. In the UK, the first co-operative retail society was formed on this basis in the last century, and the societies have since grown to form the largest single retailing organisation in the country with more than ten million members and more than 10,000 shops.

Traditionally the UK co-operative societies have also pursued political and social objectives. They finance and organise educational programmes and support political movements which seek to extend the ideas of worker and consumer control of industry.

A worker or producer co-operative is a group of workers who organise themselves into a collective group in order to produce and sell goods. The main principle behind worker co-operatives is that the enterprise should be owned and controlled by the workers engaged in it. The workers provide the capital, take all the management decisions, either collectively or by electing managers from among themselves (although occasionally a manager who is an outsider might be appointed) and they share out the profits on some agreed basis.

There are a number of potential advantages of co-operatives.

(a) Through consumer co-operatives buying in bulk at a relatively low price and cutting out the 'middle man' retailer or wholesaler, consumers benefit from lower prices for goods purchased;

(b) producer co-operatives and consumer co-operatives enable their members to pool their resources and equipment, and can provide a capital base which many individuals would not be able to achieve on their own;

(c) producer co-operatives have sometimes been established to take over the running of a factory after its previous management has announced its decision to close it down. The co-operative might therefore be a means of providing continuing employment;

(d) members of co-operatives are able to pool their specialist skills. Especially in developing countries, co-operative organisation can provide training of members in appropriate skills, such as husbandry or business management.

(e) producer co-operatives may be able to provide a more efficient and orderly system of supplying goods to their eventual markets. Particularly in developing countries, there may be gains in buying seeds or fertiliser, and transport may be shared. Co-operatives of small wine growers, for example, or agricultural co-operatives of small farmers, can help to control supply to their markets;

(f) a well established co-operative might provide a means of providing government aid to individual members.

In the UK the co-operative principle has been applied more successfully to consumer control than to worker control. This is probably because most of the disadvantages of co-operatives have applied more to worker co-operatives than consumer co-operatives. Worker co-operatives set up to keep a failed enterprise going do not have much record of success in the UK. The disadvantages of co-operatives are set out below.

(a) The total amount of capital they can provide through co-operation might be relatively small, restricted by the limited wealth and number of individual members. For a worker co-operative this might mean that there are inadequate funds for the necessary plant and machinery. Also if there is a lack of financial resources this might prevent the business from operating long enough for its products to establish themselves in the market.

(b) Co-operatives may lack the required management skills to be run effectively. There is likely to be a lack of management experience among the workers and specialists and skilled managers can often earn a higher income in alternative employment. Also, if management is elected from the ranks of the workers this may result in the election of popular figures rather than effective managers.

(c) There may be a tendency to distribute profits amongst the owners of the co-operative rather than reinvesting any surplus to ensure the long term growth and viability of the business.

(d) A large co-operative can become too unwieldy and difficult to manage. If various retail societies amalgamate, for example, the local base can be lost and members become more remote from management. The management committee may then have little effective accountability to individual members, most of whom probably do not take an active interest in its affairs, while on the other hand it may be unwilling to allow a free enough rein to the executive managers it appoints to enable the organisation to compete with private enterprises. These problems may prevent a co-operative from obtaining the advantages from economies of scale which competitors may have gained.

13 ECONOMIC FACTORS

Tutorial note: although you might be able to draw on your general knowledge to answer this question, make sure that the points you make concern the *economic* factors involved. The impact of government regional policy is clearly a factor which should be discussed.

Suggested solution

The geographical location of the enterprise is usually a fundamental decision for an entrepreneur. There will be a number of influences on this decision including social factors. For example, the top management might prefer to live in a particular part of the country and hence locate the firm in what they consider to be a pleasant area to live. There are a number of other economic factors which influence the choice of location.

It is usually assumed that firms will wish to minimise their costs of operation, so firms will be mainly concerned with the effects of different location on the cost of production. Usually, several locations are possible sites from which the firm might operate and the management will thus choose that site which minimises the costs of production. Such a decision may not be as easy as it sounds. However as in deciding what to produce, a firm may face a number of trade-offs; for example its needs as a manufacturer might conflict with its requirements as a seller. Although one location might be optimal in relation to the source of major raw material inputs, another site might be more favourable in relation to access to markets. The ultimate decision of where to locate will depend on the assessment of the maximum net advantages of alternative sites.

The advantages of different localities may be considered in terms of natural advantages, acquired advantages and government policy. The natural advantages may be considered in terms of transport costs and proximity to markets. The two main ways in which transport costs affect the location of a firm are in the movement of its raw materials and in the movement of its finished product. Where a firm is faced with the choice of a site near to its sources of supply or a site near to its markets, the strength of the attractions of the alternative sites will basically depend on the nature of the manufacturing process carried out by the firm.

If the firm's raw materials are bulky, heavy and costly to transport while the finished product is light, compact and relatively cheap to transport, the firm will be attracted to the sources of its raw materials. When the manufacturing process greatly reduces the weight and bulk of the raw materials used, the quantity to be transported will be much less when the firm is located near the source of its raw materials.

On the other hand, when the transport costs of finished goods are much higher than those for the basic materials there will be a strong attraction to locations near to the market. This will clearly be the case where the manufacturing process increases bulk, as it does for instance in the furniture industry. Transport costs will also be relatively high where the product is perishable or fragile.

Access to markets may also be important for reasons other than those associated with transport costs. The development of the European Community, with the abolition of internal tariff barriers and the coming of the Single European Market at the end of 1992, has encouraged some firms, particularly Japanese owned, to locate manufacturing plants within the EC in order not to be excluded from those developments. The establishment of the Nissan car plant on Teesside is a notable example in this respect.

As far as manufacturing activities are concerned, supplies of capital and land are not usually important determinants of location, as these inputs are usually available in a number of alternative locations. The availability of labour may however be an important influence on location. Labour is relatively immobile which means that labour may be in surplus in some regions but in short supply in other areas. A firm may find, therefore, that labour costs are higher in some areas - those of labour shortage - than in other areas. Where there are regional differences in the costs of labour these will clearly influence a firm's decision on where to locate. The availability of labour with particular types of skills will also be important to many firms and the speed with which unskilled labour may be trained and retrained will influence location decisions.

Other natural advantages include physical features and accessibility. For some firms, the physical features of the site are of prime importance. Firms which require very large quantities of water in their production processes will be attracted to river locations. Those firms which have serious problems of waste disposal, especially chemical industries, are also usually located on river-bank sites, while the problem of dust control has made it necessary to site cement works in fairly remote locations.

Firms may historically have been attracted to a particular location by the natural advantages of a site, such as the availability of raw materials or access to sources of energy. When these natural advantages have disappeared, for example following the exhaustion of a mineral deposit, or have become unimportant, the location may remain attractive because it yields important acquired advantages. These acquired advantages develop as the concentration of firms, and hence the industry, grows larger. Such advantages may include a skilled labour force, communications, marketing and commercial organisation, nearby ancillary industries, training colleges in the locality and a widespread reputation for products of the region. All of these factors can help to lower the costs of production and hence make some locations more attractive than others when a firm is considering the relocation of its plant.

In the UK and in many other developed countries, the geographical distribution of industry is not decided entirely by market forces: there are often government restrictions on the freedom of managers to decide the location of their firm's operations. Since the Second World War, successive UK governments have introduced various types of measures in order to control industrial location, basically in order to try and achieve a better regional balance of economic activity. The government, therefore, has had to interfere in the decisions of firms when siting their plants. Often this has involved providing incentives by way of grants and soft loans to firms which are prepared to move to areas of high unemployment, while also curtailing expansion in the more prosperous areas by limiting the granting of Industrial Development Certificates. Over the past 10 years, however, many of the traditional features of regional policy have been removed by the Conservative government which has reduced the amount of state interference in the location decision of managers, including the abolition of IDCs and reducing the availability of grants and loans. Despite this, some government incentives do remain, for example in 1980 the government introduced the first of a number of Enterprise Zones which provide various inducements for firms to move back to city areas. Firms which locate in Enterprise Zones have a long period of exemption from rates, very favourable tax treatment of capital expenditure, and speedy planning approvals. Such inducements, as well as other continuing aspects of regional policy, will have an influence on managers contemplating the relocation of their manufacturing capacity.

14 PRICE TAKERS AND PRICE MAKERS

A company is a price-taker in a market in which there is perfect (or near-perfect) competition. The demand curve in the market as a whole is downward-sloping, but no company in the market can satisfy a significant proportion of total demand. The price taker cannot influence market supply significantly and it can only sell whatever output it produces at the ruling market price. It will not sell below this price because there would be no point in doing so, and if it tried to sell at a higher price, demand would fall to zero. The company's individual demand curve is horizontal (ie. perfectly elastic) so that at any level of output, the price (average revenue per unit) and the marginal revenue per unit are the same. The individual firm will maximise its profits by producing up to the level of output where MC = MR = AR = P.

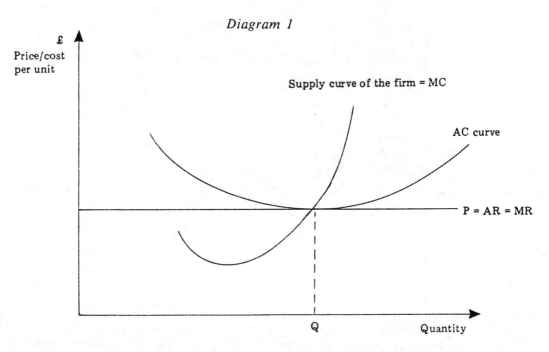

Diagram 1

In the long run, MC will equal MR where the firm's average cost curve is at its lowest point, so that no firm in the market is making supernormal profits.

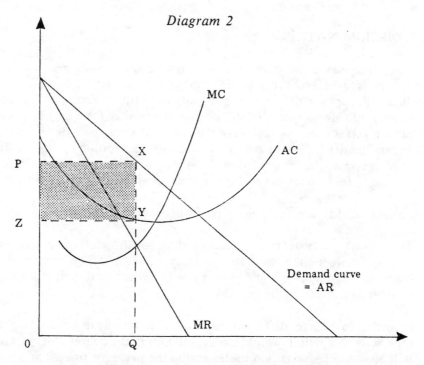

Diagram 2

In diagram 2, the monopolist maximises its profits at output Q, where MC = MR and the price will be P(=X) and average cost will be Z(=Y). Supernormal profits are earned, amounting to PXYZ, and the customer is paying higher prices than he would in a perfectly competitive market. The firm is not producing at the lower possible unit cost, and is a 'price maker'.

A comparison between a price-taker's and a price-maker's output, price and profits is shown in diagram 3. If a price-taker and a price-maker have exactly the same MC and AC curves as in diagram 3, the price-maker will be able to sell at a higher price and would produce less than a price-taker.

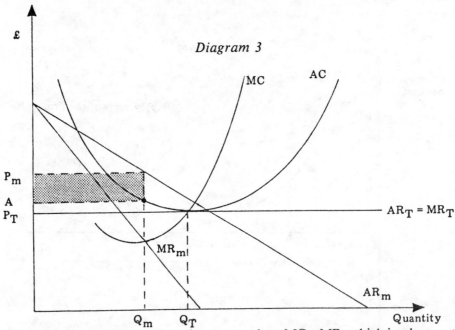

Diagram 3

In the diagram, the price-maker would produce up to where MC = MR, which is where output = Q_m, price = P_m and costs = A and supernormal profits are earned, as shown by the shaded area. The price-taker would also produce up to where MC = MR but in this case, this is where MC =AC =MR_T= AR_T, output is QT and the firm makes no supernormal profits in the long run (although an efficient firm might be able to do so in the short run).

15 PRICE DISCRIMINATION

Price discrimination is the process whereby a producer sells a given product or service at different prices to different consumers or to the same consumer at different points in time. An individual will, for example, usually pay more for a train journey to London departing before around 10 am than after 10 am. British Telecom charge more for a telephone call between 8 am and 1 pm than they do for the same call between 6 pm and 8 am. Price discrimination occurs when the supplier can identify different groups of consumers according to their willingness to pay for a given good or service, and can separate them into different sub-markets. Additionally, it must not be possible for consumers to buy in one sub-market and sell in another.

The necessary conditions for price discrimination to occur are:

(i)   There must be at least two distinct markets for the good or service and there must be no seepage between these markets. This means that it will be impossible or uneconomic for consumers to purchase in the lower priced market and re-sell in the higher priced market, ie arbitrage must not be possible.

(ii) In order to charge different prices the seller must be able to control the supply otherwise competitors would under-sell him in the dearer market. Clearly, a monopolist will be in the best position to determine the price (or prices) at which the good is sold.

(iii) The elasticity of demand must be different in at least two of the markets, ie the demand conditions in the separate markets must be different so that total profits may be increased by charging different prices.

Price discrimination as practised by a monopolist is illustrated in Figure 1, where it is assumed that there is a monopoly supplier of a given homogeneous product. It is further assumed that the monopolist can sell the product in two markets, A and B, and that demand in market A is more price inelastic than demand in market B.

220

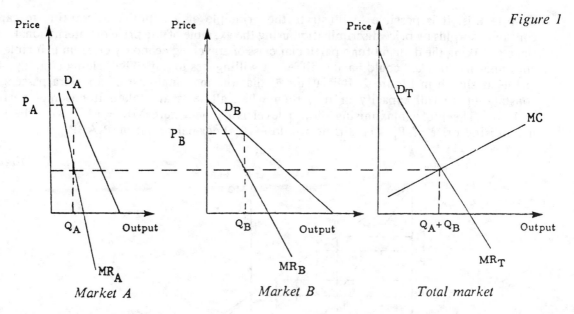

Figure 1

Market A   *Market B*   *Total market*

The first panel of Figure 1 shows market A, the second panel market B and the third panel the total market. Assuming that the monopolist aims to maximise profits he will follow the usual rule: $MR_A = MR_B = MC$, ie the marginal revenue from an additional sale in sub-market A should equal the marginal revenue from selling an additional unit in sub-market B, and this should equal the marginal cost of providing an additional unit of output.

The curve labelled MR_T in the third panel of Figure 1 is the horizontal sum of MR_A and MR_B, ie it is the combined marginal revenue curve for both markets. The monopolist therefore equates MC with MR_T to determine his total production. The total output level is divided between the two markets with Q_A being sold in market A at a price of P_A, and Q_B being sold in market B at a price of P_B. Thus consumers pay a higher price in market A where demand is inelastic than in market B where demand is elastic. As long as the markets can be kept separate, no trading between them will occur and the price discrimination will be effective.

Although this analysis helps to explain why different prices may be observed for the same product in different markets it is possible for suppliers to achieve a greater degree of price discrimination. For example, on some airline or rail journeys a large number of different prices may be charged for the same journey. The more a supplier is able to isolate every individual consumer and charge them a price equivalent to their willingness to pay then the closer the supplier comes to perfect price discrimination.

Price discrimination can be thought of as an attempt on the part of producers to capture consumer surplus. Consumer surplus refers to the difference between what a consumer is willing to pay for a good and what he or she actually has to pay to obtain it. Consumer surplus is usually measured on a diagram as the area above the price line and below the demand curve. If a supplier were able to practise perfect price discrimination it would extract the entire surplus from consumers. Perfect price discrimination occurs when the supplier isolates every individual consumer and charges them a price equivalent to their willingness to pay. If a market can be segmented in this way perfect price discrimination can be practised. However, the necessary conditions for successful perfect price discrimination are very exacting and it is rarely, if ever, observed. Clearly, there would be significant complications of identifying the willingness to pay of a large number of consumers in a given market, let alone the problems of keeping the sub-markets separate.

Despite this, it is possible to illustrate the principle of a supplier attempting to capture consumer surplus by price discrimination using the example of the price of international airline tickets. Taking the demand for a particular class of travel, eg economy class, in principle each consumer in this class could have a different willingness to pay. The pricing strategy of the airline is shown in Figure 2. It is assumed that the marginal cost of an extra passenger is constant up to full capacity of qm, then when all seats are taken it becomes perfectly inelastic. The profit maximising output level is q_1, ie where MR = MC, with the profit maximising price of P_1. The airline would earn abnormal profit of P_1ABP_5.

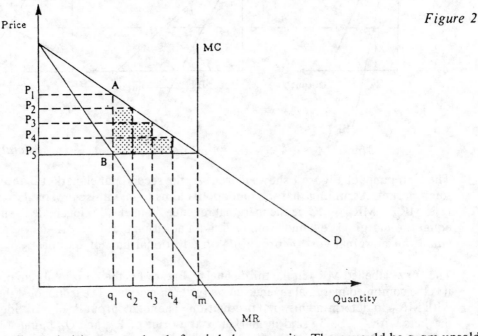

Figure 2

However the profit maximising output level of q_1 is below capacity. There would be q_1qm unsold seats. The supplier is able to fill these seats by charging different prices in different outlets. Some seats would be priced at P_2, some at P_3 or P_4, and some at the MC level of P_5. Different consumers will have a different willingness to pay, eg those who are able to book in advance but who have a relatively low willingness to pay may buy a ticket at price P_4. In contrast those who decide to travel at the last minute and have a higher willingness to pay can be charged at P_2. If there are unsold seats on the day of departure the airline may sell stand-by tickets at P_5, ie at marginal cost. If the airline is successful in discriminating between all these types of customers then it captures consumer surplus equivalent to the shaded area. This is added to the firm's abnormal profits. The more individual consumers the airline can isolate, the more they can add to abnormal profit. In this way many different prices are charged on the same flight for the same class of tickets. For this to occur however, the market conditions outlined earlier must apply, ie the airline must keep the individual markets separate and must prevent arbitrage taking place between consumers.

For price discrimination to occur, the supplier must be able to charge different prices to different consumers of similar goods in different markets. The markets may be separated from each other in a number of different ways:

(i)   *geographically* - as when an exporter charges different prices in the overseas market than in the home market;

(ii)   *by type of demand* - for example, in the market for milk where the household demand for liquid milk differs from the industrial demand for milk for making cheese;

(iii) *by time* – it is usual to charge a lower price at off-peak periods. This is the case in the telephone, electricity and travel industries;

(iv) *by nature of the product* – for example, with medical treatment, where if one person is treated he is unable to resell that treatment to another.

16 PRICE ELASTICITY OF DEMAND

The price elasticity of demand is a measure of the sensitivity of the quantity which will be demanded by consumers of a good to changes in the price at which it is available to them. The price elasticity over a particular range or 'arc' is expressed in the following equation:

$$\text{Price elasticity of demand} \ = \ \frac{\text{percentage change in quantity demanded}}{\text{percentage change in price}}$$

Because an increase in price will generally lead to a reduction in the quantity demanded in normal circumstances, and a decrease in price will lead to an increase in demand, the price elasticity of demand will be a negative number. In other words, price and quantity demanded are inversely related. Normally, the minus sign is ignored, and the absolute size of the elasticity is noted.

It can easily be appreciated from the above that in the case of goods where consumers are relatively insensitive to changes in price, the price elasticity of demand will be low: in other words, demand will be relatively inelastic. An example of such a good would be an 'essential' good for which substitutes are not readily available, such as milk or petrol. If an increase of 10% in the price of milk leads to a fall in the quantity demanded by 2%, the price elasticity of demand would be given by:

$$E \ = \ \frac{0.02}{0.10} \ = \ 0.2$$

A high price elasticity of demand indicates that consumers will cut down demand significantly when there is a relatively small increase in price. Non-essential 'luxury' items may fall into this category, or goods for which substitutes are readily obtainable such as butter. If an increase of 20% in the price of butter led to a decrease in sales of 30%, because of consumers choosing to buy margarine instead of butter, then the price elasticity of demand for butter will be:

$$E \ = \ \frac{0.30}{0.20} \ = \ 1.5$$

Unit elasticity occurs in cases where the percentage change in price is equal to the percentage change in quantity demanded which results. Where a small increase in price would lead to consumers cutting their purchases from the maximum quantity obtainable to zero, the situation is said to be one of perfect elasticity. The demand curve in such a case will be horizontal, parallel to the x axis where x is the quantity and y is the price. The term 'perfect elasticity' refers to a situation in which a change in price results in no change at all in the quantity demanded. Perfect inelasticity implies a vertical demand curve, parallel to the y axis.

A change in price will have an effect on the total revenue derived from sale of the product. If a small increase in price leads to an increase in total revenue, demand is inelastic – less than unity. If an increase in price leads to a fall in total revenue, and a decrease in price leads to a rise in total revenue, then demand is elastic – more than unity. Elasticity will vary at different ranges of price on a straight downward sloping demand curve, as illustrated in Figure 1.

Figure 1

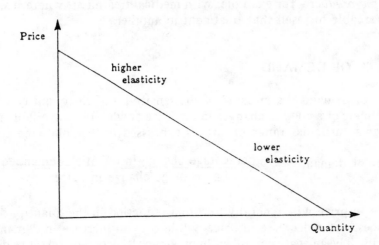

In the region of the demand curve at higher price levels, the percentage change in quantity deriving from a particular change in price will tend to be relatively high, because the quantities demanded in this region are relatively small. Similarly, at the bottom right end of the demand curve, demand is relatively inelastic because the demand quantities involved in this region are relatively high.

The price elasticity of demand indicates the effects that changes in price have on sales. If demand is relatively elastic, it may be unwise for a business to raise prices, since demand may fall significantly enough to reduce total revenue and possibly to reduce profits. If, on the other hand, demand is relatively inelastic, increasing prices may allow total revenue to be increased.

For those reasons, it is important that business people are aware of the concept of elasticity of demand. In practical situations, however, empirical data on elasticities of demand will probably not be easy to compile. Often, management's awareness of the elasticity relevant to their products consists of a general knowledge of the marketplace and pricing decisions will be a matter of informed judgement.

The price elasticity of demand will depend on a number of factors. Firstly, it will depend upon how necessary a product is for the consumer. Goods and services which are considered to be luxuries are the first which consumers cut down on if prices increase. Products which consumers perceive to be necessities will tend to have a low price elasticity. An example is petrol, around its current price range. In 1990, the Gulf crisis led to significant increases in the price of petrol, while the quantity demanded changed little. Consumers of petrol treated their use of petrol as necessary. They did not choose to consume significantly less by cutting down the number or length of journeys made or by reducing travelling speeds.

A particular brand of petrol will not necessarily show the same degree of inelasticity, since a small price increase for that particular brand can quickly lead to motorists switching consumption to other brands. This switching is likely to occur unless all brands of petrol increase in price by similar amounts at the same time.

The availability of substitutes for a product will also have an effect on its price elasticity. Goods and services which are perceived by consumers to have few acceptable substitutes will tend to have relatively low price elasticities. Petrol again provides an illustration, here of a good for which there is no readily available substitute in most cases. In cases where substitutes do exist, consumers can switch to the substitutes if prices rise.

The time period involved also affects the price elasticity of goods. The longer the time period being considered, the higher is the price elasticity. Although a motorist may not react over the short term to increases in petrol prices, in the longer term adjustments can be made to cut consumption if sustained higher price levels are anticipated. Public transport may be extended or improved to provide a better alternative to motor car use. Motorists may move to be closer to their place of work. Manufacturers may improve the fuel efficiency of motor car engines. Adjustments such as these did occur in many countries in the year following the large increases in oil prices during the 1970s, and the rise in oil consumption was curtailed as a result of measures towards greater energy efficiency.

Finally, the proportion of a consumer's income which a commodity takes up can have an influence on its price elasticity, where that proportion is significant. A motorist will probably be more sensitive to a 10% increase of price in car prices than a 10% increase in the price of newspapers for the reason that he spends a higher proportion of his income on motoring than on newspapers, which do not therefore loom so large in his perception of his pattern of spending. The 19th century economist Giffen found that poor people might increase the quantity demanded of bread, a product which took up a larger proportion of ftheir income, when its price increased. This could have occurred for the reason that the price increase would force them to reduce their consumption of other more expensive foods and therefore to consumer more bread to compensate for this.

17 ELASTICITY OF SUPPLY

Tutorial note: as with any exam question, plan what you are going to say before launching into your answer. The Stage 1 examiner suggested the following approach to this question.

'(1) Define, and explain the measurement of, elasticity of supply.
(2) Discuss the effect of time - market, short and long periods - with emphasis on the ability to alter the factors of production and the subsequent effect on costs.
(3) Explain the importance of the cost structure on supply; comment on the impact of raising output on the level and structure of costs in both the short and long run.'

Suggested solution

Supply is the quantity of goods which existing or potential suppliers would be prepared to supply to the market at a particular price. The upward-sloping supply curve illustrates the general fact that suppliers will be prepared to supply greater quantities of output as price increases.

The elasticity of supply is a measure of the responsiveness of supply to a change in price. This responsiveness is quantified as the percentage change in the quantity supplied divided by the percentage change in price. A good for which supply increases by 10% as the result of a 5% increase in price has an elasticity of 2.

The two limiting values of elasticity are infinity and zero. The elasticity of supply may be close to zero for very rare goods or services. It will not be possible to increase the quantity supplied as the price increases. Examples here would be the services of a top rock star, or a unique work of art. The supply curve will be vertical in cases where the supply elasticity is zero.

'Perfect' elasticity describes a situation where the elasticity of supply is infinite, and the supply curve is horizontal. Supply is said to be 'elastic' when the percentage change in the amount which producers want to supply exceeds the percentage change in price. Otherwise, supply is 'inelastic'.

Elasticity of supply will be determined in large part by:

(a) the time period over which its measurement is made;
(b) the opportunity cost of using the factors of production necessary;
(c) fixed costs and variable costs of production.

The effects of time on supply and to the response of supply to changes in price can be considered for analytical purposes in terms of three lengths of time period. Firstly, the market period reflects a short time period within which output cannot be altered. Supply of the commodity is limited by existing stocks of the good, and is therefore inelastic.

The 'short-run' period is long enough for output to be increased or decreased in order to alter supply of the commodity. However, fixed equipment such as plant and machinery cannot be altered in the short run. Although suppliers will be able to reduce output fairly quickly, suppliers will be able to produce larger quantities only if they are not already operating at full capacity. The degree of inelasticity in the market and short run periods will depend upon how much stock or how much spare capacity exists.

In the long run period, capital investment is possible. New factories and machines can be built, and old ones closed down. New firms can enter the industry. Over this length of period, supply elasticity will be relatively more elastic.

Costs can be analysed into fixed and variable elements, and it will be the opportunity costs of using the factors of production required in particular combinations which will determine the amount of a product which a firm will make available.

It is not surprising that an important determinant of the elasticity of supply is the change in costs as output is varied, since the basis of the supply curve lies in the costs of production. If the firm operates in perfect competition then the firm's marginal cost curve (from the point it intersects the average variable cost curve) is the firm's supply curve, as this indicates what quantities the firm will supply at different market prices. Clearly the costs of factors of production will affect the elasticity of supply. If demand for the firm's product increases, the supplier must attract more factors of production in order to increase output. If the cost of attracting new amounts of the factors is high then the costs per unit of output will rise rapidly as output expands. The stimulus to expand production from any given price rise would therefore quickly be choked off by increasing costs and supply would tend to be rather inelastic.

Conversely, if costs per unit of output rise only slowly as production increases, for any given increase in the price of the product there will be a larger increase in the amount supplied before the increase in costs halts the expansion in output. Supply in this case would therefore tend to be rather elastic.

Supply in the market period cannot be varied beyond the stocks which are available. Production costs have already been incurred, and an unanticipated difference in price will result in windfall gains or losses when judged against opportunity costs.

In the short run, increases in supply must come from greater output from existing capacity. This will involve additional variable costs, which must be met from sales revenue for supply to be worthwhile. Obtaining extra output may be more costly than existing output if plant is more efficient at the existing level of output.

In the long run, fixed costs as well as variable costs may change. Fixed costs may rise as capital investment occurs. The new capital investment necessary to increase supply in the long run may lead to economies of scale being gained, which will reduce unit costs. This may permit a large increase in supply over the long run period. However, it should be recognised that capital investment over this time scale - typically, several years - may be influenced by various factors other than the price mechanism. Demographic or other market changes foreseen by entrepreneurs, and corporate strategic objectives, are as likely to influence the investment decision as changes in current price levels.

18 SHORT RUN AND LONG RUN COSTS

Tutorial note: Avoid the pitfalls noted by the Stage 1 examiner: 'A common error was to identify the main costs and then to suggest which of these were long and which were short term costs. Other candidates omitted any reference to diminishing returns or returns to scale and produced very confused answers. A few interpreted the short and long run in terms of the equilibrium of the firm and the rise and fall of revenue and profits.'

The examiner suggested the following approach.

(1) Definition of and distinction between fixed and variable costs.

(2) Explanation of the short and long run.

(3) Analysis of fixed, variable, average and marginal cost in the short run - with appropriate diagrams and reference to the law of diminshing returns.

(4) Analysis of long run average cost curve - with diagram and reference to scale economies/diseconomies.'

Suggested solution

Economists base their estimates of production costs on the concept of opportunity cost, which is measured in terms of foregone alternatives. The opportunity cost to a firm of using resources in the production of a good is the revenue foregone by not using those resources in their best alternative use.

When considering production it is usual to distinguish between the short run and the long run. The short run is defined as that period of time over which the input of at least one factor of production cannot be increased. If the quantity of a factor cannot be increased in the short-run, it is called a fixed factor. A factor whose quantity can be increased in the short run is known as a variable factor. Corresponding to this division, total costs can be broken down into fixed costs and variable costs. As the firm has to pay the costs associated with the fixed factors whether or not the firm produces, these costs are called fixed costs. Examples are rent and rates, and interest payments on loans. As fixed costs do not vary as the level of output rises they are obviously the same whether output is zero or several thousand units. Those costs that do change as output varies are known as variable costs, for example, the cost of raw materials, power and labour. Total variable costs increase as the level of output increases.

The short run costs may be summarised as follows:

TC = TFC + TVC

where TC is total costs, TFC is total fixed costs and TVC is total variable costs.

Assuming that in the short run labour is the only variable factor and assuming a fixed capital stock, the firm will eventually encounter the law of diminishing returns and the average productivity of labour will begin to fall. Further, assuming that the firm buys its factors of production in perfectly competitive factor markets, factor prices will be constant no matter how much the firm buys. This implies that the eventual decline in the average productivity of labour must push up the average variable cost of production, as average variable cost and average labour productivity are opposite sides of the same coin.

Average variable cost (AVC) is obtained by dividing total variable cost by the quantity produced (Q), ie

$$AVC = \frac{TVC}{Q}$$

AVC reaches a minimum when the level of output is at the point where average productivity of labour at a maximum, because at this level of output the proportions between the fixed factor and the variable factor are at an optimum. At levels of output above the optimum the variable factor has progressively less of the fixed factor to work with and its average productivity declines. This results in higher AVC as output increases. Conversely, AVC falls until output reaches the optimum level, because at low levels of output the variable factor has too much of the fixed factor to work with. Thus, as shown in Figure 1, the AVC curve is U-shaped.

Average fixed cost (AFC) is obtained by dividing total fixed cost by the quantity produced, ie

$$AFC = \frac{TFC}{Q}$$

AFC declines continuously as output increases as shown in Figure 1, because the given level of fixed costs will be spread over a bigger level of output.

Average total cost (ATC) is obtained by adding together average fixed costs and average variable cost, ie

ATC = AFC + AVC.

Alternatively it can be obtained by dividing total costs by the level of output, ie

$$ATC = \frac{TC}{Q}$$

As shown in Figure 1 ATC is U-shaped. Initially, ATC declines as the fixed costs are spread over a larger output and initially the firm benefits from increasing returns to the variable factor. Eventually ATC increases as the influence of diminishing returns which pushes up AVC outweighs the decline in AFC.

Marginal cost (MC) is defined as the change in total costs resulting from changing the level of output by one unit, ie

$$MC = \frac{DTC}{DQ}$$

The shape of the MC curve is related to the behaviour of the marginal product (MP). At low levels of output the firm benefits from increasing marginal returns to the variable factor (ie increasing MP), thus MC will be declining. MC reaches a minimum at the level of output at which MP is at a maximum. When the firm encounters diminishing marginal returns (ie MP is falling), MC begins to rise. Hence, as shown in Figure 1, the MC curve is U-shaped. The MC curve cuts the AVC and ATC curves at their minimum points.

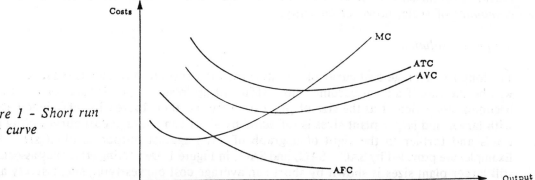

Figure 1 - Short run costs curve

The long run is defined as that period of time over which the input of all factors of production can be varied. Thus all factors are variable in the long run. The long run average cost (LRAC) curve shows the lowest possible cost of producing different levels of output given the production factors and factor prices. Figure 2 shows a LRAC curve. It indicates the minimum possible average cost of producing any level of output on the assumption that all factors are variable. The LRAC curve therefore indicates the minimum average cost of production for each level of output, given that plant of the appropriate capacity has been constructed. In Figure 2, the minimum average cost of producing output Q_1 for example is C_1.

If having built a plant appropriate to minimum long-run average cost at a given level of output, the firm varies its output, it will move along a short-run average cost (SRAC) curve. In Figure 2, as the firm changes its level of output with the plant appropriate for minimum long-run average cost of production at output Q_1, it works along $SRAC_1$. There is a SRAC curve tangential to every point along the LRAC curve. Figure 2 shows three such SRAC curves. Each SRAC curve lies above the LRAC curve except at the point at which it is tangent. The LRAC curve is sometimes known as an 'envelope curve' for this reason.

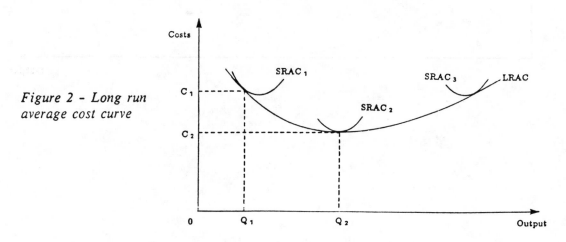

Figure 2 - Long run average cost curve

Figure 2 shows that the LRAC curve reaches a minimum when Q_2 units of output are produced. Up to this point the LRAC curve is declining because the firm is experiencing economies of scale. Economies of scale are those factors which bring about a reduction in average costs as the scale of production of the firm rises. As output is increased above Q_2, the LRAC curve rises, indicating that the firm is experiencing diseconomies of scale, which occur mainly because managerial functions become increasingly difficult to perform effectively as the size of plant increases.

19 DISECONOMIES OF SCALE

Tutorial note: like all examination questions, this one should be read carefully. The question is asking for an account of *diseconomies* of scale - don't be tempted to elaborate at length on *economies* of scale, however cogently.

Suggested solution

The long run average cost curve of a firm is usually considered to be a U-shaped curve. This will be the case if a firm becomes more efficient up to some specific size of plant and then becomes less efficient as the size of plant increases further. Increasing efficiency associated with larger and larger plant sizes is reflected by short run average cost curves lying at lower levels and farther to the right of a graph of costs against output as plant size increases. Examples are provided by SAC_1, SAC_2 and SAC_3 in Figure 1. Decreasing efficiency associated with still larger plant sizes is shown by short run average cost curves lying successively at higher levels and further to the right, for example SAC_4 and SAC_5. The resulting long run average cost curve (LAC) thus has a general U-shape.

Figure 1

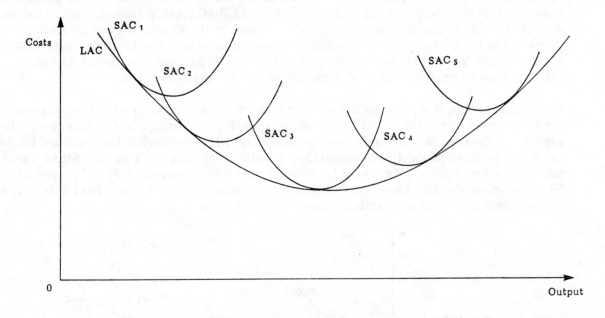

The forces causing the LAC curve to decrease for larger outputs and sizes of plant are called economies of scale. Among the more important economies of scale are (1) increasing possibilities of division of labour, (2) increasing possibilities of taking advantage of advanced technological developments and (3) the benefits of using larger machines.

The question arises as to why, once the plant is large enough to take advantage of all economies of scale, shown by SAC_3, still larger plant sizes are likely to result in less efficiency. Those factors which cause the LAC to rise are called diseconomies of scale.

There are a number of diseconomies of scale which relate to plant. The greater the physical space over which a plant is spread, the greater the likelihood of bottlenecks and the higher the costs of moving materials, labour and semi-finished goods from one place in the plant to another. Moreover, the larger the plant and thus the greater the volume of output the more likely it is that raw materials will have to be sourced from more distant suppliers, thereby driving up the transportation costs of incoming materials. Similarly the larger the output of a plant, the farther distances the finished product may have to be shipped to reach potential buyers, thereby raising the costs of transporting the product from the point of manufacture to the final consumer.

Another type of diseconomy of scale relates to the increasing difficulties and costs of managing ever larger enterprises. Management, like any other factor of production, is variable in the long run. However, it is argued that, beyond a certain stage, increases in management lead to less than proportionate increases in output and thus cause an increase in the long run average costs. It is argued that as the scale of output increases beyond certain levels, management becomes complex, managers are overworked and the decision making process becomes less efficient.

The decrease in the efficiency of management is associated with two factors. Firstly it is argued that there is loss of control of the top management once the firm has exceeded a certain size. Decisions may be delayed by the bureaucratic red tape of large firms. Also information can be deliberately or accidentally distorted as it passes through the hierarchical layers of management or may even be stopped for various reasons, for example because a certain group of managers have performed poorly and do not wish this information to be passed to a higher level. Clearly, decisions of top management will not be optimal if the information which is used to arrive at the decision is inaccurate or comes with time lags, during which crucial changes in the competitive environment of the firm may have taken place. Secondly, it is maintained that the uncertainty of the environment in which the firm operates - arising from the market conditions and the reaction of competitors - increases with firm size and that this greater uncertainty leads to less efficient decision-making.

The nature of industrial relations is also likely to change as plant size increases. The proportion of workers belonging to a trade union tends to increase with plant size, partly because the trade union finds it easier to organise a large number of workers in one location compared to the same number of employees spread over a number of small plants. The greater unionisation may partly account for the evidence that larger plants suffer from more strikes and other labour disputes than do smaller size plants. The greater the trade union power the more effective the union leaders will be in bargaining over wage rates with the result that large firms will pay higher hourly wage rates than small and medium sized firms. Thus, to the extent that larger size is accompanied by an increase in the ability of trade unions to secure higher wage rates, the large enterprise may find itself confronted with diseconomies of scale unless it takes steps to offset them by means of automation or some other productivity-increasing strategy.

The greater automation associated with large scale organisations may cause problems and may partly account for the greater incidence of labour disputes in large plants. A typical worker in a large plant is more likely to consider himself as a 'cog in a machine' with no individual identity. A worker in a large manufacturing plant is also likely to be considerably removed from the centre of decision making and may not feel highly committed to the firm and hence there may be a greater willingness to strike or engage in other disruptive activity. A related problem with large integrated plants, for example a steelworks, is that an industrial dispute involving only a few key workers may lead to a complete halt in production, as all the stages in the production process are interdependent.

It should be noted, however, that diseconomies of scale, especially those arising from managerial diseconomies, are not a necessary consequence of the increase in the scale of the plant. Positive features of the decentralisation of the decision-making process, the mechanisation of various managerial tasks, the improvements in budgeting of the activities of the various departments, a regular system of reporting at the different levels in the hierarchy, and the use of computers providing rapid access to information all tend to offset the problems of managing complex organisations, so that managerial diseconomies may not be a problem in the modern industrial world. Indeed, the empirical evidence from various studies of costs shows that the LAC curve is L-shaped. In other words, these studies do not provide evidence of diseconomies of scale in large scale operations.

20 PRECISE RELATIONSHIP

Utility is the satisfaction or pleasure that an individual derives from the consumption of a good or service. As used by economists, the term utility is not a property of a good or service, but the derivation of satisfaction from the use of such a good or service. Thus, for example, bread has the same property whether in a period of glut or famine. However, bread's true utility is to the consumer: the consumer's utility will vary according to the state of body and mind. Utility is therefore a condition unique to each individual.

The value of a good or service is its money worth. Economists in the nineteenth century, such as Alfred Marshall, argued that the utility of a product to a consumer determined its value. Today, economists accept that both supply and demand factors are important in determining the value of a product. For modern economists, therefore, the money value of a good is the same thing as its price, and in most markets price will be determined by the forces of supply and demand.

For each consumer the relationship between utility and price will determine the equilibrium of the consumer. From this it is possible to derive the consumer's demand curve for individual products. The cardinalist approach to the theory of demand postulates that utility can be measured. Various suggestions have been made for the measurement of utility; the most convenient measure is money, ie utility is measured by the monetary units that the consumer is prepared to pay for another unit of the commodity. Other suggestions are that utility may be measured in subjective units, called utils. So, for example, a consumer may obtain 20 utils of utility from a helping of beans, but only 10 utils from a helping of peas. It would be concluded from this that the consumer obtains twice as much utility from the beans as from the peas, and that the absolute difference between the utility derived from the beans and that derived from the peas is 10 utils. Clearly utility measured in utils is an abstract subjective concept, hence the most convenient measure is money.

Central to this approach to consumer equilibrium and the derivation of the demand curve is the concept of marginal utility and the hypothesis of diminishing marginal utility. Marginal utility is the extra utility derived from the consumption of one more unit of a good, the consumption of all other goods remaining unchanged. The hypothesis of diminishing marginal utility states that as the quantity of a good consumed by an individual increases, the marginal utility of a good will eventually decrease. Consider, for example, the utility derived by a thirsty consumer from successive glasses of milk. The first glass will yield a great deal of utility, ie the marginal utility of the first glass is very high. A second glass may be welcome, but is unlikely to yield as much utility as the first, and a third glass of milk is likely to yield even less utility. Once his thirst is quenched, the consumer may have no further desire for liquid refreshment and any more milk would yield disutility. The hypothesis of diminishing marginal utility appears to be a valid generalisation about consumer behaviour: the more a consumer has of a commodity, the less utility he is likely to derive from the consumption of an additional unit.

In the simple example of a single commodity, the consumer can either buy the commodity, eg good X, or retain his money income. Under these conditions the consumer is in equilibrium when the marginal utility of good X (MUX) is equated to its market price (PX), that is:

$$MUX = PX$$

If the marginal utility of X is greater than its price, the consumer can increase his welfare by purchasing more units of X. Similarly if the marginal utility of X is less than its price the consumer can increase his total satisfaction by cutting down on the quantity of X and keeping more of his income unspent. Therefore, he attains the maximisation of his utility when $MUX = PX$.

If now the consumer has to choose between two goods, X and Y, which have prices PX and PY, then he will maximise his total utility, subject to the size of his income, when he has allocated his income in such a way that the utility derived from the consumption of an extra penny's worth of X is equal to the utility to be derived from the consumption of an extra penny's worth of Y. That is when the marginal utility per penny of X is equal to the marginal utility per penny of Y. Only when this is true will it not be possible to increase total utility by switching expenditure from one good to the other. Hence the condition for equilibrium of the consumer is:

$$\frac{MUX}{PX} = \frac{MUY}{PY}$$

In order to derive the individual's demand curve for good X, consider what happens to this condition when the price of X falls:

$$\frac{MUX}{PX} > \frac{MUY}{PY}$$

The consumer can now increase his total utility by consuming more units of good X. This will have the effect of decreasing the marginal utility of X (because of the hypothesis of diminishing marginal utility) and he will continue increasing his expenditure on X until the equality is restored. Hence a fall in the price of a good will, *ceteris paribus*, lead to an increase in the consumer's demand for it, so the demand curve will slope downwards from left to right.

This result is illustrated in Figure 1. Panel (a) shows the total utility function of good X, which increases, but at a decreasing rate up to quantity qm, and then starts declining. Accordingly, the marginal utility curve of good X, shown in panel (b), declines continuously, and becomes negative beyond qm.

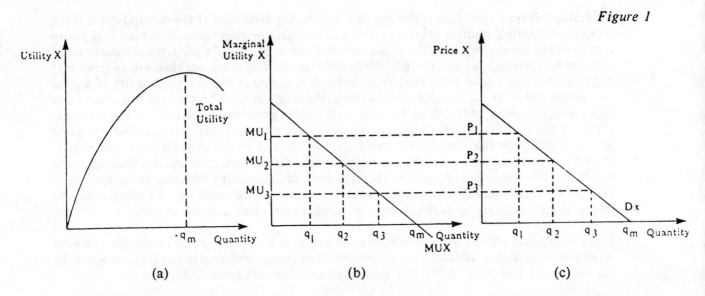

Figure 1

If the marginal utility is measured in monetary units, the demand curve for X, shown in panel (c), is identical to the positive segment of the marginal utility curve. At q_1, the marginal utility is MU_1. This is equal to P_1, by definition. Hence at P_1, the consumer demands q_1 quantity. Similarly at q_2 the marginal utility is MU_2, which is equal to P_2. Hence at P_2 the consumer buys q_2, and so on.

Clearly, marginal utility is not to be confused with total utility. Total utility is the sum total derived from all the units consumed. Marginal utility is derived only from the last unit consumed. It is this difference which explains what is known as the paradox of value. Early economists attempting to discover the relative prices of goods encountered what they considered to be a paradox: very necessary commodities such as water were observed to have prices that were low relative to the prices of many luxury commodities such as diamonds.

The paradox of value arose because the early economists believed that expensive goods should be ones with high total utilities and cheap goods ones with low total utilities. They were thus arguing that market values should be related to total utilities. However, in considering consumer equilibrium, the relevant concept is marginal utility, not total utility. Utility maximisation depends on equating market prices with marginal utilities not total market values with total utilities.

Water has a low price because it is in plentiful supply compared to the demand. Hence people consume water to the point where its marginal utility is very low, and they are not prepared to pay a high price to obtain a little more of it. Water therefore has a high total utility but a low marginal one and a low price. The value or price of water is determined by the demand and supply of water. Diamonds have a high price because they are in short supply - being relatively scarce - compared to the demand for them. Hence people must stop consuming diamonds at a point where marginal utility is still high. Diamonds therefore have a low total utility but a high marginal one and a high price. The value or price of diamonds is determined by the demand and supply of diamonds.

21 OLIGOPOLY

(a) An oligopolistic market is one in which a few firms supply the entire market for a particular good or service. Oligopoly means literally 'a few sellers'. An extreme form of oligopoly is known as duopoly, ie just two firms supply the entire market. Oligopolistic firms tend to be large leading to highly concentrated market structures. Oligopoly is the dominant form of organisation in the manufacturing sector of the economy.

The main effect of the small number of firms is to give each firm such a prominent market position that its decisions and actions have significant repercussions on rival firms. What one firm does affects the others. If one firm changes price, brings out a new product or steps up its advertising, the rival firms will take note and consider whether and how to respond. As a result, competition becomes highly personalised, with each firm recognising that its own best course of action depends on the strategies followed by its rivals.

Rivalry among oligopolists may involve either standardised or differentiated products. If the firms in an industry produce a standardised product, the industry is called a pure oligopoly. Such markets would include those of steel, aluminium, lead, copper, cement and newsprint. If a few firms dominate the market for a differentiated product, the industry is called a differentiated oligopoly. This is the case in the production of cars, cigarettes, television sets, toothpaste, soap, soft drinks and beer. There are usually considerable barriers to entry in oligopolistic markets. A common barrier to entry is the presence of substantial economies of scale. Where minimum average costs occur at output rates so large that a firm has to be big to be competitive, small scale firms incur unit costs so much higher that entry to the industry is generally not profitable. Also, the fact that existing firms produce well known highly advertised products and sell them through established marketing outlets works against the successful entrance of new firms.

(b) The characteristic of competition in oligopoly is that the product price tends to be 'sticky' ie it is slow to change with rival firms choosing to compete on terms other than price. This situation is considered in the kinked demand curve model of oligopoly behaviour. Figure 1 illustrates the situation where the firms in an oligopoly sell at a common price of P_1. At this price Firm A's sales volume is shown as Q_1 units. If Firm A independently lowers its selling price to P_2, rival firms are likely to react by lowering their prices to prevent Firm A from gaining sales, market share and profits at their expense. Figure 1 shows that if other firms match A's price cut then A's sales will be at Q_2 units. Thus A's demand curve for lower prices is shown along the path of the solid line extending down from point K in Figure 1.

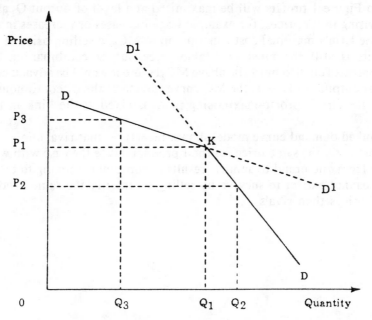

Figure 1

If Firm A should attempt to raise its selling price above P_1, for example to P_3, it is likely that rival firms will not follow the price increase. Firm A will thus become a high price seller and lose sales to rival firms. Figure A shows that at a price of P_3, Firm A's sales fall to Q_3 units. The higher price would not cause Firm A to lose all of its customers because some buyers will have strong enough preferences for A's brand that they are willing to pay the higher price.

Figure 1 thus shows that there is a kink in the demand curve facing Firm A, shown at point K, which occurs at the established price level of P_1. The demand curve above price P_1 is relatively elastic showing that rivals will ignore price rises and hence Firm A will lose sales if it raises price. Below price P_1 the demand curve is relatively inelastic, showing that rivals will follow price decreases and hence Firm A will not increase its share of the market if it cuts price below P_1.

When the firm's demand curve is kinked, its corresponding marginal revenue curve consists of the disjointed segments as shown in Figure 2. The upper segment corresponds to the more elastic portion of the demand curve, whereas the lower segment corresponds to the less elastic portion of the demand curve. The vertical discontinuity in the MR curve is at the prevailing price and output rate.

Figure 2

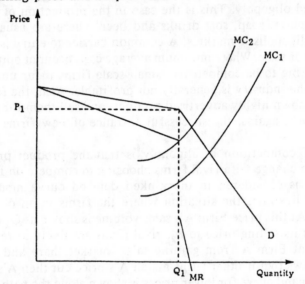

In Figure 2 the firm's marginal cost curve is MC_1. As profits are maximised where MC = MR, then in Figure 1 profits will be maximised at a level of output Q_1 and the price will be P_1. If rising input prices, for example wage increases or increases in raw material prices, shift the firm's marginal cost function up to MC_2, a selling price of P_1 and an output of Q_1 units is still the most profitable price-output combination. In fact, the firm's marginal cost function must rise above MC_2 before it would be advantageous to change either price or output. As long as the MC curve intersects the discontinuous portion of the MR curve, the firm's profit-maximising point is fixed at the kink in the demand curve.

The kinked demand curve model shows, therefore, that rival oligopolists will charge the same or nearly the same price for their products since the ease with which consumers can switch from one brand to another results in consumers moving to the low-priced sellers. Firms cannot expect to survive by selling essentially the same product at significantly higher prices than rivals.

For many firms in oligopolistic industries, the most attractive strategies for gaining sales, profits and market share are therefore found in market variables other than price. Successful non-price strategies are harder to duplicate and tend to have a longer-lasting effect on strengthening a firm's market position. Thus there exists a tendency among rival oligopolists to channel the main thrust of their competitive efforts into forms of product differentiation, for example product innovation, customer service, quality, performance, convenience of use, terms of credit, styling and design, advertising and sales promotion. In oligopolistic industries many millions of pounds are spent each year in efforts to maintain and promote differentiation.

Another aspect of behaviour in oligopoly is that of collusion, where a group of oligopolists make an agreement relating to the prices to be charged and/or the output level. The oligopolists attempt to act like a monopolist, by restricting output and raising price, thereby sharing amongst themselves the maximum profits that can be earned in the industry. The details of the agreement to collude - often known as a cartel agreement - will usually only be known to the oligopolist firms as such agreements are usually counter to legislation relating to competition.

In Figure 3 it is assumed that firms in an oligopoly have combined to act as a cartel. The cartel sets total production at Q_m, which is sold at a price of P_m. This is the output level and price that would result in the case of a monopoly.

Figure 3

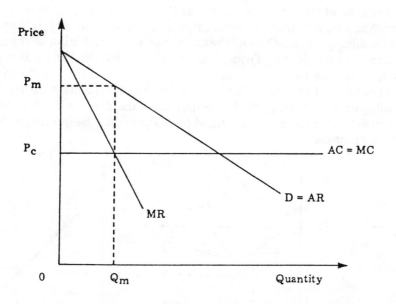

It is argued that cartels are likely to break down in the long term because individual firms have an incentive to cheat by producing in excess of their quota and by undercutting the agreed price. Where the individual oligopolist believes that other firms will adhere to the cartel agreement there will be an incentive to obtain a higher profit level by producing a greater output level than that agreed in the cartel arrangement and similarly lowering the price below that agreed with the other firms. However, the individual firm can only increase profit at the expense of other firms because the original agreed output and price level represents the maximum profit situation for the industry. Where the price cuts of the individual firm become known to others, then the market price may be driven down to the competitive price P_c, if rival firms also increase their output level and reduce their price. Maximum benefit for firms in the oligopoly is only achieved, therefore, if all parties to the cartel agreement agree not to cheat.

22 CHARACTERISTICS

A cartel, a merger and a holding company represent different ways by which firms may integrate their activities in order to exert control over the market in which they operate. There are fundamental differences however, in each of these three concepts.

(a) *A cartel*

A cartel is a form of collusive activity which is particularly associated with the desire of firms operating in an oligopolistic industry to secure joint profit maximisation. Such collusive activity may be either overt or tacit. A cartel arrangement which is overt usually takes the form of either an express agreement in writing, or an express oral agreement arrived at through direct consultation between the firms concerned. Alternatively, a tacit agreement is one of 'unspoken understanding' arrived at through firms' repeated experiences with each other's behaviour over time.

Under a full cartel arrangement, a cartel administration agency would determine the price and output of the industry, and the output quotas of each of the separate member firms in such a way as to restrict total industry output and maximise the joint profits of the group. The price and output level of the industry would then be the same as that of a profit-maximising monopolist.

This situation is illustrated in Figure 1, where it is assumed that the firms appoint a central agency, to which they delegate the authority to decide not only the total quantity and the price at which it must be sold so as to attain maximum profit, but also allocation of production among the members of the cartel, and the distribution of the maximum joint profit among the participating firms. Figure 1 shows that the marginal cost curve of the market is derived from the summation of the marginal cost curves of the individual firms. The central agency will set the price by first finding where the industry MR curve and industry MC curve intersects, at this output level the price will be obtained from the industry demand curve. Output level Q_3 and price P_1 are thus the industry profit maximising price-output combination.

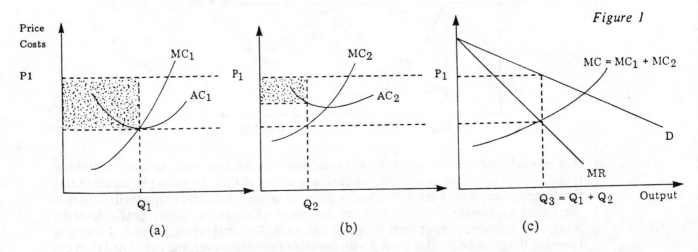

Figure 1

Figure 1 shows that (for simplicity) there are only two firms in the cartel. Each firm's cost structure is shown in Figure 1(a) and Figure 1(b) respectively. The central agency will allocate the production among the two firms by equating the MR to the individual MCs. The firm in Figure 1(a) will thus produce Q_1 units while the firm in Figure 1(b) will produce Q_2 units. Figure 1 shows that the firm with the lower costs produces a larger amount of output. This does not mean, however, that this firm will also take the larger share of the attained joint profit. The total industry profit is the sum of the profits from the outputs of the two firms, denoted in Figure 1 (a) and (b) by the shaded areas. The distribution of profits is decided by the central agency of the cartel.

Cartel agreements among competing oligopolist firms are aimed at reducing the uncertainty arising from their mutual interdependence. Cartels are likely to break down in the long run, however, as individual firms have an incentive to cheat by producing in excess of their quota and by undercutting the agreed price. If an individual firm believes that other producers will adhere to the cartel agreement then the firm will have an incentive to increase its own profit by selling more at a lower price. An individual firm can only increase its own profit at the expense of its competitors, because the cartel arrangement represents the maximum profit situation for the industry. In the long run the breaking of the cartel agreement will, if practised by all cartel members, result in lower profits for all members.

(b) *A merger*

A merger is the amalgamation or combining together of two or more firms. From the point of view of the firms a merger may have the advantage of enabling the firms to reduce production and distribution costs or it may enable it to expand its existing activities, or move into new markets. A merger may also enable the firm to remove unwanted competition and increase its market power.

Three major forms of merger activity can be identified.

(i) *Horizontal merger*

This occurs when firms combine at the same stage of production, involving similar products or services. Horizontal merger may provide a number of economies at the level both of the plant and the firm. Plant economies may come from the rationalisation made possible by the merger, for example production may be concentrated at a smaller number of enlarged plants so allowing technical economies of scale to be achieved. Hence there will be a reduction in cost per unit as the size of plant output increases. Firm economies result from the growth in size of the whole enterprise, permitting economies via bulk purchase, the spread of administrative costs over greater output, the cheaper cost of finance, and so on.

(ii) *Vertical merger*

This occurs when the firms combine at different stages of production of a good or service. Firms will benefit from such a merger by being able to exert control over quality and delivery of supplies if the vertical integration is 'backward' ie towards the source of supply. Inputs might also be cheaper, obtained at cost instead of cost plus profit. Vertical integration may also be 'forward' ie towards the purchaser. This may allow the firm more control of wholesale or retail pricing policy and provide more direct customer contact. Clearly, through vertical integration the firm will be able to obtain increased control of the market.

(iii) *Conglomerate mergers*

This refers to the merging of firms which produce different types of products ie there is a diversification into products with which the acquirer is not directly involved. The major benefit for the firm is that it allows the spreading of risk, in that the firm is in effect cushioned against adverse movements in demand against particular products. The various firm economies, noted above, may also result from a conglomerate merger.

A number of theories have been suggested in an attempt to explain merger activity. It is often argued that the achievement of lower average costs - and thereby higher profits - through an increase in the scale of operations is the main motive of merger activity. Plant and firm level economies have already been noted. To these may be added the 'synergy' effect of merger. This is the apparent '2 + 2 > 4' effect, where merger increases the efficiency of the combined firm by more than the sum of its parts. Synergy could arise from combining complementary activities as, for example, when one firm has an effective production division while another firm has effective marketing skills. It should be noted however, that the empirical evidence does little to support the view that there are specific and substantial benefits to either the economy or the acquiring firm's shareholders arising from merger activity.

(c)   *A holding company*

This is a company that controls another company or companies. Ownership may be complete (100%) or partial, with a shareholding of less than 100%. In its most extreme form a holding company is really an investment company. It may simply consist of shareholdings in a variety of individual, unconnected, business operations over which it exercises little or no control. The term also applies, however, to an enterprise which itself operates a portfolio of virtually autonomous business units. Although part of a parent company, these business units operate independently and probably retain their original company names, as is the case with Hanson Trust. The role of the parent company may be limited to decisions about the buying and selling of such companies with very little involvement in their operations or strategy. However, where the holding company is a substantial shareholder, then it will have the power to control the policies of subsidiary companies.

Holding companies are most frequently used as a means of achieving diversified growth, with the firm operating separate companies in different lines of production activity. There are a number of attractions to the firm from following a policy of diversified growth:

(i)   it allows the spreading of risks; a one product firm is extremely vulnerable to fluctuations in sales. A diversified company can expect growth in some product market areas to offset declines in others. Diversified firms are thus able to cross-subsidise temporary losses in a particular market with profits earned elsewhere;

(ii)   diversification allows the firm to reorientate its activities towards new areas of high growth and profit potential and away from mature and declining markets. As new products are invented and new consumer demands created a one product firm will be particularly vulnerable to both product and market obsolescence.

The advantages that a holding company can offer to the constituent businesses are based on the idea that each firm will operate to its best advantage if left well alone. These businesses will not have to carry the burden of a high central overhead since the head office staff of the parent company is likely to be small. The business units can, however, benefit from their membership of the group in such ways as the offsetting of profits against others' losses and the benefits of cheaper finance for investment from the parent company.

In reality, however, there may not be the skills at the centre to provide help since the aim is to keep the centre as slim as possible. The greatest weakness of the holding company structure is through its lack of internal strategic cohesion. There may be duplication of effort between business units or there may be very little synergy between the business interests.

23 VARIOUS TYPES

(a) Inflation is an increase in the general level of prices, which thus reduces the purchasing power or real value of money.

Inflation is a term that is associated with a situation in which there is a *continuous* tendency for prices to rise, and the increase in output of goods and services is continually less than the increase in spending in money terms.

Extremely high rates of inflation are sometimes referred to as runaway inflation or hyperinflation.

The two basic types of inflation are *demand-pull* inflation and *cost-push* inflation.

(i) *Demand-pull inflation* describes a situation in which there is excessive demand for goods and services, which 'pulls' prices up to a higher level.

One way in which demand-pull inflation occurs is an increase in credit lending by building societies and banks (including credit card companies). Borrowers use their loans to spend more, and there is an increase in the money supply because the money lent by the banks (which is an asset of the banks) finds its way back into the banks as customers' deposits (and these liabilities of the banks are included in various definitions of the money supply). Another way in which demand-pull inflation occurs is excessive borrowing by the government (also from banks), caused by government expenditure exceeding government income from taxation and other sources.

(ii) *Cost-push inflation* occurs when the cost of factors of production increases at a rate in excess of the current rate of inflation.

Wages costs are often regarded as a major cause of cost-push inflation. There is an *expectations theory* of inflation that the work force will try to achieve wage increases in anticipation of what inflation will be; this anticipation becomes a self-fulfilling prophecy, since actual wage increases themselves become a cause of inflation. Firms that award higher wages without improvements in productivity taking place must either accept a reduction in profits or pass on the higher costs to customers in the form of higher prices. Unless the workforce becomes more productive, and is able to create more output in exchange for higher wages, it is argued, inflation will be caused by this process of passing on higher costs into higher prices.

Imports are another possible cause of cost-push inflation. The UK is heavily dependent on imports, and if there is a fall in the foreign exchange value of sterling, the cost of imports will rise. Higher import costs either add to the cost of raw materials of UK manufacturers, who must pass on the higher costs into higher prices, or else directly affect the price of goods in the shops.

(b) Inflation can only be measured broadly because:

(i) individuals buy different goods and services and in differing quantities and so the rate of inflation for one individual will not be the same as the rate of inflation for another;

(ii) it would be impossible to monitor the prices of all goods and services.

An inflation index (or price index) can be constructed by taking a selected 'basket' of items and monitoring their prices at regular intervals (typically monthly). A base year (eg. January 1981) is selected for a price index level of 100 and subsequent changes in prices are measured as a monthly change in the index level.

In the UK, the main index for measuring inflation is the Retail Price Index which measures prices of a 'basket' of hundreds of items including the cost of housing, such as mortgage repayments for an average-sized mortgage.

Although the RPI is a very broad measure of inflation, it is nevertheless an indicator of inflation which receives wide publicity and attention from the government, trade unions and employers. It is also used for such purposes as the updating of social security benefits and the calculation of capital gains for taxation purposes.

24   IMPORTANCE OF MONEY

Money may be defined as any generally acceptable medium of exchange, ie it is necessary that a high proportion of the population should be willing to accept a particular commodity in exchange for their goods or services before that commodity may be regarded as being a money substance. Thus, for the benefits of a monetary market economy to be obtained, there must be a widespread confidence in the money substance established.

Many different substances have been used as money throughout the world, eg cowrie shells, cattle, gold and silver. The early forms of money were usually 'commodity moneys' ie they possessed an intrinsic use value, in addition to their value as a medium of exchange. Money in the modern economy has little intrinsic value, and is known as 'representative money', its value lying in its purchasing power rather than in any use to which the money substance itself may be put. Bank notes and coins are representative money, and widespread confidence in their purchasing power is vital to the successful operation of the monetary system. In the modern economy bank notes and coins only comprise a relatively small proportion of the total money supply, the main component being bank deposits.

The importance of money lies in the functions that it performs. It is possible to identify four different functions of money:

(i) *A medium of exchange*

As already stated money acts as a medium of exchange or means of payment. Money is unique in performing this function, since it is the only asset which is universally acceptable in exchange for goods and services. This is the most important function of money in an economy, because without money, the only way of exchanging goods and services would be by means of barter, ie by a direct exchange of goods or services.

A barter economy has severe limitations. The exchange of goods by barter will only occur when there is a 'double coincidence of wants', ie when two people at the same time have goods that the other wants and is willing to barter in exchange. A barter economy would tend to be a localised economy. It is unlikely that international trade would occur, for example, on anything other than a very limited scale.

It would be impossible to have an advanced economy based entirely on barter. An economy develops through the specialisation of individuals in a particular type of product or service ie through the 'division of labour'. By specialising, an individual is able to produce goods or services more efficiently and in greater quantities. This also applies to business organisations as a whole. These tend to specialise in particular types of product or service, for example in the production of capital goods such as machine tools, the provision of consumer durables like washing machines and televisions, or the provision of services such as banking, insurance, hairdressing and motor repairs. It would be impracticable for any advanced society in which so many specialised organisations exist to trade with each other and with consumers by barter.

As business organisations develop, they require people to work for them as employees. The division of labour within an organisation means that individual employees specialise at one particular job. In a monetary economy, employees are rewarded mainly by money wages or salaries. In a barter economy, however, there would be no obvious way of rewarding employees regularly with goods or services that the employees would be happy to accept; a steel worker, for example, would be reluctant to accept a girder in payment for a week's work. In a barter economy, therefore, people would not organise themselves into large stable business units.

For these reasons, barter trade is inefficient. It involves high transaction costs, for example in searching out the double coincidence of wants, and limits the willingness of individuals and organisations to specialise, hence they need to become more self-sufficient. The result is likely to be a sub-optimal use of resources. A monetary economy overcomes the drawbacks of a barter economy. There is no requirement in a monetary economy for a double coincidence of wants before exchange takes place, because someone giving goods or services will always be prepared to accept money in exchange. This is because the money so received can then be used to obtain goods or services they want from someone else either immediately or at some later date. Money, therefore, greatly reduces transaction costs, facilitates trade and reduces the risks of specialisation, which encourages greater specialisation, leads to more efficient use of resources and thus encourages economic growth and development which ultimately leads to higher living standards.

(ii) *A unit of account*

This refers to the use of money as a common denominator for the valuation of all goods, services and assets. This function of money is associated with the use of money as a means of exchange. Money is able to measure exactly what something is worth. It provides an agreed standard measure by which the value of different goods and services can be compared.

It is extremely convenient to be able to compare directly the relative values of all traded goods whatever their absolute values. This may be seen with the example of four products traded in a market, for example pigs, sheep, hens and corn. The relative value of these products must be agreed before exchange can take place. It might be decided that:

```
1 pig            = 0.75 sheep = 3     hens  = 1.5 bags of corn
```

It therefore follows that:

```
1 sheep          = 1.33 pigs  = 4     hens  = 2    bags of corn
1 hen            = 0.33 pigs  = 0.25 sheep  = 0.5  bags of corn
1 bag of corn    = 0.67 pigs  = 0.5  sheep  = 2    hens
```

There are thus twelve exchange rates in a market with four commodities. With money, however, it is possible to establish a common unit of 'value measurement' or 'account' by which the relative exchange values or prices of goods can be established. In the example above it might be established that:

```
1 pig            = 3M  (where M is a unit of money)
1 sheep          = 4M
1 hen            = 1M
1 bag of corn    = 2M
```

Clearly, transactions will be greatly facilitated as consumers need to acquire information on only four exchange rates. The use of money in this way also allows the valuation of assets, for example, for insurance or taxation purposes.

(iii) *A standard for deferred payment*

Money is extremely useful where a transaction involves an agreement to make a payment at a future date. When a good is bought the purchaser might not want to pay for it immediately, perhaps because he doesn't yet have the money, and instead asks for credit. Although selling goods on credit is not an essential feature of an economy it is an important aspect of all modern industrial economies. The use of money facilitates the credit mechanism and stimulates trade. The function of money in this respect is to establish, by agreement between buyer and seller, how much value will be given in return at some future date for goods provided now. A promise to pay a certain amount of money in the future is likely to be more acceptable to a creditor than a promise to hand over real goods or assets which might not even exist at the time of the initial transaction.

(iv) *A store of value*

Money acts as a store of value, or wealth, ie wealth may be held in the form of money. Money is not the only asset which acts as a store of wealth: assets such as land, buildings, machinery and works of art also perform this function. A major advantage in holding wealth in money form is that it is immediately spendable ie it may be used to purchase directly other forms of wealth or goods or services without delay. Money is thus a liquid store of value. Liquidity is the ability to transform an asset into a means of exchange with minimum delay and without significant penalty or loss of face value.

A liquid store of wealth can therefore be drawn on by its owner to obtain goods and services whenever he wants, and without having to wait to convert the store of wealth into a means of exchange. A house is a store of wealth, but if its owner wishes to use this wealth to buy something else, he must first sell the house and then use the proceeds from the sale to make his purchase. Clearly a house is not a liquid asset.

In order that it performs these functions effectively it is important that money should maintain its value over a period of time. The major cause of money losing its value is inflation. With low inflation money will adequately perform the function of a means of exchange. With very high inflation (and especially hyper-inflation) people might prefer not to use money at all. Instead they might prefer to revert back to a barter economy, or use alternatives to money such as gold.

Money should be a stable unit of account. However, the relative value of different goods and services varies over time because individual products or services do not each rise in price by the same percentage amount. Hence the relative value of goods becomes distorted which may cause confusion to producers and consumers.

Inflation undermines the function of money as a standard for deferred payment. During a period of inflation someone who incurs a debt will gain at the expense of the lender or creditor, because when the debt has to be repaid, its real value will have declined. For the same reason, a lender or someone who allows credit will lose out, and might therefore be reluctant to extend credit at all or lend money except at high interest rates. Also, long term contracts may only be agreed if they contain a clause whereby the buyer must pay the seller for the cost of any price inflation over the period of the contract.

Money is a poor store of wealth in a period of inflation. During inflation money loses some of its purchasing power or real value. This may cause people to store their wealth in different assets such as property or works of art which they do not expect to lose value.

25   THE BANK OF ENGLAND

Almost every country with a developed financial system has a central bank, and the Bank of England is the central bank of the UK. Basically, a central bank is responsible for the organisation and operation of its nation's official monetary and financial policies. The origins of the Bank of England may be traced back to 1694, when the Bank received its charter as a joint stock company. It was established specifically with the objective of raising a loan for King William III who required funds to finance a war which was being waged against France. Until after the Second World War the Bank remained a private company, which in theory pursued commercial profit-making objectives. However for many years prior to that time the Treasury had been the dominant force behind the Bank's activities. The Bank of England Act 1946 nationalised the Bank, with the state's acquisition of the whole of the Bank's capital.

The Bank of England has a very wide range of functions, probably as wide as those of the central bank of any other major industrial country:

(a)   *Banking role*

The Bank of England offers a wide range of conventional banking services to its customers. However, the composition of its customer base is very different from that of a typical commercial bank. There are relatively few private customers, such as the Bank's own staff, as well as some domestic institutions and private individuals. The Bank also maintains accounts for over a hundred overseas institutions, including the Bank for International Settlements, the International Monetary Fund and the World Bank.

The Bank holds a substantial volume of bankers' deposits. About 20% of these funds are made up of operational deposits, held mainly by the clearing banks to cover interbank fund flows arising from the cheque clearing process, and to be used for the purchase of notes and coin from the Bank. The remainder are non-operational non-interest bearing cash ratio deposits, which must be made by all authorised banking institutions under the conditions of the August 1981 monetary control provisions.

The British Government is also a customer of the Bank. The balances of the Government's accounts are centralised at the Bank. It is the responsibility of the Bank to ensure that any net deficit is financed and that any surplus funds are used to repay outstanding debt.

Budget deficits are usually covered in the long run by issuing gilt-edged securities; short term financing is covered by the issue of Treasury Bills. For day-to-day deficits the Bank makes available to the Government 'ways and means advances'.

(b) *National Debt management*

Following its role as banker to the Government, the Bank has responsibility for managing the National Debt. Thus the Bank has responsibility for financing the PSBR each year as well as funding a steady stream of maturing instruments arising from the large outstanding National Debt.

(c) *Production and distribution of bank notes*

The Bank has the exclusive right to produce and issue bank notes in the UK (the exceptions to this rule are the notes issued by the Scottish and Northern Ireland clearing banks). New notes (and coin) may enter the financial system through withdrawals of funds by the clearing banks from their accounts with the Banking Department of the Bank of England.

(d) *Lender of last resort*

A very important function of the Bank of England is to act as lender of last resort to the domestic banking sector. This role is considered crucial to the stability of the financial system as a whole. This does not mean, however, that the Bank guarantees the solvency of every banking institution in the UK. The situation is that the Bank is ready to accommodate shortages of cash in the banking sector. The assistance is provided against the background of the Bank's monetary control objectives. This means that assistance will only be provided in a manner which avoids excessive interference with the achievement of any official money supply growth or interest rate targets. So, for example, while the Bank will not deny cash to the banking system, it may charge a high and punitive rate for the provision of that cash, in an attempt to put pressure on interest rates and thereby undermine the root cause of the initial cash shortage. In general the Bank acts as lender of last resort by purchasing (rediscounting) commercial or Treasury bills from the banking sector. This assistance is provided via the discount houses, which act as intermediaries between the Bank and the commercial banks.

(e) *Management of the Exchange Equalisation Account*

The Bank manages the Treasury's Exchange Equalisation Account (EEA), which contains the UK's gold and convertible currency reserves. These reserves, together with the EEA's sterling capital, are used as the basis for the Bank's foreign exchange market intervention. For much of the period 1945 to 1972 the role of the Bank was to maintain a fixed exchange rate. From 1972 the pound was allowed to float on the foreign exchanges. There has been periodic intervention to smooth exchange rate movements. Under Nigel Lawson's Chancellorship in the late 1980s, this intervention was directed at a policy of 'shadowing' the mark. Under the European exchange rate mechanism (ERM) which sterling joined in October 1990, the Bank is required to take action if sterling drifts beyond 'divergence indicators' against other currencies.

(f) *Control of monetary policy*

Probably the most important function of any central bank is to undertake monetary control operations, with the view of achieving specified monetary policy objectives. In relation to monetary controls, the Bank of England has a large array of operational methods and instruments available for its use. The major activities are:

246

(i)   *Market intervention*

Through the use of open market operations, the Bank enters the market and buys or sells bills or securities, thus influencing the financial asset portfolio held by the private sector. In this way the Bank influences the level of liquidity within the financial system, as well as the level and/or structure of interest rates.

(ii) *Lender of last resort*

For monetary control purposes, it is the conditions of lending, and particularly the rate of interest charged, which are crucial. If funds are provided only at a penal rate, this may push interest rates upwards, thus depressing the demand for loans and hence money supply growth.

(iii) *Non-market controls*

The Bank may use a number of instruments which are designed to attack directly the creation of bank credit. For example, special deposits, involving banks being required to place funds with the Bank equal to a certain percentage of a subcategory of their sterling deposits, were used throughout much of the 1960s and 1970s. While special deposits earned interest from the Bank, they could not be used as part of the reserve base of the banks. Formal directives, incorporating interest rate ceilings on deposits, lending ceilings and qualitative guidelines, were implemented periodically until the late 1970s. Also, informal 'moral suasion' has occasionally been used to bring pressure on the banking sector, with the objective of persuading institutions to follow a particular course of action.

(g) *Supervision of authorised banking institutions*

Under the terms of the Banking Act 1987, any institution within the UK which wishes to take deposits from the general public is legally obliged to register with the Bank of England, and must obtain authority from the Bank in order to operate a banking business. The Act places upon the Bank a formal duty of broad supervision over the activities of all authorised institutions. Within the requirements of the 1987 Act the Bank may be seen as supporting, advising and controlling the institutions of the UK domestic banking sector. Above all, however, the Bank's efforts are directed towards maintaining the integrity of the financial system and hence the confidence of the general public in its stability and continuity. In particular the Bank seeks to ensure that individual institutions follow prudent policies of liquidity management, which provide secure liquidity without undue exposure to excessive costs.

(h) *Other supervisory responsibilities*

The Bank performs a broad supervisory role in relation to the activities of UK financial institutions. In particular, the Bank seeks to maintain the good conduct of City institutions, in accordance with their established traditions. The Bank also attempts to keep open the channels of communication between all of the major sectors of the financial system and the government.

26 DEPOSIT CREATION

Bank deposits can come into being in three ways:

(a) *When a bank receives a deposit of cash (notes and coin)*
When a person deposits cash in his bank he receives a bank deposit of the same money value. The bank's assets and liabilities have increased by equal amounts. A bank's liabilities consist of claims against the bank. The bank's deposits are liabilities because it is committed to meet all its depositors' demands for cash and to honour all cheques drawn on these deposits. The cash is an asset because it is a claim against the Central Bank.

(b) *When a bank buys securities with cheques drawn on itself*
The seller of the security (usually government bonds) will pay the cheque into his bank account and his deposit will increase by the amount he has been paid for the security. There has been no transfer of funds from any other depositors, and so the total of bank deposits will increase by the amount paid by the bank for the securities, while the assets of the bank will rise by the value of the securities held.

(c) *When a bank makes a loan*
The most important method by which bank deposits come into being is by means of a bank's lending operations. On any particular day only a relatively small portion of the funds held by banks will be withdrawn. There may be a very substantial outflow of funds, but there is also likely to be a very substantial inflow. Hence, the net change in a bank's holdings of cash on any particular day is likely to be relatively small. The banks are therefore able to lend a substantial part of the funds deposited with them. As lending is the most profitable of a bank's activities (it charges interest on its loans), it is to be expected that all banks in the system do this. The effect will be a multiple expansion of credit following an initial deposit of cash.

This process may be illustrated in the following example. It is assumed that banks wish to maintain a cash ratio of 10%, ie they maintain a ratio of 10% cash to total deposits. This means that banks will lend 90% of all cash deposited with them. If therefore a bank receives a cash deposit of £10,000 it will lend £9,000 in the form of advances. The effect of these transactions in the bank's balance sheet is set out below:

Liabilities	£	Assets	£
Deposits	10,000	Cash	10,000
Deposits	9,000	Advances	9,000
	19,000		19,000

The bank has not made the loan in cash, but simply credited the sum of £9,000 to the borrowers. Bank deposits have increased by £9,000 but so have the bank's assets in the form of a claim against the borrowers. Having been granted loans, borrowers will seek to spend them, with cash being withdrawn from the bank to meet these expenditures. The £9,000 used by borrowers to make purchases will flow back into the banking system as someone else's deposits. A further 90% of these deposits (ie £8,100) will be re-lent. Again, this will flow back into the banking system with 90% of these deposits (ie £7,290) being re-lent.

It is apparent that this process will continue, and as a result of the initial cash deposit, there will be an expansion of bank lending in the form of a diminishing series:

£10,000 + £9,000 + £8,100 + £7,290 + + . . .

Clearly, the initial deposit of £10,000 leads to an eventual increase in bank deposits many times greater than the initial cash deposit. The increase in bank deposits comes about because of the lending activities of the banks in their search for profits. Hence the relevance of Hanson's quote that 'Bank deposits . . . are largely created by the commercial banks themselves'.

If banks always maintain cash reserves equal to some given proportion of their deposits, then their ability to create bank deposits is determined by the amount of cash they can acquire. If we express the cash ratio as r, the level of bank deposits as D and the amount of cash held by the bank as C, then:

$$D = \frac{1}{r} \times C$$

The effect of any change in the cash reserves may therefore be expressed in the form:

$$\Delta D = \frac{1}{r} \times \Delta C$$

In the example used above we have:

$$\Delta D = \frac{1}{0.1} \times 10,000$$

Hence an initial cash deposit of £10,000 leads to an eventual increase in bank deposits of £100,000. A cash ratio of 10% therefore implies a credit multiplier of 10.

Banks are therefore able to create deposits to a much greater value than the cash in their possession. However, because they must maintain some safe ratio between their cash reserves and the level of total deposits, the size of the cash ratio sets the upper limit on the extent to which bank deposits can be expanded following an initial deposit of cash.

It should be noted that an individual bank does not create credit simply by expanding its deposits by some multiple of its cash reserve. An individual bank doing this would quickly experience a net outflow of cash, as it was forced to honour cheques drawn on these deposits and such a situation could not continue for long. Instead, each individual bank simply re-lends a part of whatever is deposited with it. The effect of this, however, is to create a situation where the combined total level of deposits held by all banks is a multiple of their combined cash reserves.

The process outlined above is somewhat simplified and in practice may be different, although it is true that when a single bank makes a loan it is likely to lose cash to other banks. A rise in the cash reserve is, however, likely to affect all banks at the same time. Thus they will all be making loans so that inter-bank indebtedness will tend to cancel itself out. The individual bank is not likely to lose cash to other banks unless it pursues a lending policy very much out of line with these other banks.

It has also been assumed that bank customers tend to hold a constant amount of cash. This is not very realistic as both cash and bank deposits are used as a means of payment. It is much more likely that an increase in the money supply (associated with an increase in the level of bank deposits), especially if it is associated with an increase in income, will lead to an increase in the public's demand for cash. A cash leakage at each round of lending and spending will substantially reduce the size of the multiplier. If it is assumed that the total amount of cash held by the public increases or decreases as the total volume of bank deposits rises or falls, then the effect of the credit multiplier on total bank deposits is not $\Delta D = \frac{1}{r} \times \Delta C$, as devised above, but:

$$\Delta D = \frac{1}{c+r} \times \Delta C$$

where D, r and C are as above, and c is the ratio of cash held by the public to the volume of bank deposits.

Thus with r = 10%, and the public choosing to have cash:bank deposits ratio of one-fifteenth (6.67%), then the total increase in bank deposits arising from an initial increase of £10,000 would be

$$\Delta D = \frac{1}{0.0667 + 0.10} \times 10,000 = £60,000$$

Hence the credit multiplier is reduced to 6.

This explanation has also assumed that banks stick closely to the given cash ratio. If banks choose to maintain cash reserves above the conventional (or legal) cash ratios, an increase in cash reserves may have little or no effect on the level of bank deposits.

Finally, it has been assumed that banks can extend loans because there are willing customers eager to borrow from banks. This must be qualified in two ways: firstly, customers might not want to borrow at the interest rates charged by banks; secondly, banks may not wish to lend to high risk customers - there must be prudent management of lending operations by the banks themselves. These factors would constrain the growth of a bank's deposits.

27 CONFLICTING AIMS

A commercial bank is a profit-making organisation, and will therefore seek to make a satisfactory return on its investments and lending. At the same time, another function of a bank is to provide a mechanism whereby depositors can transfer funds - eg. by writing cheques or by standing order and direct debit payments - and the bank must be able to meet calls for withdrawals and for transfers of funds to other banks. The need for some liquidity means that a bank must have enough liquid assets to meet these demands from its short-term creditors/liabilities.

The system of paper money and credit transfers between bank accounts has its origins in the activities of credit creation which developed from the seventeenth century onwards. Banks would receive deposits of silver, and provide paper certificates to the owner crediting the amount of the silver to the depositor. The depositor had the right to withdraw the silver if he wanted to, but otherwise the banks would retain it. The banks discovered that they could lend some of the silver out and receive interest, since they could be confident that the depositors would not all require their silver at once, but enough needed to be retained to meet the immediate potential needs of depositors. Hence the need for the modern banker to keep sufficient liquid assets to meet likely demands of customers for cash.

The Bank of England will monitor the ratio of a commercial bank's liquid assets to its total assets, to ensure that the liquid asset ratio remains suitably high. Experience will show what proportion of its total assets a bank ought to keep in liquid or near-liquid form. Liquid assets on the whole earn a lower return than not-so-liquid assets because interest yields tend to be higher for investors in longer term investments. Thus a bank will make bigger profits from longer term investments (eg. loans to companies and personal loans) but at the same time it must retain sufficient liquidity.

Some bank lending and investments involve greater risks of default by the borrower. A bank will be willing to take some risks with its lending; if it did not, it would lose good business as well as bad customers. To compensate it for the higher risk of default, a bank will normally charge a higher rate of interest to the borrower. Provided that bad debts are not a serious problem (as they appear to have been with much UK bank lending to developing countries) high-risk lending is more profitable. However, banks are the guardians of depositors' money and they must be able to retain the confidence of their depositors who might otherwise withdraw their funds from the bank.

Banks must therefore demonstrate prudence in much of their lending, avoiding excessive high-risk lending and, in many cases, insisting on security for a loan. Companies might be expected to give a fixed and a floating charge as security for a loan, for example. If the borrower defaults, the bank will then be able to sell off the secured assets in order to recover the debt. A drawback to secured lending is that it can discourage borrowers, and so banks can lose business and profits by insisting on security for loans. Several US banks have succeeded in taking business away from the UK clearing banks in recent years by not demanding security for large loans they have made to companies.

Liquidity, profitability and security are therefore conflicting aims, and commercial banks must try to reconcile them so as to achieve a satisfactory balance between the three. This is evident in the asset structure of the banks.

Every bank keeps some till money and operational deposits with the Bank of England (which act as the bank's own bank accounts). These are fully liquid assets which earn no interest but which are needed to meet the demand for cash withdrawals by customers and transfers of funds to other banks (to settle the balances on net transfers by cheque etc. between customers of the banks). In total these are perhaps 2% of a bank's total assets.

A bank will also hold near-liquid reserves which it can convert into liquid resources very quickly and with little risk, should it need to do so. These consist of:

(i)   investments in bills of exchange (mainly bills issued by other banks, but also some Treasury bills of the government and bills issued by local authorities) which are held to maturity or sold if need be in the money markets;

(ii) money market loans, especially deposits of funds by the bank with the discount houses, and also certificates of deposit issued by other banks, and local authority debt instruments.

Banks also buy British government securities (gilts), which may have a short period to go to maturity but which, if they have a longer term to maturity, can be sold on the stock market - albeit at some risk of a capital loss. Gilts tend to give a bigger yield than bills or market loans, but the risk of the investment is a little greater.

About 20 to 30% of a bank's total assets will take the form of these liquid or near-liquid (and relatively secure) items.

About 70% of a bank's assets consist of loans to customers, mainly in the UK private sector (company loans and personal loans). Most loans are short to medium-term, although the banks do have some mortgage lending over a longer term. This lending offers the biggest returns, but at comparatively high risk; hence the insistence in many cases on suitable security. The loans are mainly fixed term, so that the bank cannot insist on immediate repayment on demand, and so they are relatively illiquid. However, since up to 30% of the bank's assets are in liquid or near-liquid form, the bank should not expect to need the remaining 70% in liquid form.

Note. A bank's assets also include its premises and equipment, which are its fixed assets for use in banking operations, but these essential items are a very small proportion of a bank's total asset structure.

28 NBFIs

Tutorial note: a good answer to this question requires knowledge of the nature of the *concept* of 'financial intermediary' and of the *institutional structure* in which NBFIs are placed, and an explanation of the relationship of the NBFIs' services to the long term financial market.

Suggested solution

The NBFIs are those financial intermediaries excluding the banks. The NBFIs may be classified as follows:

(1) Deposit-taking NBFIs
    (a)   Building societies
    (b)   Finance houses
    (c)   National Savings Bank

(2) Non-deposit-taking NBFIs
    (a)   Insurance companies
    (b)   Pension funds
    (c)   Unit trusts
    (d)   Investment trusts

Financial intermediation refers to the activity of channelling funds between those who wish to lend and those who wish to borrow. Where an individual passes money to an institution which will lend or invest it on his behalf, eg when he puts money into a building society or finance house, pays insurance premiums or buys shares in an investment trust or unit trust, these institutions are the financial intermediaries.

An intermediary buys 'primary securities', eg shares, mortgages, or promises to repay loans, from the 'ultimate borrowers' with funds obtained from 'ultimate lenders' to whom it issues claims on its behalf, eg insurance policies, deposit accounts, unit trust units, investment trust shares. These claims, its own liabilities, are 'secondary' or 'indirect' securities. Financial intermediation can thus be defined as the purchase of primary securities from ultimate borrowers and users of funds and the issue of indirect claims to ultimate lenders and investors.

Basically, then, financial intermediaries come between lenders and borrowers not as agents for one or the other but as independent operators, seeking profits themselves (except for mutual societies which are non-profit-making), and making separate contracts between themselves and lenders and borrowers. Their essential function therefore is to organise a vast flow of funds.

Building societies are 'mutual' institutions, owned by their members, and not by shareholders. The exception to this is the Abbey National Building Society which became a public limited company owned by shareholders following its flotation in July 1989. The role of the building societies is still very specialist even though there has been movement in recent years by some of the larger societies into non-traditional activities. The building societies specialise in the provision of loans for the purchase of dwellings and related expenditure, eg home improvements, with the security being the mortgage on the property involved. The building societies dominate the provision of mortgage loans in the UK, accounting for about 75% of the total outstanding mortgage debt. Most building societies offer a wide range of assets to savers, including normal deposit accounts, ordinary share accounts, high interest (limited access) accounts, subscription shares, term shares, save-as-you-earn (SAYE) facilities, and accounts with money transmission facilities. The objective of the major societies appears to be the attraction of the widest possible range of savers, including those from the corporate sector.

Finance houses specialise in the provision of medium term credit, both to individuals and to the corporate sector. Historically straightforward hire purchase facilities have dominated their activities but the scope of their business has expanded and today many finance houses provide facilities relating to contract hire, leasing, factoring, and personal loans. In recent years finance houses have emphasised the industrial and commercial aspects of their business rather than the consumer side. Finance houses commonly operate through branch networks and often provide their facilities through retailers as commercial dealers at the point of sale. The retailer or dealer will arrange the credit terms to suit the customers' requirements. Finance houses raise the bulk of their funds from banks and other financial institutions.

The National Savings Bank provides its facilities through post offices, and these facilities are available to individuals and a variety of specialised bodies including building societies and government departments. The NSB offers ordinary accounts, which guarantee a fixed rate of interest with part of the interest payment being tax exempt, and investment accounts which pay competitive interest rates with funds subject to one month's notice of withdrawal. All monies deposited with the National Savings Bank are invested by the National Investment and Loans Office. Ordinary account funds are invested in government and government-guaranteed securities and any financial surplus remaining after interest has been paid to depositors is paid to the Treasury. Investment account funds are paid direct to the Treasury's National Loans Fund. The funds deposited with the National Savings Bank contribute to the financing of the public sector borrowing requirement.

The basic operations of the insurance companies relate to the spreading of risk, both between individuals and companies and through time. There are two broad categories of activity:

(1) General business, which involves the provision of insurance against specific risks such as fire, theft or accident. The policy holder subscribes a premium covering a fixed period of time, and in return will be compensated if a loss is incurred. Inflows of funds are placed mainly in short term assets which may be realised quickly and without danger of significant capital loss.

(2) Long-term business relates to the provision of life assurance, which pays a capital sum on the death of the person whose life is insured, and to long-term savings schemes, which may involve an element of life cover should the person named in the policy die before the policy matures. As the liabilities arising from this business are generally longer-term, the insurance companies utilise the inflows of premium payments to purchase primarily long term securities, and investments which are likely to generate capital growth, as well as a continual stream of income payments. The insurance companies are large holders of gilt-edged securities and equity shares, and their activities are very important to the successful operation of the Stock Exchange.

Occupational pension schemes collect payments from contributors during their working lives in order to provide a regular pension after retirement age has been reached. The evaluation of an individual's life expectancy and the acceptance of the risk attached to this calculation are crucial to the calculation of the regular amount of an individual's pension. The large membership of most funds which bear this risk allows for the spreading of the risk, as well as for the familiar risk-spreading from asset portfolio diversification. During the 1980s, pension funds have grown rapidly partly because of the favourable tax treatment of contributors to their funds. Also the government has encouraged individuals to join occupational pension schemes in order to reduce individuals' reliance on State pension provisions. Traditionally pension funds have purchased large volumes of company securities. They also hold substantial amounts of government securities and have large investments in land and real property in the UK. The assets structure of pension funds is very much as would be expected given the nature of their liabilities, which are basically long-term and which tend to rise broadly in line with the incomes of their contributors.

Unit trusts are open-ended funds in which individuals and companies may invest in order to obtain a share in the income and capital gains generated by the trust's assets. They are 'open-ended' in the sense that they may expand or contract according to customer demand for 'units'. There is no secondary market in units; rather the unit trust will create new units according to demand, and will sell them directly to the purchaser. Furthermore, the unit trust will repurchase units from holders on demand. Unit trusts thus provide a convenient means for individuals and companies to obtain a share in a much larger and more diversified portfolio of assets than they are likely to be able to hold directly. The assets of units trusts are predominantly in the form of ordinary shares in companies.

Investment trusts are limited companies whose business largely relates to investment in financial assets. These institutions obtain funds through the issue of equity shares, through borrowing, retained income and realised capital gains from previous investments. Their asset portfolios are dominated by holdings of equity shares. The broad objectives of an investment trust company will determine the general nature of the assets portfolio held. Some funds are general, whilst others specialise in particular geographical areas or industries; some aim for capital growth while others seek high income levels. Shares in listed investment trusts may be bought and sold in the Stock Exchange. The investor in an investment trust does not buy the underlying assets held by the trust (which is the case for an investor in a unit trust); rather he purchases shares in the investment trust company, and thus holds indirectly a diversified assets portfolio under professional management.

29 FORMS OF BUSINESS CREDIT

Tutorial note: in discussing the importance of forms of credit, you should try to consider the issue both from a broader economic viewpoint and from the point of view of the business itself.

The following comment made by the Stage 1 examiner may also be useful if you made the mistake which he refers to:

> 'The main mistake made was the confusion of credit with finance. There are several methods of financing a business which do not fall within the definition of credit. Credit is the granting or use of goods or services without immediate payment, and it implies a debt which has to be repaid. Thus, an issue of debentures is a form of credit but an issue of shares is not.'

Suggested solution

Credit enables firms and individuals to purchase goods and services without paying for them immediately. Credit may be defined as any form of deferred payment for goods and services.

Credit is available to businesses in a variety of forms. As a general rule, the length of credit should not exceed the life of the asset which it finances. The various forms of credit differ in the time scale over which they are provided. Credit may be categorised as taking the forms of trade credit, bank credit or consumer credit.

For the purposes of short-term credit, almost all businesses make use of trade credit, which is the credit provided by suppliers of raw materials, components and other goods and services in the normal course of trade. Trade credit is typically granted for 30, 60 or 90 days before invoices must be paid. Trade credit permits a producer to defer payment until after materials or services purchased have been used in production, and thus reduces the level of working capital which would otherwise be necessary for the business to operate. If the business supplies on trade credit to other businesses, it will effectively be providing short-term finance through trade credit to its customers on the one hand, and receiving short-term finance from suppliers on the other hand. Many retail businesses can gain a significant cash flow advantage from the fact that they receive payment from customers in cash at the time of sale, but do not need to pay their suppliers promptly.

Bank overdrafts offer an alternative form of short-term credit. Bank overdrafts will be more flexible than trade credit in terms of amount, within the limits which a bank will permit for the business, but interest must be paid. Bank overdrafts should not be treated as a permanent or long-term form of credit. In general, short-term credit should enable a firm to retain sufficient liquidity, and a firm should keep its current ratio (the ratio of current assets to current liabilities) at a sufficiently high level.

A further form of short-term credit which is important to a business is the credit which a retailer is able to provide to customers through informal credit arrangements, customer credit accounts, credit cards and charge cards. These forms of consumer credit can provide a way for a business to increase sales. In many retail markets, a major retailer could lose sales significantly if it did not provide the various forms of credit which its competitors provide.

Medium-term and long-term credit is available to businesses to finance fixed assets with a comparable or longer life. For example, medium-term credit might be used to finance the purchase of cars or items of plant and machinery. Bank loans, hire purchase and leasing finance offer alternative means of financing such purchases. A firm may borrow from a bank in a foreign currency as well as in the domestic currency: such 'eurocurrency' loans could be used as part of an arrangement whose objective is to hedge the risks of exchange rate movements.

A business may make use of sources of long-term credit as an alternative method of finance to equity shares. Larger companies can issue debentures or loan stock which may be quoted on the Stock Exchange. Such loans will normally be secured with a fixed or floating charge over the company's assets. The largest firms can raise capital on worldwide markets in the form of eurobond issues, or for short- and medium-term borrowing through commercial paper or medium term notes respectively. If a company is able to generate returns on the capital which exceed the cost of capital, it will be able to secure the benefits of higher dividends for its shareholders. However, if the costs of capital exceed returns made, shareholders in a firm with a high 'gearing' or debt/equity ratio may suffer heavily. Mortgages offer a form of long-term finance which is secured on land and buildings.

Levels of credit are of great economic importance because of their implications for the money supply and in turn for the level of demand in the economy. Higher levels of credit are likely to result in higher levels of bank deposits and hence to an increase in the money stock. Credit provides for the consumption of goods and services now in anticipation of future income. Increasing levels of credit can increase consumer demand and create inflationary pressures which a government may seek to control, for example by increasing rates of interest or by direct credit controls.

30 COMPANY FINANCE

Tutorial note: it's easy to forget the most important and cheapest source of finance - retained profits. The importance of gearing - the proportion of loan finance to equity - should be mentioned in order to gain the highest marks.

Suggested solution

A public limited company ('plc') is able to finance its activities by various combinations of equity and debt. Equity refers to ordinary share capital and reserves while debt refers to long-term and medium-term liabilities. Preference share capital falls between the two. The proportion of equity and debt in the capital structure of a firm varies from one company to another, and for a particular company over time. Major differences between equity and debt relate to risk and profit. From the holders' point of view, ordinary shares are riskier than loans, but their potential profit - either in dividends or in residual market value - may be much higher. Equity holders receive any residual profit after tax and after the fixed commitments to pay interest on loans and dividends on preference capital. From a company's point of view the reverse is true - debt capital is cheaper than equity, partly because interest is tax-deductible; but it is also riskier because of the fixed nature of the legal commitments.

Ordinary shares are shares in the ownership of the company and give ultimate rights of control over its effects. The number of shares which a company is authorised to issue is indicated in its constitution (memorandum of association) which also specifies the nominal amount of each share, eg ordinary shares of £1 each. Once issued, ordinary shares represent permanent capital, not normally redeemed during a company's existence. If an individual shareholder wants to recover his capital investment while the company continues in business, he must sell his shares to someone else. Such a sale does not affect the company directly, unless it changes the controlling interest.

A plc may increase its ordinary share capital in order to raise further finance in two ways:

(i) *Issues for cash or other assets*
     The directors of the company may decide to issue a further tranche of ordinary shares in order to acquire more assets. Members of the public and investing institutions such as pension funds would be invited to offer to buy the shares.

(ii) *Right issues*
     The company may make a rights issue to existing shareholders. This involves the company offering additional shares to existing shareholders at a price which is generally a little below the current market price. Rights are issued to existing shareholders in proportion to their existing shareholdings, eg on the basis of a '1 for 5' rights issue. If a shareholder did not wish to invest more cash, he could sell his rights in the market. If he did neither, the company could normally sell the rights in the market on his behalf. The buyer of the rights would then be able to subscribe for the new shares.

The extent to which new equity issues to new or existing shareholders can be carried out will partly depend on the valuation the stock market places on the company, which in turn will be heavily influenced by the dividends paid out and/or expected and prospects for future growth of the company.

A plc may obtain finance from retained earnings, ie retained profits or undistributed profits. These are any after-tax profits that are reinvested - or ploughed back - into the firm rather than being paid out to the shareholders in dividends. Such retained earnings form a valuable source of capital which may be invested in additional fixed capital and current assets. They serve to swell the value of the company to the shareholders and increase shareholders' capital employed by adding to revenue reserves any profit not paid out in dividends or added to the accumulated retained earnings figure on the balance sheet.

Preference shares fall between ordinary shares and debt. Legally they form part of a company's share capital, but with limited rights to participate in profits. Preference dividends are normally 'cumulative', so that no ordinary dividends can be paid until all preference dividends due (including any arrears) have been paid. Preference shares have lost favour with investors and with companies seeking to raise capital. Although preference shares are still common they are usually a relatively unimportant source of finance.

Apart from equity a company may borrow in order to finance its activities. Such borrowing may be considered in terms of long-term liabilities and medium-term liabilities. Companies may raise long term debt from merchant banks, insurance companies or other institutions and for large companies from the stock exchange. In certain cases government loans may be available for companies unable to borrow commercially.

The company must repay the amount borrowed at the promised time and pay interest outstanding on the debt in the meantime. Failure to do either entitles the lender to take legal action to recover the amount due; and in the event of a company going into liquidation, all debts must be paid in full before any amounts can be paid to preference or ordinary shareholders. Sometimes a loan will be 'secured' by a charge or mortgage on some or all of the assets of the company. In the event of a liquidation this will entitle the lender to recover his debt in full before trade and other 'unsecured' creditors can receive any proceeds from the charged assets.

The terms of a long term loan can vary considerably, but will often be for a period between 10 and 20 years. The rate of interest will depend on prevailing conditions and expectations in the market at the time of issue, and on the financial status of the borrower. The greater the risk perceived by the lender, the higher the interest rate that will be required for a loan, or the more stringent the other conditions that may be insisted on.

A special category of debt can be 'converted' on pre-arranged terms with ordinary share capital at the holder's option, after which it is indistinguishable from other ordinary share capital. If not converted during the option period, convertible debt simply becomes straight debt capital when the conversion rights lapse.

Loans payable between 1-5 years from the balance sheet date are sometimes referred to as 'medium-term'. Apart from loans with a specified repayment date, certain overdrafts may also be classified as medium-term. Although in theory bank overdrafts are repayable on demand, it is not unusual for companies to go through refinancing cycles in which overdrafts fulfil a bridging role between the dates at which the company raises more permanent capital - either equity or long term debt.

The proportion of debt and equity within a company's capital structure is decided by its directors. A company with a large proportion of debt in its capital structure is said to be highly 'geared'. The higher the financial gearing the greater the risk for owners of equity capital, but the greater their prospect of profit if all goes well.

ECONOMICS

OBJECTIVE TESTS

SELECTION 1

1 Which one of the following statements is false?

 A Division of labour was characteristic of pre-industrial societies in which individuals were not organised together to work for an employer

 B Specialisation of labour is said to occur where one individual restricts his activities to particular products or services

 C Economies of scale can arise from the increased specialisation of labour possible in a larger enterprise

 D Division of labour is a form of specialisation of labour.

2 A production possibility curve (frontier) indicates the

 A attainable combinations of commodities for a community using all its available resources
 B allocation of the supply of commodities among the members of a community
 C quantities which a community decides to produce of various commodities at various possible prices
 D efficiency with which a community's resources are being used.

3 A demand schedule for a product is constructed on the assumption that all of the following remain constant *except*

 A the price of other products
 B consumer's tastes
 C the price of the product
 D incomes

4 An indirect tax imposed on sausages (and not on any other foods) would

 A decrease the consumption of sausages and raise the price
 B decrease the consumption of sausages and so depress the price
 C not affect the consumption of sausages but raise the price
 D neither affect the consumption of sausages nor affect the price

5 A consumer's demand curve for a good is generally downward-sloping. Which of the following statements helps to explain this?

 I As the price falls, the consumer buys more of the good and less of other goods whose prices are now relatively higher.

 II As the quantity supplied increases, suppliers suffer diminishing returns to scale.

 A I only
 B II only
 C Both I and II
 D Neither I nor II.

6   Consider which of the following events would result in a shift of the demand curve for bottled mineral water to the right:

I   the start of a period of hot weather
II   a rise in the price of mineral water
III   a fall in consumers' income
IV   a campaign advising consumers that tap water is unhealthy to drink.

Select one option:

A   event I only;
B   events I and III only;
C   event II only;
D   events III and IV only.

7   The demand for cars should be reduced by a fall in the price of

I   petrol
II   multi-storey car parks
III   motor-cycle road-fund licences
IV   train services
V   road construction

A   I, II and III
B   III, IV and V
C   III and IV
D   II and III

Diagram for questions 8 - 10

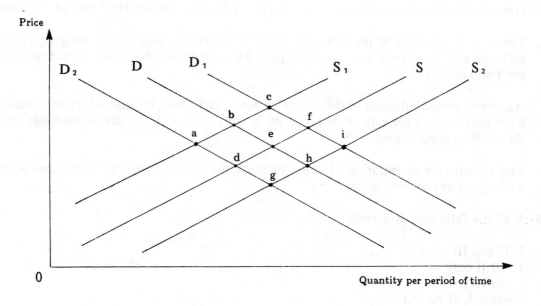

8   A market is in equilibrium at point e. The government imposes an import duty upon the imported goods which contribute to market supply whilst also easing policy on consumer credit in the economy in general. The new equilibrium will be

    A   i
    B   a
    C   c
    D   g

9   A market is in equilibrium at point e. Following a rise in the price of a substitute at the same time as a rise in the costs of producing the goods, the new equilibrium position will be

    A   g
    B   c
    C   b
    D   i

10   A market is in equilibrium at point e. If producers of the good received a subsidy at a time of rising real incomes and the income elasticity of demand for the good is equal to one, then the new equilibrium position would be the price and quantity combination shown by

    A   h
    B   i
    C   g
    D   e

SELECTION 2

1   The 'basket' of goods and services on which the United Kingdom Retail Prices Index is calculated includes mortgage interest payments and the community charge or 'poll tax'. A measure of inflation which excludes these two items is usually called the 'underlying' rate of inflation.

    I   The rate of inflation as measured by the RPI always exceeds the underlying rate of inflation when both are measured over a period in which both mortgage interest rates and the poll tax increase.

    II   An annual rate of inflation of the RPI of 9.8% and an underlying annual inflation rate of 6.4% indicates a 3.6% rate of inflation of interest rates and poll tax taken together in their RPI-weighted proportions.

    III   The annual rate of inflation of the RPI must always 'peak' at the same time as the underlying annual rate of inflation.

    Which of the following is correct?

    A   I, II and III
    B   I and II only
    C   I and III only
    D   Neither I, II nor III

2 A positive cross elasticity of demand between two goods indicates that

   A the goods are substitutes
   B the goods are complements
   C one good is income elastic and the other is income inelastic
   D one good is price elastic and the other is price inelastic.

3 In year 1 a clothing manufacturer was charging £15.50 for a pair of fashion jeans and demand reached 54,000 pairs for the year. In year 2 the price went up by 20 per cent and demand was reduced by 6,000 pairs. The price elasticity of demand for jeans is

   A 0.111
   B 0.555
   C 0.647
   D 1.546

4 An 'inferior good' is

   A a good of such poor quality that no demand for it is expected
   B a good which is not scarce
   C a good for which the demand rises constantly with income
   D a good for which the demand falls as household income rises

5 A supply schedule which has a price elasticity of supply equal to one will be

   A a rectangular hyperbola
   B a straight line drawn from the origin
   C a parallel to the x axis
   D a line parallel to the y axis

6 Which of the following statements are true?

   I   If the price elasticity of demand is less than one then a fall in price will result in a reduction in total expenditure on the product

   II The income elasticity of demand will only be less than one in the case of inferior goods

   III The cross-elasticity of demand for complements is positive

   A I only
   B III only
   C I and II only
   D II and III only

7 The total utility which a consumer derives from n units of a commodity minus the total utility he derives from $n - 1$ units is

   A the consumer's surplus from n units
   B the marginal utility of the nth unit
   C the price elasticity of the consumer's demand
   D the consumer's equilibrium demand

8   Which of the following changes will *not* affect the positioning and shape of a supply curve?

    A   A change in the price of labour
    B   A change in the distribution of household incomes
    C   Changes in technology
    D   Increased costs in transporting goods.

9   Bandaland is the main exporter of a recently developed and highly prized variety of citrus fruit, the Bandalo. An excellent crop this year has resulted in a much larger quantity of supply than last year. The Bandalo Export Corporation has considered two alternative courses of action.

    I   Dispose of sufficient quantities of bandalos (by leaving them to rot) to prevent a fall in the world market price of bandalos.

    II   Sell the entire crop at a lower price, which will cover the costs of production, storage and shipping.

    What must be the result of I, compared to II?

    A   Lower bandalo growers' real income
    B   Higher bandalo growers' real income
    C   Higher Bandaland real income
    D   Lower world real income

10 Which one of the following is *not* an 'externality'?

    A   The increased traffic congestion arising from the building of a new supermarket
    B   The availability to a professional firm of qualified staff trained by other firms
    C   Higher prices for rail travel at peak periods
    D   Higher turnover from a filling station following the re-routing of a road.

SELECTION 3

1   Which of the following is the most likely consequence of raising bank base rates?

    A   Less overseas investment in sterling
    B   Depreciation of the currency
    C   Slower growth in the money supply
    D   Higher house price inflation.

2

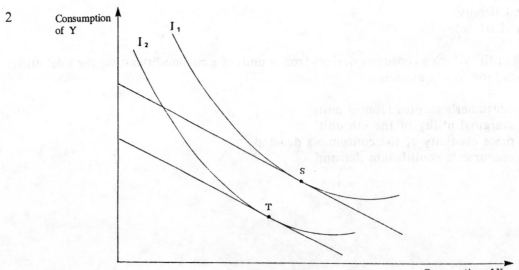

In this indifference map, points S and T are both points on the consumer's

A   income consumption curve
B   alternative price line
C   individual demand curve
D   budget line

3   Assume that there are only three commodities for a consumer to purchase. The table below shows the price of each commodity, and the marginal utility derived from the consumption of each up to and including the fifth.

Commodities	Price per unit	Marginal utility from each unit				
		1st	2nd	3rd	4th	5th
X	10p	25	20	12	10	9
Y	15p	30	15	10	2	1
Z	20p	60	50	40	20	10

How would the rational consumer distribute 95p between X, Y and Z?

A   2 units of X, 1 unit of Y and 3 units of Z
B   1 units of X, 3 units of Y and 2 units of Z
C   0 units of X, 1 units of Y and 4 units of Z
D   4 units of X, 1 units of Y and 2 units of Z

4   The optimum population is the level of population at which

A   output per capita is maximised
B   the marginal efficiency of labour is maximised
C   population has just started to decline
D   population is neither increasing nor decreasing

5   A profit maximising firm in a market with a constant wage rate w experiences a shift in its marginal revenue product of labour curve from MRP_1 to MRP_2.

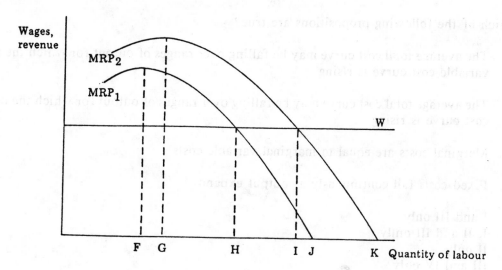

The quantity of labour employed will

A   change from F to G
B   change from H to I
C   change from J to K
D   remain unchanged.

6   Jordan McCall earns £6,000 per year working in a shop selling sheet music and compact discs. In his spare time, he plays in a band called Exodus which has played at charity and other events but has not yet earned Jordan any money. Bluegrass Management are impressed by a demonstration recording produced by the band and offer a contract which will pay £24,000 per year to Jordan. £14,000 of this relates to payments for live performances; the remaining £10,000 is an annual payment in consideration of the performance rights of recordings. If Jordan and the rest of the band take up the offer, Jordan will have to give up working in the shop to devote himself to the new contract full time. The new contract means that Jordan will receive

A   economic rent of £10,000 and transfer earnings of £18,000
B   economic rent of £10,000 and transfer earnings of £24,000
C   economic rent of £18,000 and transfer earnings of £6,000
D   economic rent of £24,000 and transfer earnings of £18,000

7   The supply of skilled bricklayers is inelastic but not perfectly inelastic. Which of the following would you expect to result from an improvement in the productivity of bricklayers?

A   The number of bricklayers in employment will fall, but their wages will rise
B   The number in employment will rise, and their wages will rise
C   The number in employment will rise, and their wages will fall
D   The number in employment will stay the same, and their wages will rise

8   The term 'marginal cost' (MC) can best be described as

A   the reduction in profits from selling an additional unit
B   an opportunity cost
C   the addition to total costs from producing an additional unit
D   the total variable costs at each level of output

9   Which of the following propositions are true?

I   The average total cost curve may be falling over ranges of output for which the average variable cost curve is rising

II   The average total cost curve may be falling over ranges of output for which the marginal cost curve is rising

III   Marginal costs are equal to marginal variable costs

IV   Fixed costs fall continuously as output expands

A   I and III only
B   I, II and III onlly
C   II only
D   III and IV only

10 In the theory of costs the term 'long run' can be best defined as

A   the period during which only one factor of production can be varied

B   the period during which technology can vary

C   the period during which it is possible to vary all factors of production within the existing technological constraints

D   the period during which the law of diminishing marginal returns (variable proportions) operates.

SELECTION 4

1   The figure below represents a monopolist seeking to maximise profits.

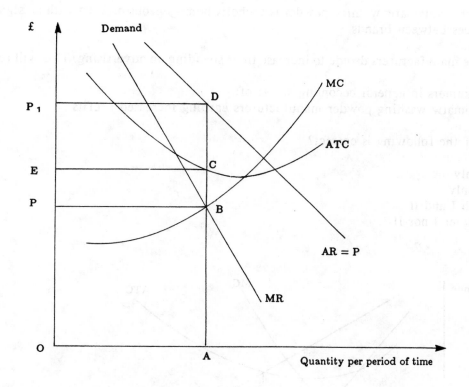

Which of the following statements will be true?

I   The monopolist's price will be *OP*

II   Supernormal profits equivalent to the area of *ECDP₁* will be earned

III The introduction of cost-saving techniques will not cause the monopolist to lower price

A   I only
B   II only
C   I and II only
D   I, II and III

2   Price discrimination is

A   the practice by which a firm charges different prices to different markets

B   the imposition of tariff barriers on imported goods

C   the government policy by which a nationalised industry is forced to raise its prices despite the absence of any change in market forces

D   illegal price-based rationing practised by black marketeers

3   In Pirhania, automatic washing powder is sold under eight different brand names. The washing powder manufacturers know that more automatic washing powder will be bought if prices fall and less will be bought if prices rise. They also know that advertising will not increase the amount of the product bought although it will increase the choice of brand. Changes in manufacturing and other costs in the industry are partly passed on to the consumer through changes in prices.

Assume that automatic washing powder is a wholly homogeneous product with no significant differences between brands.

All of the manufacturers decide to increase their spending on advertising. This will result in

I   consumers in general becoming worse off
II   automatic washing powder manufacturers earning increased profits

Which of the following is correct?

A   I only
B   II only
C   Both I and II
D   Neither I nor II

4

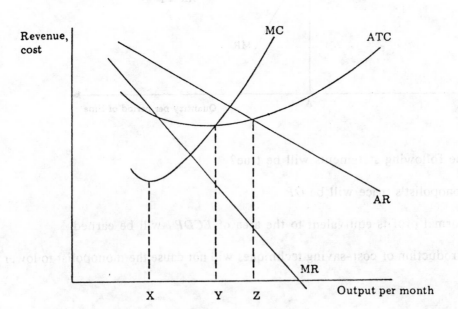

In the diagram above:

I   The technically optimal output for the firm is at output X
II   The firm will maximise total revenue at output Y
III   The firm only makes normal profits at output Z

Which of the following is correct?

A   I only
B   III only
C   I and II only
D   II and III only

5   In conditions of monopolistic competition, a profit maximising firm should produce the quantity of output at which

A   marginal revenue equals marginal cost
B   marginal revenue equals zero
C   marginal cost equals average total cost
D   marginal cost equals marginal revenue.

6   I   A firm in conditions of monopolistic competition will eventually reach equilibrium output at a level less than that at which average total cost is at a minimum.

    II   For a firm in perfect competition, the output level at which marginal revenue equals marginal cost is that at which the firm's average variable costs are minimised.

Which of the following is correct?

A   I and II
B   I only
C   II only
D   Neither I nor II

7   Which of the following can be barriers to entry which help to protect monopolies?

I   Product differentiation
II   Product patents
III   Economies of scale

A   I and II only
B   I and III only
C   II and III only
D   I, II and III

8   Which of the following monetary aggregates represents notes and coins in circulation with the public, plus residents' sterling deposits with banks and building societies?

A   M0
B   M2
C   M4
D   M4c

9 All of the six banks in a small country maintain a liquidity ratio of 8%. One bank receives additional cash deposit of £1 million. There will now be a further increase in total bank deposits up to a maximum of

A £480,000
B £6 million
C £11.5 million
D £12.5 million

10 The broad money supply in a certain country was:

Year	$ million
1989	18,760
1990	20,420

Between 1989 and 1990, the velocity of circulation of broad money fell from 6.0 to 5.8. The volume of transactions remained unchanged: the country's economy did not grow or decline in real terms. What is the annual rate of inflation between the two years?

A 3.45%
B 5.22%
C 8.85%
D 12.60%

A brief explanation is given with each solution

SELECTION 1

1   A   Division of labour refers to the specialisation of labour within particular parts or operations in a production process, and can be seen as having led to the development of the exchange economy.

2   A   The production possibility curve shows opportuities for increasing the output of one good by reducing output of another where resources are limited.

3   C   A demand schedule shows the quantity of demand at different prices of the product. All of the other factors are assumed to remain constant.

4   A   The tax will increase suppliers' costs and consequently move the supply curve upwards, raising prices. Other goods will have become relatively cheaper, and so consumers will substitute some sausage consumption with other consumption. Some increase in price will occur because demand is not perfectly elastic.

5   A   The demand curve indicates the quantity of a good which the consumer would buy at different prices. By the substitution effect, the consumer will buy more of the good as its price falls relative to other goods, and therefore statement I is correct. The demand conditions illustrated by the curve are independent of conditions of supply: statement II is incorrect.

6   A   A rise in the price will not affect demand conditions. Events III and IV will both lead to a leftward shift of the demand curves, if any.

7   C   III and IV are substitute products for car travel. I, II and VI are complements of cars.

8   C   The import duty raises the supply curve (S_1). Easier credit enhances demand (D_1).

9   B   More expensive substitutes increase demand (D_1), while higher production costs raise the supply curve (S_1).

10   B   The subsidy moves supply to S_2. Since the good is 'normal' (not 'inferior'), rising incomes enhance demand to D_1.

SELECTION 2

1   D   If increases in mortgage interest and poll tax are small compared with other price increases, the underlying rate will exceed the RPI inflation rate: therefore I is incorrect. By the same reasoning, it can be seen that II must be incorrect. The peaks of RPI inflation and underlying inflation may occur at different times, depending upon the influence of mortgage interest and poll tax changes.

2   A   Cross elasticity of demand is a measure of the responsiveness of demand for one good to changes in the price of another. If the two goods are substitutes, the cross elasticity will be greater than zero. If the goods are complements, the cross elasticity will be negative.

271

3   C   If quantity demanded q changes from q_1 to q_2 when price p changes from p_1 to p_2, then:

$$\text{Price elasticity of demand} = \frac{\text{Change in q}}{\text{Change in p}} \times \frac{(p_1 + p_2)}{(q_1 + q_2)}$$

$$= \frac{6{,}000}{3.10} \times \frac{(15.5 \times 18.6)}{(48{,}000 + 54{,}000)}$$

4   D   Inferior goods contrast with normal goods, for which a rise in income leads to a rise in demand.

5   B   The elasticity of supply is equal to 1 when the supply of goods varies proportionately with the price.

6   A   An inferior good will have a negative income elasticity of demand. The cross elasticity of demand for complements will be negative. II and III are therefore incorrect.

7   B   This follows from the definition of marginal utilitiy.

8   B   A change in the distribution of household incomes may well affect demand, but the supply curve would be expected to remain unchanged.

9   D   The effect on bandalo growers' real income will depend upon the elasticity of demand for the product.

10   C   A consumption externality exists where the consumption of a good or service has a direct effect on the welfare of someone other than the consumer. A production externality exists where production activities of one firm affect those of another. The key point to remember about externalities is that their cost or benefits are not reflected in market prices. This is the case with A, B and D. C is an example of how 'price discrimination' is applied.

SELECTION 3

1   C   Higher interest rates should discourage borrowing, and since bank and building society borrowing is the main cause of increases in the broad money supply, there should be a slowing down of money supply growth. A, B and D are all the opposite of what would be expected. Higher interest rates should attract overseas investment funds and strengthen the value of the domestic currency. Inflation in house prices is very sensitive to interest rate changes because most houses are purchased using borrowed money: higher interest rates mean higher mortgage costs and should therefore dampen house price inflation.

2   A   The income consumption curve joins the points of tangent between the consumer's indifference curves and corresponding budget lines. It shows what combination of goods will be consumed at different levels of incomes, and may not be a straight line.

3   A   The consumer will purchase the combination for which the margial utility gained from the last penny spent on each commodity is equal.

4   A   Maximisation of output per capita is the criterion for optimality which an economist would usually use.

5   B   A profit maximising firm will employ labour up to the point at which MRP falls to the wage rate, at H and I respectively.

6   C   Transfer earnings are the reward which a factor of production would receive in its next best employment. Economic rent is the difference between a factor's transfer earnings and its actual reward for its present use.

7   B   The diagram below shows how a shift in the MRP of labour resulting from productivity improvements from MRP_1 to MRP_2 will lead to a relatively small increase in numbers employed from L_1 to L_2 and a relatively large increase in wages from W_1 to W_2.

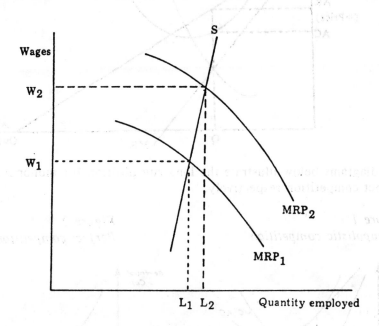

8   C   This is simply a definition of marginal cost.

9   B   Fixed costs remain unchanged as output expands (IV is therefore incorrect).

10   C   The answer provides the definition of the economist's term 'long run'.

SELECTION 4

1   B   The monopolist's price will be OP_1, not OP (I). III is incorrect since the monopolist will produce at the output at which marginal cost equals marginal revenue. Lower costs will lead to a price being set which is lower down the demand curve, at a correspondingly lower price.

2   A   An example of price discrimination is the practice of charging lower fares for passenger travel at off peak times than at peak periods.

3   A   The same amount of automatic washing powder will be consumed as before, but the prices will be higher as a result of increased advertising expenditure. Consequently consumers will be worse off. Manufacturers pass on part of the increase in advertising costs but bear part themselves: therefore, their profits will be reduced.

4   B   I is incorrect: the technically optimal output is the output at which average total costs are minimised (Y). II is also incorrect: sales revenue is maximised when MR = O. III is correct: normal profits only are earned at the level of output at which price equals average cost (AR = ATC).

5   A   A firm's short-run equilibrium in conditions of monopolistic competition is shown below.

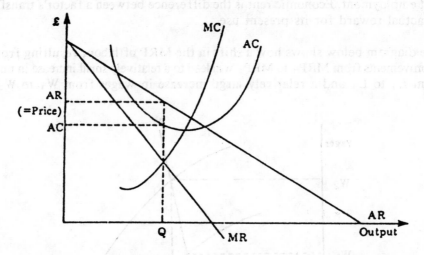

6   B   The diagrams below illustrate the long run position for monopolistic competition and perfect competition respectively.

Figure 1
Monopolistic competition

Figure 2
Perfect competition

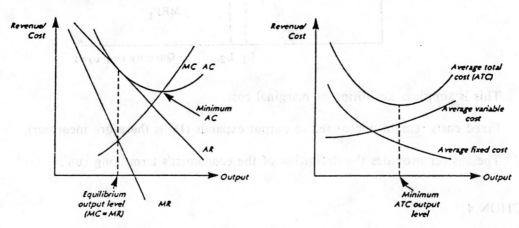

In monopolistic competition, a firm's equilibrium is where MR = MC, and this is at an output level below minimum AC. For a firm earning no supernormal profits, the equilibrium situation is illustrated in Figure 1 above. Statement 2 is false because although average *total* cost is minimised, average *variable* costs are not at a minimum and diminishing returns apply. Figure 2 shows this.

7   D   All of the items could operate as barriers to entry, as could a government-awarded franchise. Natural monopoly is really a special case of economies of scale.

8   C   M4 is a wide definition which includes all residents' sterling deposits with both banks and building societies. M4c is like M4 but includes foreign currency deposits.

9 C A cash ratio of 8% means that the credit multiplier for any initial increase in cash deposits will be 1/8% = times 12.5.

Maximum increase in bank deposits   = £1 million × 12.5
                                       = £12.5 million

This £12.5 million includes the initial deposit of £1 million, and so the *further* increase in bank deposits is £12.5 million - £1 million = £11.5 million.

10 B The quantity theory of money gives us MV = PT

MV in 1989 = 18,760 × 6.0 = 112,560
MV in 1990 = 20,420 × 5.8 = 118,436

T remains unchanged. The rate of increase in price level P is:

$$\frac{118,436 - 112,560}{112,560} = 0.0522, \text{ ie } 5.22\%$$

FURTHER READING

You may like to obtain further practice in tackling short questions in multiple choice format. BPP publish the *Password* series of books, each of which incorporates a large collection of multiple choice questions with solutions, comments and marking guides. The relevant Password titles for this paper are Foundation Business Mathematics, Business Law and Economics. These are priced at £6.95 each and each contains about 300 questions.

To order your *Password* books, ring our credit card hotline on 081-740 6808 or tear out this page and send it to our Freepost address.

To: BPP Publishing Ltd, FREEPOST, London W12 8BR   Tel: 081-740 6808

Forenames: (Mr / Ms) _____

Surname: _____

Address: _____

_____

Post code: _____

Please send me the following books:	Quantity	Price	Total
Password: Foundation Business Mathematics		£6.95	
Password: Business Law		£6.95	
Password: Economics		£6.95	

Please include postage:

UK: £1.50 for first plus £0.50 for each extra book

Overseas: £3 for first plus £1.50 for each extra book

I enclose a cheque for £_____ or charge to Access/Visa

Card number ☐☐☐☐☐☐☐☐☐☐☐☐☐☐☐☐

Expiry date _____ Signature _____

If you are placing an order, you might like to look at the reverse of this page. It's a Review Form, which you can send in to us with comments and suggestions on the kit you've just finished. Your feedback really does make a difference: it helps us to make the next edition that bit better. So if you're posting the coupon, do fill in the Review Form as well.

CIMA BUSINESS STUDIES

Name: _____

How have you used this kit?

Home study (book only) ☐ With 'correspondence' package ☐

On a course: college_____ Other _____ ☐

How did you obtain this kit?

From us by mail order ☐ From us by phone ☐

From a bookshop ☐ From your college ☐

Where did you hear about BPP kits?

At bookshop ☐ Recommended by lecturer ☐

Recommended by friend ☐ Mailshot from BPP ☐

Advertisement in _____ ☐ Other _____ ☐

Have you used the BPP Study Text for this subject?   Yes/No

Your comments and suggestions would be appreciated on the following areas.

Study guide and quiz

Content of solutions

Errors (please specify, and refer to a page number, if you've spotted anything!)

Presentation

Other